MARTIN BUBER'S FORMATIVE YEARS

JUDAIC STUDIES SERIES

Leon J. Weinberger

General Editor

MARTIN BUBER'S FORMATIVE YEARS

From German Culture to Jewish Renewal, 1897–1909

Gilya Gerda Schmidt

The University of Alabama Press

Tuscaloosa and London

The University of Alabama Press
Tuscaloosa, Alabama 35487-0380

Manufactured in the United States of America

The paper on which this book is printed meets the minimum requirements of American National Standard for Information Science-Permanence of Paper for Printed Library Materials, ANSI Z39.48-1984.

Library of Congress Cataloging-in-Publication Data

Schmidt, Gilya Gerda.
Martin Buber's formative years : from German culture to Jewish renewal, 1897–1909 / Gilya Gerda Schmidt.
p. cm. — (Judaic studies series)
Rev. version of the author's thesis (Ph.D.)—University of Pittsburgh, 1991.
Includes bibliographical references and index.
ISBN 0-8173-0769-9
1. Buber, Martin, 1878–1965—Childhood and youth. 2. Jews—Germany—Intellectual life. I. Title. II. Series: Judaic studies series (Unnumbered)
B3213.B84S36 1995
296.3′092—dc20 94-24877

British Library Cataloguing-in-Publication Data available

In memory of Mordecai Gustav Heiser (1905–1989) ע"הש
and in deep gratitude to
John Neubauer and Alexander Orbach

CONTENTS

LIST OF FIGURES

Figure 1. *Ex libris*: "Mein ist das Land" (Jerusalem, National Library, Buber Archives, Ms. Var. 350 A/7a).

PREFACE

When I was a child in post–World War II Germany, my father brought home wallpaper samples for me to draw on. At a time of extreme material and spiritual poverty, I created on scrap paper worlds of richness and beauty that I had never seen but was sure existed. Later, I began to realize the dreams I held step by step, some already at a young age, others not until I was a mature woman. One dream, I was told, I would never fulfill—that of becoming a teacher, perhaps a university professor. I didn't believe the pessimistic forecasts but held on to my inner vision. Already well on my way to graduate school, I encountered Martin Buber. In his writings, I found my own worldview confirmed as a path to fulfillment but on a much broader scale than I had envisioned. It was not a question of following him blindly—I, too, am not a herd animal—but of experiencing the courage I already had for a nobler purpose, a greater task than personal gain. Martin Buber taught me to have the courage to be myself and to be not only for myself. He loved the two cultures that are also mine and reminded me of where I had been and where I had to go.

During my undergraduate years, Professor John Neubauer skillfully guided me through the maze of German literature. His sensitivity and brilliance set a standard for my own teaching and scholarship. In an effort to free me from the grasp of Franz Kafka's world, my first mentor introduced me to Buber's writings. Then Cantor Mordecai Heiser, of blessed memory, a Holocaust survivor, who had studied with Leo Baeck and was a schoolmate of Emil Fackenheim's at the Hochschule für die Wissenschaft des Judentums in Berlin, epitomized the lovable "Yekke" of the early twentieth century, bringing to life for me a people and a culture that I never knew and that had been destroyed by the Nazis. The odyssey came to a conclusion of sorts under the skillful and patient guidance of Professor Alexander Orbach, who managed to keep me on track through a number of metamorphoses. Without his encouragement, persistence, and mentorship, my dream would have failed already in sight of the goal.

This book, which contains aspects of my work over a twelve-year period, may be enjoyed by those who are familiar with German idealism, Vienna, and the various early twentieth-century avant-garde movements, and by those who take pride in Zionism and believe in the regeneration of Judaism and the need for a spiritual center in Eretz Israel. It is a book for the historian, the philosopher, the theologian, the Germanist, and the Judaic Studies professional because Buber was himself any and all of these. The reader does not have to agree with Buber's perspectives but ought to engage his arguments, and mine, in a lively dialogue.

I owe the chance to write this version of the book to my colleagues Rabbi Leon Weinberger and Richard Cohen, who invited me to Alabama for a postdoctoral fellowship in Judaic Studies. The friendly and congenial atmosphere of the Religious Studies Department at The University of Alabama and the quaint campus environment, as well as collegial support, greatly enhanced my creativity and desire to finish this project.

Earlier financial support was provided by a University of Pittsburgh Israel Heritage Room graduate scholarship for dissertation research at the Buber Archives at the Jewish National and University Library in Jerusalem in 1988 and a scholarship from the Keren L'Dorot Foundation through the efforts of Rabbi Bernard Mandelbaum. I am extremely grateful to Margot Cohn and her staff at the Buber Archives for their invaluable assistance in locating the materials I was interested in and their help with copying what I needed. Over the years, the personal support of Rabbi Simon and Betty Greenberg of blessed memory was a treasured source of strength for me. I will always gratefully remember the gracious hospitality of my friends Dr. Avraham and Iris Shapira and their children Yaniv, Sivan, and Yonat during my visits to Israel. A special note of thanks to Nicole Mitchell of The University of Alabama Press for her consideration and sensitivity during the final stages of this project and to Joan Riedl for her patience in proofreading the text. I acknowledge with gratitude the fine assistance of Diane Spielmann and the Leo Baeck Institute in New York and the masterful copyediting of Trudie Calvert.

I hope that this book will encourage readers to research some of the Buber materials mentioned and discussed and to study German Jewish culture beyond the introductory level.

MARTIN BUBER'S FORMATIVE YEARS

Figure 2. Picture of Martin Buber from *Die Stimme der Wahrheit—Jahrbuch für Wissenschaftlichen Zionismus*, 1, ed. Lazar Schön (Würzburg: N. Philippi, 1905), 205. Courtesy of Leo Baeck Institute, New York.

PROLOGUE
The Problem of Individuation and Community

In 1897, Martin Mordecai Halevi Buber (1878–1965), who was an Austrian citizen by birth, returned to Vienna from Lvov, Galicia, where he had been raised by his grandparents, Salomon and Adele Buber, to pursue university studies.[1] From 1897 to 1904, Buber continued his higher education at the universities of Vienna, Leipzig, Zurich, and Berlin. He studied art history and philosophy and, in 1904, completed a doctor of philosophy degree with a dissertation titled "Zur Geschichte des Individuationsproblems: Nicolaus von Cues und Jakob Böhme" ([Contributions to] the History of the Problem of Individuation: Nicholas of Cusa and Jakob Böhme).[2]

This book presents an account of the struggles and explorations which Buber undertook, often simultaneously, during the period from 1897 to 1909.[3] Each chapter highlights a particular concern of Buber's which he pursued in the form of an apprenticeship, covering many disparate areas. My goal is to create a composite picture of Buber's development, paralleling his own goal in his work. Each of the apprenticeships contributes a piece to the mosaic that was the early Martin Buber. Yet it is hoped that one can see that the mosaic reflects a unity that already then existed within Buber. This unity informed his moral imperative to search for the right components for a new type of Jewish personality and eventually Jewish community.

Buber's earliest papers, his earliest activities, and his many tentative probings in different directions were the first, and therefore authentic, expressions of his struggles and concerns, and they reflect his spontaneous responses upon encountering an issue. Buber was an activist of the word. He considered this activism legitimate, for "the narrative word is more than [just] speech, it actually transmits the event to future generations, the telling itself is event, it is consecrated as sacred action."[4]

When I first contemplated this project, I hoped to examine how

Martin Buber went about developing a new type of Jewish community for post-Emancipation German Jewry, but when I began to gather and to read the materials for the early years, I realized that Buber's occupation in the years from 1897 to 1909 was not so much with the community as with the individual. While Buber's goal was community, the challenges he encountered were precommunity, dealing with matters of an individual and societal nature.

The organization of this book is organic in nature. Buber's interests were in German culture, in Jewish renewal, and in the renewal of humanity, in that order. Hence I begin in Chapter 1 by illuminating his claim that contemporary society was undergoing a crisis both of culture and of community. These crises, in turn, he believed had been caused by a crisis of personality that resulted in the absence of strong, autonomous personalities with a vision. This lack led to a glaring void of leaders capable of shaping contemporary culture and community. Buber looked to culture rather than to politics or religion for a solution because he was infatuated with the thought of Friedrich Nietzsche (1844–1900). Nietzsche advocated a transvaluation of the very basis for human values from morality to aesthetics. Buber suggested that people who shared a desire for togetherness beyond economic and religious associations should form a new type of community. The question not yet resolved was whether the approach to this new venture should be through art or through life. Previous attempts to transform society, such as those of the romantics, had been primarily through art. Buber likewise explored artistic approaches, but he also learned about a new form of art that occurred in life—the socialist community of Gustav Landauer (1870–1919).

Chapter 2 deals with Martin Buber's academic career. Not surprisingly, in his university studies Buber occupied himself with those subjects that most interested him at that time in his life—art and philosophy. Hence, dualism as an intellectual problem dominated the material he encountered—from Aristotle to Nietzsche. The philosophical debate on the topic of dualism manifested itself in a discussion of aesthetics. Yet Buber's exploration of aesthetics moved away from contemporary philological considerations (Ludwig Wittgenstein and Ernst Mach) and toward a contemplation of the soul. He began by an exploration of the soul through the mediated experience of philosophy and art, not through faith, leading him to search for thinkers who also searched for ways to overcome this "human condition." He found leads to the unity of the soul in the theology of Nicolas of Cusa (1401–64) and Jakob Böhme (1575–1624). They believed not only in the existence of God, but in the goodness of creation. Such a perspective necessitated the belief in a unity between the Creator and the created world, not the dualism current in Western thought. Buber drew on Cusa's and Böhme's schemes of the microcosm for his own philosophy of a harmonious universe.

Concurrent with his university life and literary activities, Martin Buber became interested in renewing his ties to Judaism. Buber's attraction to Zionism can be seen as part of his general dissatisfaction with contemporary German society. This dissatisfaction prompted him to reestablish the connection with his Jewish context, although he did not choose to return to the established tradition or the existing community. Rather, he chose Zionism as his point of departure. Buber's entrance into the world of Zionism brought him into direct contact with the views of Theodor Herzl (1860–1904) and Ahad Ha-Am (1856–1927) and the movements they spawned. Their work inspired Buber to express his own views on Zionism and to work for a Jewish cultural renewal. I shall explore Buber's commitment to what he termed the relative life in Chapter 3.

This encounter with the relative life in the form of Zionism encouraged Buber to search for what he perceived to be the missing dimension—the absolute life. In Chapter 4, I explore Martin Buber's literary encounter with Hasidism, the form of Jewish mysticism that emerged in the eighteenth century in parts of Poland and the Ukraine. Along with Micah Joseph Berdichevsky (1865–1921), Rabbi Abraham Isaac Kook (1865–1935), Samuel Hayyim Landau (1892–1928), Judah Leon Magnes (1877–1948), Aaron David Gordon (1856–1922), and others in this period who were also interested in spirituality in the Jewish context, Buber looked for a way to reintroduce the spirit as the major building block for a new Jewish way of life. Buber's work was seminal to the serious study of Jewish mysticism. Not only did he introduce the study of Jewish mysticism to a new generation of scholars such as Gershom Scholem, he also brought attention to the Hasidim in a novel and positive way. Heretofore, Hasidism had been maligned as an anachronistic, pietistic, Jewish movement that stood in the way of modernization. As Steven Aschheim has pointed out, after Buber, German Jewry's encounter with the East was nothing short of a venerated cult.[5]

In the Epilogue, I will sum up how Martin Buber's various efforts provided building blocks for his future worldview and what this meant for the future of Jews, Judaism, and humanity. By 1909, only about a decade since the beginning of his Zionist activities, Buber had considerably matured in his conception of what mattered in life. No longer did he aim simply to awaken the people to the cause of Judaism, for that had been accomplished in the years between 1897 and 1904. He now demanded a total commitment of body and soul to Judaism in the form of Jewish knowledge, the Hebrew language, and the land of Israel. All these efforts were to lead to communal revitalization, an idea on a higher level than that of personal redemption which Buber advocated during his primary Zionist period. Redemption was perhaps the key concept in Buber's philosophy of this period—of the self and, through it, of the people. It was, however, a redemption wrought by humanity, not bestowed by Divine grace, resulting from a union of past and present in anticipation of the future.

Martin Buber was a complicated and complex young man. His views were always enthusiastic, often brilliant, sometimes too polar, at times frustrating and circular, sometimes contradictory, and at times the somewhat inflexible attitude of the "Yekke" clearly obscured his objectivity. Nevertheless, drawing on European, Jewish, and Oriental insights, Buber during these years was one of the bright young stars on the horizon of Jewish renewal who fashioned a synthesis that was to serve him and a new generation of European Jews until the rise of Adolf Hitler. His commitment to human rejuvenation through communal revitalization became the basis upon which he developed the views for which he became famous after World War I. He would not have been able to do so without the preceding struggles, which are discussed and analyzed in this book.

I

A TIME OF CRISIS
Contemporary Cultural Concerns, 1897–1901

TURN-OF-THE-CENTURY Vienna was unique in every respect. Politically, it was the center of the multiethnic Austro-Hungarian monarchy; culturally, it was at once fiercely Austrian nationalistic and proudly European, influencing the entire German-speaking domain.

The period known as Viennese Modernity lasted from about 1890 to 1911.[1] A host of culture critics such as Karl Kraus (1874–1936), Sigmund Freud (1856–1939), Max Burckhard (1854–1912), Henrik Ibsen (1828–1906), Peter Altenberg (1859–1919), Hermann Bahr (1863–1934), Hugo von Hofmannsthal (1874–1929), and Arthur Schnitzler (1862–1931) wanted to bring about change for the sake of progress.[2] According to sociologist Max Burckhard, the word *modern* was given currency by Hermann Bahr[3] and came to signify progress.[4] The four Viennese poets Bahr, Altenberg, von Hofmannsthal, and Schnitzler belonged to an elite literary group, Jung Wien (Young Vienna) and considered themselves the conscience of contemporary Vienna. This "circle of young poets, focused around Arthur Schnitzler and Hermann Bahr . . . the most distinguished of them being Hugo von Hofmannsthal and Stefan Zweig"[5] (1881–1942) and met at the Cafe Griensteidl.[6] They had been raised in a society that thought it natural "to center its life upon the theater, which formed the standards of speech, dress and mores; . . . and in a city in which the standards of journalism were exceptionally high." These artists were interested in contemporary issues such as dilettantism, decadence, narcissism, neuroticism, alienation, fragmentation, and resignation, as well as the consequences of imitation. Such key words of the period identified what Bahr called a "romanticism of the nerves."[7] The language reflected the "sickness" of the culture, and the literature disseminated the message of the fin de siècle. There was a concerted effort to bring about a renaissance of earlier periods such as romanticism or neoclassicism, which were perceived to have been more authentic. But instead of a re-creation, contemporary thinkers achieved only an imitation of the ideal. The enfeebling mood of "imitation" that had pervaded nineteenth-century Europe, and which Karl Immermann (1796–1840), Nietzsche, and others called the period of the *Epigonen* (imitators),[8] carried over into the twentieth century. The Young Vienna literary circle under the leadership of Hermann Bahr endeavored to turn the trend around.

When Martin Buber came to Vienna in 1897, he already held an appreciation for the great critical minds of the late nineteenth century, especially Friedrich Nietzsche, whose Zarathustra served as a hero model for him.[9] Nietzsche's assertion that God is dead had opened the door to a complete transvaluation of values. No longer was a Divinely based morality the only possible foundation for life. In *The Birth of Tragedy* (1872) Nietzsche claimed that aesthetics could serve as a better foundation for modern life than morality.[10] Therefore, Buber found a ready-made context for his intellectual and cultural curiosity as well as for his energies in the lively exchange of contemporary cultural criticism that occurred in the coffee houses as well as the literary journals of the period. During his first year in the city, Wittgenstein's Vienna became Buber's Vienna as well, for, as he himself told us, he did succumb to the power of the Burgtheater.[11]

Buber nevertheless saw the problem of the individual in a society in crisis sharply and clearly. This is apparent from his critical 1897 essay "On Viennese Literature" about the four Young Vienna writers Hermann Bahr, Hugo von Hofmannsthal, Peter Altenberg, and Arthur Schnitzler.[12] In this article, written in Polish, for a Polish journal, Buber attempted to come to grips with the nature of the crisis of personality that he perceived.

Buber's analysis of the worldview of these four poets illuminated his perception of the contemporary cultural situation in Vienna. Buber was most fascinated by Hermann Bahr, who was the decisive figure of this period, the founder and leader of the Young Vienna literary circle. Although Bahr took exception to the pessimism of such contemporaries as Ernst Mach (1838–1916), who maintained that "the self cannot be saved," Bahr's stand lacked fortitude.[13] Buber criticized Bahr as a butterfly, who "has taken to heart all the trends of our time" and indiscriminately flitted from one topic to another. This dynamic way of remaining forever on the move provided a vitality that made Bahr "the apostle of a slogan yet unborn."[14] This lack of depth was significant to Buber, however, who declared that Bahr "puts on a new I every day, like a new tie" and that "his individuality is really an utter lack of individuality."[15]

Although Buber recognized in Bahr several of the qualities he associated with the personality of an artist—dynamism, flexibility, the ability to point to topical themes—Bahr's individuality differed in quality from that Buber found in the individuals he chose as models—Cusa and Böhme, Johann Wolfgang von Goethe, and the romantics. Buber complained that Bahr "shows no development; all his 'mental states' . . . are of equal value."[16] The quest for self-knowledge was not an easy one, and modern individuals, who tended toward superficiality, required a proper guide for their pursuit of the quest for deeper knowledge. Consequently, although "the traits of contemporary intellectual life in Europe . . . have found vivid and dazzling expression" in Bahr, Buber did not consider him and his approaches appropriate for the quest he himself was embarking on. Rather, attitudes such as the "absence of unity and harmony" and "impotence, sterility, lassitude, [and] a wide, but superficial curiosity," which were visible in Bahr, had contributed to the decadence that characterized the downward spiral of contemporary culture.[17]

Bahr wrote that the decadent individual tried to discover the inner human being, as the romantics once did. But in contrast to the romantic, the decadent person did not wish to express the spirit or the feeling, but only his nerves.[18] Thus decadence discovered new art forms unknown to earlier generations. The decadent individual also has a tendency toward artificiality, moving away from nature. Decadence further expresses its "feverish passion for the mystical" in allegories and obscure images. Decadent individuals abhor all that is usual, frequent, normal. They endeavor to find the strange exception.[19]

In contrast to Bahr's expressed dilettantism, Hugo von Hofmannsthal was a nineteenth-century "Werther," a Goethean character who turned inward to the point of knowing no more about external life than that he was born in Vienna in 1874. Buber explained that through his poetry, von Hofmannsthal "wishes to examine and to explain the essence of life, of the life that he, shut up within himself, knows only through intuition." Buber implied that von Hofmannsthal could not write about life from experience because he did not have any. Again, von Hofmannsthal had the potential for personality, but because his outer and inner lives were completely separate, he "never struggles for his I."[20] He made no attempt to live what his inner eye perceived; he was satisfied to write about it, leaving the realization to others.

For Buber, this was not what life was all about. Despite his friendship with von Hofmannsthal, he perceived a different priority than did the resident of this decadent age, the precocious child who matured early, whose "unmasculine lassitude" made no demands, and for whom it was sufficient that "his soul always remains unaltered, the delicate, weary soul of an aristocrat who has not [yet] tasted life, and who [also] no longer demands anything from it." The resigned individual of von Hofmannsthal's type was old before his time; he was stagnant, not dynamic, incapable of change and growth. It is the dilemma of the modern human being that he has no feeling, does not struggle, and makes no progress—he is satisfied merely with intellectualization of themes and with finished form. "Like Bahr, he [von Hofmannsthal] does not grope for words; each thought attires itself for him in full, noble words."[21] If Buber objected to the fact that the philosopher used a system, he also objected to the fact that the poet forced his words into an existing perfect form. In Buber's mind, every individual ought to strive for his or her own form of expression, not merely follow the established conventional mode.

Peter Altenberg differed significantly from Bahr and von Hofmannsthal. He commented that individuality is a justification to be the first, the herald of some organic progress of human qualities with the possibility that it will become progress for humanity. "To be the first, that's what matters! For this person has a mission, he is a leader, he knows that all of humanity comes after him! God sent him ahead of time!"[22] Such ideas were truly in the spirit of Buber. He admired that Altenberg, like Dante before him, "does know that Divine laugh, does know anger as destructive as a hurricane and passion that burns like a simoon." This was much in contrast to Bahr, whose superficiality deprived him of any depth, and to von Hofmannsthal, whose dream existence separated him from life and whose poetry did not result from a struggle. But, alas, Buber lamented, the Viennese Dante wanted to be like Bahr and von Hofmannsthal. "He sees something beautiful in their pallid life and imitates them."[23]

To Buber's utmost despair, Altenberg pretended a lack of true emotion, even though he was capable of it. "He strives to conceal his love, he feigns lassitude, languor, decadence, he assumes a tone of salon irony, which smiles easily and indulgently, but does not know a full, divine laugh." Buber here described the modern, decadent individual, who was only a pale imitation of the true individual. In Buber's opinion, the authentic individual was epitomized in the earlier German romantics. Even Altenberg succumbed to the spirit of "our times, which makes men small and weak" and has "warped this beautiful soul and taken the halo of apostleship from its brow."[24] In other words, all the apparent qualities of the decadent individual were only imitations of the real thing. Thus, though Altenberg was capable of being an authentic human being, he chose not to because it did not suit the trend of the time.

Although the times had imposed an enfeebling state of mind on Altenberg, Buber was not willing to let go of him. Altenberg was a man who had "embraced all of nature with his love."[25] The two men shared the same Blakean approach, "to see a world in a grain of sand."[26] Altenberg's emphasis was on the ordinary; he dealt with minute everyday life events—an approach Buber himself later employed when retelling the tales of the Hasidim. Underneath the unsuitable shell of fin-de-siècle Vienna shone the kernel Buber yearned for—"an individual . . . one of those who are the leaven of humanity"[27]—one of those, one might add, whom Martin Buber could envision as a component of the community he desired, if only Altenberg had the desire to be such an individual.

If Buber saw Altenberg as a prophet in disguise, Arthur Schnitzler embodied the prophet of doom who heralded the death of the human species. In a last effort at self-preservation, "each of our feelings, each urge, each passion is presented in a mild and subdued form so that we never lose the conviction that all of this fervor is nothing but a beautiful illusion."[28] Buber lamented how far culture had declined to equate self-preservation with feebleness rather than with struggle. This way of viewing the world was an illusion, a way of creating seeming harmony where no harmony was possible. It was a way for the artist to invert inner and outer worlds, to turn things upside down. If humanity were not dying, these images would stir people into action. Instead, the muted quality of Schnitzler's art was thought to reflect the whimper of an age no longer capable of roaring like a lion.

Therefore, when Martin Buber lamented the crisis of humanity, he recognized that the outward manifestation of this crisis, namely isolation, had an inner cause, the human being's alienation from his self, his inability to know himself. The absence of *Gemeinschaft* which Buber perceived in his age was a direct result of human inability to come to grips with the individual self, to reflect and to grow, to develop a personality that could serve as a building block for community.

Schnitzler, von Hofmannsthal, Bahr, and Altenberg were in various degrees products of modern society, protesting meekly against the death of humanity. The older generation considered them to be revolutionaries because they offered criticism of contemporary culture, but Buber went one step further. Rather than agreeing with their perception of themselves as the conscience of fin-de-siècle Vienna, he turned their criticism of contemporary culture upon them, including them among the decadent dilettantes of modern Vienna. "In all of them is found that typically Viennese lack of the heroic, revolutionary element."[29] Although he found their efforts commendable, the source of their labors did not generate a Nietzschean Dionysian dynamic that could turn humanity around. Thus, ultimately, Buber had to look somewhere other than contemporary Viennese *litteratëurs* for suitable models for the new Jew and for the new human being.

The individualism of modernity was not based on the same concept as the self-realization Buber was looking for. In Buber's view, all people who adopted "the substitute religion" of individualism became weak and ineffective like the decadent Austrian poets he had described in his 1897 article. This individualistic ideology pervaded both the masses and the bourgeois middle class. Thus society now consisted of shallow and apathetic single individuals who, in Buber's view, hungered after material riches without concern for either spiritual well-being or the welfare of their fellow human beings. Franz Kafka expressed this view well when he wrote: "Human beings are connected among themselves through ropes, and it is a tragedy, when one's ropes loosen and a person falls lower than the others into empty space, and it is horrible when the ropes that tie a person to the others tear, and he falls. Therefore, a person must stay close to the others."[30] But what if the ropes have torn for most human beings? Then clearly the net is no longer capable of catching those who fall because it has too many holes. And one by one, these individuals are lost.

The realization that the net of community had been irreparably damaged emerged among isolated thinkers in Europe at the turn of the century. Buber was one of these individuals who pleaded for personalities with an authentic vision who could help form the kind of community that would try to realize a common ideal. His sensitivity to the negative aspects of the modern individual had great significance for his future work in searching for a different and fresh path for contemporary German Jewry. This effort became his primary concern. Thus Buber at this time did not offer as sharp and detailed a critique of current society and civilization as did some of his contemporaries. He was also vague in offering an alternative, namely the community of the future as well as a new culture. As we will see from the following two sections of the chapter, he made it clear only that the new community would hail from a different source than the old and would inevitably emerge from the decadence of contemporary culture. For the German Jew, decadence was not yet a problem. Buber saw it as his task to keep German Jewry from such a direction and, as we shall see in Chapter 3, he took this self-imposed charge seriously.

On Old and New Community

Buber was a herald figure, ahead of his time. He was "an anticipator" (*ein Ahnender*), like Friedrich Nietzsche and Jakob Böhme, or, as he put it in another context, a John-the-Baptist figure, a forerunner. Already during his student days, he belonged to an organization called Die Neue Gemeinschaft (the New Community).[31] This utopian/humanistic organization, heavily imbued with Goethean ideology, was cofounded and frequented by Buber's friend Gustav Landauer. Landauer, a philosopher, literary critic, and scholar, was also a passionate socialist. Eight years older than Buber, Landauer was already well established in his work and reputation when Buber met him. Landauer was highly political and at the same time thoroughly mystical. He hoped to create a socialism that would renew the human spirit, a vision Buber happily adopted and adapted to his own work in Zionism.

At one of the group's gatherings in Berlin in 1901, Buber spoke on the topic of old and new community.[32] The two types of community Buber discussed differed in that the old one was the community that humanity had known to date. This he considered basically utilitarian. The new type of community would lie in the future and would be idealistic. The old community was useful either to an economic group, in which case its purpose was this-worldly (*diesseitig*), or to a religious group, then its purpose was otherworldly (*jenseitig*). We see here Buber's problem with the existing dualistic concept of community. He objected to the fact that the historical community was not governed by high-minded ideals but by practical purposes. He was further concerned that if humanity's activities were governed only by utilitarian principles, then humankind's morals would also be informed by these same utilitarian principles. He thought that such utilitarian human morals primarily served to subdue the human instinct for self-assertion and preached instead usefulness to society as our only goal and the only norm for society.[33] Thus in the old community, socialization takes precedence over self-preservation, yet self-preservation has to be the first step in the process to self-realization, which, in turn, will lead to true community. Ideally, successful socialization in the modern world is, of necessity, preceded by self-realization.[34] Buber pointed out that in a world in which community occurs without individualization, the members of that community are bound together by statutes and dogma, which are meaningless to them because these statutes fail to reflect their individual needs.[35] In an age when the individual is so important, such a community could not possibly survive. And it did not survive. Many people did what Buber did: they left the familial fold and the familiar moorings and became shipwrecked, free from the old constraints but totally without new ideals or new guidelines for behavior.[36] Often, along with the old community, the center of the traditional community, God, was now also dead, and the new god of modern humanity—extreme individualism or narcissism[37]—reflected the values of the contemporary age, namely materialism and egotism.[38]

Buber made it clear that in his view the new community would consist of a voluntary association of individuals who shared a desire for togetherness beyond (*jenseits*) economic and religious associations. The terminology reminds us of Buber's intellectual indebtedness to Nietzsche and especially of *Jenseits von Gut und Böse* (*Beyond Good and Evil*) (1886), in which Nietzsche left behind the moral, though not aesthetic, categories of contemporary thought. Likewise, Goethe's novel *Wahlverwandtschaften* (*Elective Affinities*)

(1809) stressed voluntary association over traditional bonds. Nietzsche and Goethe were authentic personalities of the kind Buber wished for. Both men severely criticized the culture of their respective periods, calling for new creative approaches to human relations and a new foundation for these relations.

The primary difference between Buber's cultural models and his own evolving strategy was in approach. All of Buber's historical models struggled with contemporary problems through art. Buber likewise started on this path. But he simultaneously learned the path of social action from his friend Gustav Landauer. Inspired by Landauer, Buber labored for his own version of Jewish socialism, namely Zionism, at the same time that he struggled theoretically with his cultural ties to Nietzsche and Goethe.[39] The art of modernity was not original and genuine, not "of one piece," and Buber eventually left behind the artistic ways of German culture and its discontents, though not its heroes. He proceeded to build a strong program of social action, although it can be considered a program only in retrospect.

One can tell from Buber's lecture that this community of the future was not yet an experience for him, despite his membership in Die Neue Gemeinschaft and his efforts for the Zionist cause, but rather a hope he presented in a somewhat vague and tentative manner. He began by an attempt at formulating the ideals of this new entity. The new community would be one of freedom and choice, of individual self-realization and life. For Buber, community, which is "the alpha and the omega of life," has a twofold purpose: "itself and life."[40]

Building on his rejection of the contemporary personality, Buber had as his first goal a certain vision of the individuals who would make up this new community. They would be people who are "equally happy to give and to take, because both are the same action, one from the mover [giving] and the other from the one being moved [receiving]." This lived reciprocity "of whole and solid individuals" would form the basis for their resolution "to be united . . . by a common bond—for the sake of greater freedom." In other words, he felt that they could live and grow only in an environment in which reciprocal giving and creative commitment abounded: "That is community, that's what we want."[41]

The second goal of community is life. In contrast to the first goal, which is idealistic, this goal is practical. Not words but deeds matter.

These deeds "liberate the human being from the slavish rigidity of thought . . . and allow him to consolidate all of his energies for living." Die Neue Gemeinschaft was the prototype of this new community, and for members of this organization, "community and life are one."[42]

Instead of the dualistic tendency which Buber acknowledged as a characteristic of modern life, we see here a focus on unity as necessary for a life of community. Buber wrote that "like a wild, wonderful mountain stream that plummets to the depths in wild, excessive abandon," community and life together create, not for utilitarian purposes, but "a work of beauty."[43] This notion of life as a work of art resurfaced in different ways in Buber's contemplations on the relationship between the body and the soul.

What Buber did not and perhaps could not make clear at this point was that the self-actualized individual who would participate in this community of choice would have overcome the problems of alienation and fragmentation and would have created for himself, via the pain of the struggle, a harmonious worldview which he would be willing to share with like-minded others. Yet in a world of opposites, this serenity cannot be reconciled with the "wild, excessive abandon" of the Dionysian mountain stream. Therefore, this future community must stem from a different source than the present one.[44] Buber attempted to discover this source in a variety of different experimental groups.

In this speech, Buber addressed himself to the ultimate purpose of Die Neue Gemeinschaft. "We belong to this group because we share a specific necessity of life, in our time." This necessity differed from the one of society. The philosophy of the group treasured diversity of opinion and required that deed supersede ideology and religion. Buber continued, "We are guided by the personal revelation of each individual process of realization instead of by dogma and creed of faith."[45] Through their union, these like-minded individuals develop ultimate freedom. Thus, while Buber described an extreme stage of individualism freed from all conventional limiting factors, this ultimate, futuristic individualism was to allow the person a new type of bonding, which would be facilitated by self-realization.

The universalistic nature of Buber's perception is clear from these statements. Dogma and religion had no place in such a philosophy; they would have been limiting and therefore dividing factors. He pointed out that the members of Die Neue Gemeinschaft had chosen art over dogma because "art was capable of expressing creation in its infinite variety."[46] Here we meet the modern Buber, the student of aesthetics who, like his contemporaries Franz Kafka and Thomas Mann (1875–1955), and before them Goethe and Novalis, saw art as the ultimate vehicle of expression of the human spirit. Yet most modern art no longer expressed the authentic self or the Divine and was therefore impotent. Hence Buber's critique of the four Viennese poets. But what if one could again find a way to reach the authentic self or the Divine so that art would once more be able to effect a transformation of the spirit?

Individualism was an important aspect of Buber's quest for community. Everyone has to develop his or her own personal philosophy, for "what unites us [in Die Neue Gemeinschaft] is a common experience [of life], not a common philosophy." In support of this theory, Buber quoted his mentor, Gustav Landauer, who employed Goethe's Faustian imagery to conjure up the unifying depths of "the mothers." "If we differentiate ourselves thoroughly, when we as individuals descend deeply into ourselves, then we'll eventually find, in the innermost core of our hidden being, the most ancient and most general of community: with humanity and with the universe."[47] This conviction that unity can be found when one gets beyond all the differences sustained Buber through the doubts and uncertainties of his own struggle with life in modern society.

Die Neue Gemeinschaft wanted to set an example for humanity. "Our Gemeinschaft . . . wants to transform, not reform," Buber wrote.[48] Thus it would be a community which, created beyond (*jenseits*) society, would consist of original ideas. It would be a genuine work of art.[49] No longer would there be the modern dichotomy between life and art, but "this life, in which the creative power glows and throbs, becomes a work of art . . . : it is a new type of art, which creates a totality from eternity and bestows on every day the aura of a [sacred] festival." To think in this way itself is creative, for to realize an idea in a practical form, such as a community, is not the accepted notion of art. For this reason, Buber called the concept of Die Neue Gemeinschaft "*post-sociale* . . . for it goes beyond [current] society and its norms." This idea was no accident; the philosophy of Die Neue Gemeinschaft was nurtured by the classical image of a utopian community found in Part II of Goethe's *Faust*. When Buber envisioned "a far-off, pristine spot for new homes and new sacred places, somewhere, where we can commune with nature," he recalled Faust's vision just before his soul was spirited away. Buber firmly asserted, "Our community does not want a revolution, it *is* a revolution. . . . We want to live new things, to create—in a small circle, a sheer community, a new way of life."[50]

In light of the foregoing, it is not surprising that another Faustian element permeated Buber's thinking as well—action comes before theory. In the beginning is the deed, not the word. Buber made the point in the speech that, by realizing its self, the community would also realize life. The two, self-fulfillment and fulfillment of life, originate from the same source: "In this new life . . . people come together . . . through love, desire for community, and through a desire to share."[51] As a result, unity would be reestablished *within* the individual and *between* individuals, creating in the community the harmonious beauty God intended. Because the community would be wrought from humanity's struggle for self-understanding, its creation would be an original human work of art unlike any ever before.

The place of formal religion was not explored in the essay, and as Paul Mendes-Flohr and Bernard Susser pointed out, the only sentence in the manuscript that spoke of religion as "saturating our new life" was deleted in the final version.[52] The reason for this change may well have been connected with Buber's uncertain personal stand on religion and the problematic role of religion within culture. Buber considered existing religion to have become lifeless and stagnant, no longer inspired by a living relationship with God.[53] In fact, Buber did not offer a new formula for religion in culture until his publication of *Die Geschichten des Rabbi Nachman* in 1906.

On Culture and Civilization

During this period, the concept of culture was a topic of much debate and speculation. Again, the father of such critical inquiry had been Nietzsche, who railed against the degeneracy of contemporary culture in all of his work. Sigmund Freud, Wilhelm Dilthey (1833–1911), and Georg Simmel, as well as Rudolf Eucken (1846–1926),[54] Kurd Lasswitz (1848–1910),[55] and many others joined in this major debate of the time. The thrust of the debate centered on the nature and role of culture, *Bildung*, and civilization.

In his article "Kultur und Civilisation," published in the journal *Kunstwart* in 1901, Buber pointed out that there are times of cultural maturity and times of cultural gestation. During a period of cultural maturity, cultural life is set in its form and begins to show signs of rigidity that will lead to its eventual death. The time of cultural gestation, by contrast, is "filled with a boundless fire that moves in struggle and yearning and bursts all existing forms; harmony is still unrealized, the enormous productivity of opposites still rules the process."[56]

The new community which Buber proposed in the same year as an authentic work of art could come about only in a time of "alleged cultural maturity." At the same time, however, Buber considered Greek-based, dualistic European culture to be on the decline in his time, and he prophesied that "in the chaos of our days an epoch of cultural gestation . . . is on the horizon." What sort of cultural gestation this might be he did not say, but in retrospect it is clear that this was a time of Jewish cultural gestation. It was Buber's contention that "harvest time and seed time" always meet and that, in all of history, "we can discern such epochs of gestation and transition to which ours also belongs." Epochs of transition in European history included the Renaissance, the Baroque, and the Enlightenment. In this organic process, "the old trees of the forest rotted," but "again and again a new forest grew: in all times there was a decaying and an emerging world."[57]

Such a genuine work of art as the new personality and the new community he envisioned could come about in the current period of transition. Buber perceived human beings among his contemporaries "who prophesy the spirit and the living fire and prepare the way for the new future even while the ax is set to the trees. In their works we see new energies, new ways of seeing and of creating, new creations, new developments."[58] These fiery spirits did not include the Young Vienna circle, but they did include such underrated visionaries as Theodor Herzl and Ahad Ha-Am, as well as Gustav Landauer and Martin Buber.

Buber asserted that the culture of a period is formed by those creations which "heighten the character of life, elevate life values, enrich life possibilities and participate in the more noble and more intensive shaping of life."[59] The problem was that, as Nietzsche had already stated, values had been stood on their head.[60] The quality of German culture was not what it used to be, and neither was its individual counterpart, *Bildung* (personality development). "*Bildung* originally stood for a strong and beautiful unfolding [*Entfaltung*] of the personality, a quiet harmonizing of all energies and a noble unity of expressive style in all matters, but now *Bildung* means merely a colorful admixture of unrelated, thoughtlessly amassed knowledge."[61] Like the concept of culture, the concept of *Bildung* evolved in the age of idealism with Johann Gottfried Herder, Gotthold Ephraim Lessing, Friedrich Schiller, and Goethe. *Bildung* is "basic education of the whole human being—intellect, will, and feeling—within the totality of being." *Bildung*, of necessity, encompasses religion. The ways or methods of acquiring this education are not limited. The primary principle of *Bildung* is the notion of freedom—a sense of what it means to be a free human being and the possibilities contained therein.[62] In Buber's view, *Bildung* holds the place for individuals that culture holds for periods and nations.[63]

Buber asserted that at the turn of the century, the terms *culture* and *civilization* were confused because his contemporaries did not significantly distinguish between them. He charged that "culture is currently being terribly misused" because "the large mass of contemporaries" lacked "purity of thought and delineation of concepts," or, if they possessed these qualities, they despised them as did the poet Altenberg. Instead of providing "a new and personal content and a continued harmonization of energies which manifests itself in a larger or smaller degree of harmony in one's life-style, depending on the stage of culture," the word *culture* "is deprived of its proud and eloquent meaning and is reduced to a collective term for the so-called 'achievements of modernity.' "[64] Buber's criticism reflected Nietzsche's thought in *Zarathustra*. Convinced that Nietzsche was the philosophical prophet of a new age, Buber applied his lessons to his own perception of the world.

For Buber, culture and civilization fell into the same distinctive categories schematically as did the new and the old community. Culture is idealistic while civilization is practical. Both are necessary for life, but one—culture—is the leaven, while the other—civilization—produces the concrete results.

Culture has one purpose only, and that is to create beauty. The labors of culture are never practical by intent; rather, they are the bountiful overflow of the soul. Though God is not mentioned in the essay, for Buber culture emanates directly from God, the ultimate creator of beauty. In culture, the creative principle rules. "The products of culture are not utilitarian, but beautiful, they are the creation of a surplus of the soul."[65]

Culture lavishes, that is, no expense of time, energy, or resources is too great, for the creation of culture is an outpouring of Divine grace on humanity.[66] God lavishes His energy on the world, never diminishing the source, and the artist or other human creator does the same.

Culture is something distinct, ruled by its own laws. It does not follow the laws of common sense or any other laws we know; it is beyond human law. Culture elevates and ennobles life—it gives life an extra dimension beyond the ordinary—through art, music, or spirit. We must therefore accept culture as a gift, even if we do not understand it. "The masters of culture create beyond their will: something new and unexpected arises from their labors and supersedes them; they achieve something different and better than what they dreamed of; their creation is not like a human product, but like a new being, arisen from a dark region, not comparable to anything existing; like the promise of a new way of life."[67] These images come straight out of Goethe's *Faust*.

Every true creation bears the stamp of necessity; that is, it is created by a specific individual in a specific period. Every epoch and people has its own distinct culture, never to be repeated by any other period or people. Culture develops in paradoxes and without continuity; it always belongs to a certain period with whose peculiar expressiveness it arises and disappears. Artistic or social movements are therefore unique, onetime events in history and are irreplaceable. Likewise, culture has an individualizing effect on people and insists on a fuller expression of the personal elements.[68]

Culture is also only for a select few, not for the masses. "Culture cannot thrive in the broad stream [of society]." A popular movement such as Zionism, however, would be capable of creating a bridge from these "productive individuals" to the masses, thus mediating the culture to the common folk.[69]

Civilization is different. According to Buber, civilization applies itself to what is useful or utilitarian. Buber was not interested in discussing the fruits of civilization, and he did not give examples to illustrate his points. Civilization, he felt, is for the masses. It follows the broad stream, pleasing the greatest number with the minimum amount of resources. Civilization must economize; it maintains and simplifies life. The workers of civilization set goals and reach them. Civilization invents ever new means of coping with life. Although Buber stopped short of Nietzsche's dichotomy of masters and slaves, the terminology Buber applied to the person of civilization and to the person of culture will not be lost on the reader. One who labors for civilization is a worker, and one who produces culture a master. "The workers of civilization set goals which they reach; but the masters of culture achieve beyond their will." Civilization therefore deals with the infrastructure of living, the mundane, everyday tedium no human being can escape. For the creator of a new world, such as Buber, it was not worth discussing.[70]

Although Buber was purposefully rigid in separating the two spheres of culture and civilization in this essay, he did not in reality advocate such rigidity. He did so only for the sake of clarity, wanting it understood that civilization and culture are not to be thought of in the same way.

Both of Buber's essays "Alte und Neue Gemeinschaft" and "Kultur und Civilisation," are very abstract and very vague. They foreshadow more specific projects, both in Buber's life and in humanity's journey, but they were not blueprints for any particular program. At this very time, however, when the critic Buber expressed himself so vaguely and schematically on contemporary topics, the idealist Buber had already spent three years passionately contributing to Jewish cultural renewal in a major and concrete way. He had written many poems, among them "Unseres Volkes Erwachen" (The awakening of our people) (1899),[71] been a delegate to the Third Zionist Congress (1899),[72] and was producing a profusion of speeches and essays that dealt with all aspects of the Jewish cultural renaissance among German Jewry for whose realization he labored so vigorously. At the same time, Buber also was a student at the universities of Vienna, Leipzig, Zurich, and Berlin, where he struggled with contemporary cultural issues and studied the history of art and philosophy.

2

ACADEMIC BEGINNINGS

Apprenticeship in Aesthetics, 1897–1904

BUBER FIRST matriculated at the University of Vienna, the k.k. Universität, in January 1897.[1] Although he specifically stated in his *Autobiographical Fragments* that he spent the first year of his university studies in Vienna, he also concluded that

> the lectures of those two semesters, even the significant scholarly one, did not have a decisive effect on me. Only . . . the seminar as such immediately exerted a strong influence: the regulated and yet free intercourse between teacher and students, the common interpretations of texts, in which the master at times took part with a rare humility, as if he too were learning something new, and the free exchange of question and answer in the midst of all scholastic fluidity—all this disclosed to me, more intimately than anything that I read in a book, the true reality of the spirit, as a "between."[2]

Despite the positive experience of the seminar and his lasting interest in the spiritual dimension of life, it seems that during this year Buber exchanged the classroom for the theater. By his own account, the theater managed to do what the classroom could not, namely hold the young rebel's attention. He wrote:

> What affected me most strongly . . . was the Burgtheater into which at times, day after day, I rushed up three flights after several hours of "posting myself" in order to capture a place in the highest gallery. When far below in front of me the curtain went up and I might then look at the events of the dramatic *agon* as, even if in play, taking place here and now, it was the word, the "rightly" spoken human word that I received into myself, in the most real sense. Speech here first, in this world of fiction as fiction, won its adequacy; certainly it appeared heightened, but heightened to itself. It was only a matter of time, however, until—as always happened—someone fell for a while into a recitation, a "noble" recitation. Then, along with the genuine spokenness of speech, dialogical speech or even monological . . . this whole world, mysteriously built out of surprise and law, was shat-

tered for me—until after some moments it arose anew with the return of the over-against.[3]

It is obvious from both of these personal reflections that Buber was extremely sensitive to any action that seemed to him to be forced and was attracted to spontaneous discourse rather than to finished, polished declamations, whether on the stage or in the classroom. At the same time, however, he was cognizant of the living, dialogical nature of the two kinds of speech and of the need for both.

University Studies: From Kant to Nietzsche and Beyond

Given his strong interest in philosophy even before his university years, Buber's course of study was not unpredictable. In his *Autobiographical Fragments* he commented on his strong attachment to two recent philosophers—Immanuel Kant (1724–1804), who created modern, systematic philosophy, and Friedrich Nietzsche, who undid it. They "entrenched directly upon my existence—in my fifteenth and in my seventeenth year,"[4] while he still lived in Lemberg (Lvov).

At that age, he was already occupied with philosophical questions, suffering great anguish over his inability to come to terms with the existence of space and time. "The question about time had oppressed me in a far more tormenting fashion than that about space. I was irresistibly driven to want to grasp the total world process as actual, and that meant to understand it, 'time' either as beginning and ending or as without beginning and end. At each attempt to accept them as reality, both proved equally absurd." Buber credited Kant's *Prolegomena* (1783) with coming to his rescue at this time. He recounted that from it he learned that for Kant, "space and time are 'nothing more than formal conditions of our sensory faculty,' " that they are "not real properties that adhere to the things in themselves" but "mere forms of our sensory perception. This philosophy exercised a great quieting effect on me. The question was explained as unanswerable by its nature, but at the same time I was liberated from it, from having to ask it. Kant's present to me at that time was philosophical freedom."[5]

Although Buber was not interested in engaging Kant's rigorous philosophical system, while at the same time criticizing his contemporaries for not being rigorous enough in their speculations, he actually took quite a bit from Kant, without acknowledging his indebtedness. When he later posited two realities, the relative in relation to Zionism and the absolute in relation to Hasidism,[6] these two conceptions ran parallel to Kant's phenomenal and noumenal. Kant provided an invaluable service of liberation for Buber during this period, while Nietzsche had the opposite effect.

Friedrich Nietzsche: Herald of a New Dream

Buber applied Nietzsche's concept of "eternal return" to his revitalization of Judaism, evaluating Nietzsche's intent in *Thus Spake Zarathustra* (1883–91) as follows:

> Nietzsche himself wished "the basic conception" of this book to be understood as an interpretation of time: its interpretation as "eternal return of the same," that is, as an infinite sequence of finite periods of time, which are like one another in all things so that the end phase of the period goes over into its own beginning. This conception . . . is . . . the utterance of an ecstatically lived-through possibility of thought played over with ever new variations. The "Dionysian" pathos has by no means been transformed here into a philosophical one, as Nietzsche already had in mind. It has remained Dionysian, as its modern variant, produced by the enthusiasm of the Dionysian man over his own heights and depths.[7]

Buber spoke, almost with resentment, of the way Nietzsche took possession of his mind and imagination:

> About two years after that [his liberation from the category of time by Kant] *the other book took possession of me* [emphasis added], a book that was, to be sure, the work of a philosopher but was not a philosophical book: Nietzsche's *Thus Spake Zarathustra*. I say "took possession of me," for here a teaching did not simply and calmly confront me, but a willed and able—splendidly willed and splendidly able—utterance stormed up to and over me. This book, characterized by its author as the greatest present that had ever been made to mankind up till then, worked on me not in the manner of a gift but in the manner of an invasion which deprived me of my freedom, and it was a long time until I could liberate myself from it.[8]

The hero Zarathustra railed against passive resignation, projecting a strength, vitality, and optimism that had not been known in German culture since the time of the romantics. Nietzsche's powerful, persuasive, even seductive ideas in this book clothed in poetic form swept away the ultimate reserve with which the tradition had equipped the young Buber. Two years later he was on his way to Vienna, still totally under the spell of Nietzsche's powerful imagery.

In December 1900, Buber published his article "Ein Wort über Nietzsche und die Lebenswerte" (A word on Nietzsche and life values), in a women's magazine called *Die Kunst im Leben* (Art in life).[9] As we learn from Buber's later recollections, at age seventeen he decided to translate Nietzsche's *Zarathustra* into Polish because "I was . . . so taken by the book."[10] Nietzsche's Dionysian dynamics and superiority of will captured and held Buber's imagination for a long time. As late as 1913, in his work *Daniel*, Buber was still recreating *Zarathustra*. The idea for *Daniel* was inspired by his literary hero, Nietzsche, and the activism by his contemporary hero, Gustav Landauer.[11]

As we can readily see from this article, and despite Buber's reservations in *Encounter*, Nietzsche was a personality after his own heart. In contrast to Arthur Schopenhauer's apathetic human being, Nietzsche created a hero who took on Messiah-like stature in "a time of smallness." Buber compared Nietzsche to the decadent turn-of-the-century personalities for whom "the relations between human beings had become small, pitifully small, and the relationship of the human being to himself and to his own development was in the deepest core rotten." In Buber's mind, Nietzsche "fought with the finest and noblest sword of the century against the prevailing metaphysics and morality, for he saw in them tools and symptoms of decaying life."[12] In his dramatic way, Buber painted a Siegfried-like Nietzsche as the herald of truth and resurrection.[13] Of Nietzsche, Buber wrote:

> He uncovered the feeble lies of our values and our truths. But the tip of his raised sword glistened purple in the light of the rising sun. He found fresh, powerful seed corns in ancient royal crypts; from dead cultures he wrested elements for new formation. In the confused and barren turmoil of the present, he collected the authentic and the productive. He erected in front of our eyes the statue of the heroic human being who creates his own self and beyond his self. In place of a thin and lame altruism he put the egotism of his own development and the virtue of giving; in place of pity he put cooperation and shared joy [*Mitfreude*]. To those who worshiped the beyond, he taught the noble meaning of the earth and of the human body. He contrasted the ideal of a comfortable and painless life with a stormy

> and dangerous life, whose powerful beauty is enhanced by the pain. Instead of happiness for the greatest number, he considered the creation of great people and great ideas to be the purpose of humanity.[14]

This characterization sums up in a few lines the effect Nietzsche had on Buber and others in the early twentieth century. *Comfort* was a word Nietzsche abhorred because it implied complacency. In *The Genealogy of Morals*, Nietzsche unmasked the shallow values and the slave morality that had become the accepted norm, and he exposed the perverted altruism that had taken the place of true compassion.[15] He reached back to ancient civilizations very much the way Buber did, for inspiration and for guidance in authentic values. In *The Birth of Tragedy*, Nietzsche protested against the uninspired philological methods of his age, a criticism that Buber adopted.[16] In Buber's view, Nietzsche defied classification. He could not be integrated into the Germanic system.

> Is he a philosopher? He did not create a unified edifice of thought. Is he an artist? He did not create any objects. Is he a psychologist? His deepest knowledge deals with the future of the soul. Is he a poet? Only if we think of poets *as they once existed* [emphasis added]: "Visionaries who tell us what might be," who give us "a foretaste of future virtues." Is he the founder of a new *Gemeinschaft*? Many rise up in his name, but they do not unite, for each one finds a different guiding light in this blessing night sky, his own, and only that, and each owes him not thanks for general knowledge of a kind that can unite people, but the release of his own innermost powers; it was not his deepest intention to share his innermost self, but to elicit from each that which is personal and productive, the most secret treasures of his individuality, and to transform them into agitating energy; heightening of general productivity, that's what he himself called the innermost meaning of his work.[17]

Buber admired Nietzsche, not because he was accomplished in form like von Hofmannsthal and others—on the contrary, Nietzsche was the patient who, in his sickness, taught about new health—but because he had a vision, a dream, and because he glorified concepts such as the will and rebirth, concepts that dominated Buber's thought. In fact, Buber took the theoretical construct for his very vague essay, "Alte und Neue Gemeinschaft," from the poetic reality of Nietzsche's world. In addition, Buber took from Nietzsche's ideas the possibility of Jewish renewal and the courage to transport the ancient Jewish foundation to the twentieth century via his own Dyonisian dithyrambs.

Buber was so taken by Nietzsche that he wrote a preface and reading guide to his own future "Zarathustra," which, however, he did not produce.[18] The preface, in neat latinized German script, with traces of the old *Fraktur*, is undated. It appears to be an early piece, addressed to his "future friends." In it, Buber explained, "This above all: if you ever come across a book on Friedrich Nietzsche with my name on the cover, please know that this is the introduction [*Einleitung*] as well as the manual [*Anleitung*] to its comprehension."[19] A poem on the cover page indicated that it was a work for initiates only.

> To you, the daring seekers, experimenters, and all
> those who ever sailed onto the terrible seas,
> To you, drunk on riddles, bedazzled by twilight,
> whose soul has been attracted to every deceptive
> abyss by the sound of flutes;
> For you do not wish to follow a lead by a coward;
> and, you hate to decipher where you can
> guess the answer—
> To you alone I will tell the riddle which I beheld,
> —the face of the most lonesome one.[20]

This essay provides insight into Buber's methodology at the time. He wrote: "It is my peculiarity to speak of each human being in his language, and when I sing of a person's harmony, I shall do it in his own rhythm. Forgive me, therefore, for the nonmethod [*Unart*][21] of these Zarathustra-sounds, oh my friends!"[22] The nonmethod he was about to imitate was, of course, Nietzsche's, who was well-known for his aphoristic style. Parenthetically, though, Buber, as much as he wanted to write like Nietzsche, was not particularly good at it, though he was good at writing systematic expositions. Many of his essays include a systematic history of an idea or a movement.

In these notes Buber compared himself to a patient who, on the model of Nietzsche, would find his own cure for his illness, if only to become sicker with a new illness. Buber claimed that he did not really understand this until he had become "a knowing one," which did not occur until a decade later.[23] Although he felt the power of the identity crisis he was undergoing, this was not the illness from which he was suffering. He lamented, "I, too, was grasped by your devil with its broad, earthy fangs: I called it 'system.' I wanted to force your dancing irresponsibility and poetical flights of fancy into gray, death-like theories. That was my illness: I did not believe in you, I believed you." But Zarathustra saved him.

> It came over me, like a revelation. . . . It is only a beginning . . . and truly also—think about it—a birth of tragedy from the musical spirit, but soon, so it seems to me, I will lose the thread of the maze. For it came over me like a gigantic chaos illuminated by flashes of uncreated light, a Dyonisian dithyramblike laughter, a childlike euphoria, a sublime joy, a first "yes." An intimation of dancing overcame me which pulled me upward into the deep black abysses.[24]

Buber here experienced his own *ekstasis* that transported him out of the world of philosophical systems to the realm of poetic freedom. In his own way, he had come full circle with Longinus of antiquity, whose inspired philosophy he admired.

Yet to have experienced this spiritual liberation from the world of Kantian reason without being able to share it would have been the same as experiencing a vision and keeping it to himself. Buber needed to communicate this experience to other kindred spirits, namely the friends of the future addressed in this essay: "Who, but you, wants to listen to the story of an illness with its convalescence and redemption, listen to it as your own inner joyful experience. Who besides you wants to—laugh blood—with me." Very much like a young romantic, Buber felt a need to share his creative but personal intoxication with others who had not, as yet, arrived on the stage of life: "Thus, oh you comrades of Zarathustra's, 'good Europeans' that you are, listen then to this confession, this fool's confession."

> No excuses! No forgiveness!
> You happy, free soul.
> Lend to this unreasonable book
> Ear, heart, and shelter!
> Believe me, friends, my unreason
> Did not lead to my undoing.[25]

Buber began the introduction by stating that he had to say a few words for the sake of order, after which he would no longer be permitted to know order. This piece of work brought out his disillusionment, at a very early stage in his studies, with contemporary German culture and the decadence of his age. Later in the essay, he confirmed this feeling:

> I was never an ultra-positivist. There was always a certain amount of romanticism in me, a kind of artistic will to create my own God, Zeus Cronius, ideal, *Übermensch*; self, Prometheus unbound [in English]; Peer Gynt, culture of beauty. And innumerable other elements: a deep, fanatical passion for the Greek ideal, an oceanic, limitless self-consciousness/self-unconsciousness, filled with sunshine and titanic paroxisms of madness; a raging hatred pregnant with disgust of the entire atmosphere in which I lived; a grim dislike of official morality; official *Bildung*, the conventional senile smiling, whimpering, and wordplays; tigerlike desires reaching to heaven, disdain, sickening disdain of all catholicism and asceticism, in short, a young, unbounding Dionysian power which wanted to sing, to fly, to laugh, to destroy, to build—to build castles in the air.[26]

Buber's essay on Zarathustra provided a unique glimpse into the unsettled mind of a young person who tried with all his might to free himself from the shackles of civilization and tradition in order to search for his genuine self. Not only Nietzsche had intimations of the future, so too did Buber; not only Nietzsche was sick, so too was Buber; not only Nietzsche submitted to Dionysian dithyrambs, so too did Buber. Buber fully realized that Nietzsche's thunderbolt approach was the only way to shake a dazed human being out of his lethargy, but at the same time he yearned for a "culture of beauty," confessed to an intimation of unlimited unity, and wanted to unleash the boundless energy within himself to create the self of his imagination.

Buber was quick to study the role models available to him and swift in implementing his visions through actual deeds. Only as an afterthought did he analyze and describe the action, sometimes disapproving and distancing himself from his deeds. We could therefore say about him what he said about Nietzsche:

> At all times there have been human beings who did not belong in a particular category and who cannot be labeled, for every classification does them violence: Every classification defies expressing the essential in them. Too many different spheres cross in them, for too many different intimations and dawns are they the mouthpiece and the aurora, and they cannot be forced into a particular conceptual box with others. They are great and defy definition as life itself does, whose apostle they are.[27]

Such individuals are, in fact, heralds of a new age. They announce a new and futuristic form of development for humanity. Their essence defies the language available to us because it is something that has never been before. The yearning of such individuals defies the power at our disposal; we can merely sense the potential locked up within them. To these individuals belonged Friedrich Nietzsche as well as Nicolas of Cusa and Jakob Böhme, whose thoughts Buber explored in his dissertation.

Buber attributed his acquisition of a philosophical foundation to "a thorough reading of Plato (Greek was my favorite language)." Yet the reading of Kant and Nietzsche were "events which broke through the continuity—the presupposition of all genuine educational work—catastrophic events. In the first of them the philosophy confronted the catastrophic situation, delivering and helping. In the second the philosopher not only stirred me up but transported me into *a sublime intoxication* [emphasis added]. Only after a long time was I able to escape this intoxication completely and attain to a certainty of the real."[28] Philosophy thus played a crucial and stimulating, though not always positive, role for Buber from a very early age. Regrettably, in these later, reflective comments, Buber ignored the crucial role this intoxicated state played in his powerful leadership in early Zionism.

Aesthetics

Buber's interest in aesthetics, a branch of philosophy, was directly related to his study of Nietzsche and his disillusionment with Christian-based German culture and the possibility that art might provide an alternative value system to religion. He had always considered art to be a powerful medium of communication and of transformation, a trend he adopted from the German romantics. Buber therefore immersed himself in a thorough study of the philosophy of art in the hope of discovering a way out of the cultural decline and a new way to the Divine.

Having shown an early and serious interest in the human soul, Buber was held captive by this interest for the rest of his life. Yet Buber's initial access to the soul came through an intellectual appraisal of a philosophical concept intricately tied to both philosophy and art and not through a faith experience. Buber was very much a modern individual, whose access to the infinite was mediated through a secular-rational channel, philosophy, and a secular-creative channel, art, like that of his contemporaries. Both of these allowed him to break out of the narrow confines of existence via the catalyst of the sublime, whose Dyonisian-dynamic *agon* transforms perceptions. Although Buber preferred that life's motivation be generated by a person's religious experience, as that of the Hasidim for example, his vision of the future did not result from religiosity but from education. He was realistic enough to understand that religiosity was not readily accessible to his contemporaries, and thus he considered culture to be an acceptable aid to the Divine.

The modern philosopher Buber made a clear distinction between the source of creative energy and the source of vision. In Buber's view, the philosophical sublime provided the creative energy or thrust for action that was necessary to effect any transformation. The Beautiful, on the other hand, provided an ideal that was to be realized by the harmonious unfolding of the potential, as in the organic plant and the microcosm, and not in the reconciliation of differences. Thus Buber found a reason to appreciate the philosophical sublime, present all around him, but at the same time he strove for a goal beyond philosophy, intimations of which he found in Moses Mendelssohn, Johann Wolfgang von Goethe, Nicolas of Cusa, and Jakob Böhme.

Discourse on the Sublime

In an essay from his student days, "Zu Schopenhauers Lehre vom Erhabenen" (On Schopenhauer's theory of the sublime), Buber traced the concept of the nobility of the soul from classical antiquity to Nietzsche. From this essay we see that this concept experienced metamorphoses of considerable dimension along the way. Buber began his analysis by focusing on "the most eloquent mark of differentiation" of the sublime in antiquity, "the stormlike, overpowering penetration of the sublime into the soul." We recognize the Dionysian might which Buber, on the model of Nietzsche, credited with providing the creative energy for all human production. "The sublime strikes [the soul] like lightning."[29] Buber called this noble spirit, which excites and invigorates the soul, "self-esteem" (*Selbstschätzung*).[30]

The philosophical concept of the sublime can be traced to the Greek philosopher Longinus,[31] who, in Monroe Beardsley's words, "is impatient with aesthetic problems, and is satisfied to say that the 'sublime' is what produces in the reader not mere pleasure or intellectual conviction, but transport [*ekstasis*]: the sense of being carried away, as though by magic. . . . 'The true sublime,' by some virtue of its nature elevates us: uplifting with a sense of proud possession, we are filled with joyful pride, as if we had ourselves produced the very thing we heard." For Longinus, the sublime was not in any way contingent upon human pain and suffering. Consisting of "large and important ('full-blooded') ideas" and "vehement emotion," *ekstasis* is capable, in Longinus's mind, "of creating great literature," a literature that is "intense and elevated in its qualities" or "moves the reader deeply and yet nobly."[32] Buber explained that the teaching of aesthetics experienced a decline during the first century C.E., and then the concept of *ekstasis* was forgotten.

The dualistic concept of the sublime reemerged only in the sixteenth century, and in the eighteenth century it received royal treatment by the famous British parliamentarian Edmund Burke.[33] In Burke's essay *A Philosophical Inquiry into the Origin of Our Ideas of the Sublime and the Beautiful* (1757), the feeling of the beautiful and the feeling of the sublime derive from different basic powers in the soul. The beautiful derives from the desire to be social (*Geselligkeitstrieb*),[34] while the sublime emanates from the desire for self-preservation.[35] This distinction was of the utmost importance for Buber's future conception of priorities. He accepted Burke's assertion that the desire for self-preservation was initially more important than the desire to be social, but he rejected Burke's definition of *social* altogether. Buber considered sociability to be very important, yet one cannot be social if one does not first know how to survive. Hence self-preservation, a precondition of self-esteem, became the single most important characteristic of Buber's new concept of personality. Buber welcomed the return to the "dualistic theory" in Burke's writings because of its ability to jolt people into action,[36] although he did not like the turn which discussions of the sublime took with Kant and later philosophers.

Buber was disturbed by Kant's negative perception of the will, an energy source Buber considered to be Divine and therefore positive and good.[37] God created the world by fiat, by His Will, and human beings, who are created in His image, can also create worlds if we allow our imagination free reign; but we certainly cannot do so when we perceive the model, namely God, to be negative. With Kant, new imagery entered into the discussion, namely a negative perception of creation. Nature as well as the senses were fear-arousing and dangerous, and humanity, as a moral entity, had to subdue both by brute force, not by a synthesis forged by the creative imagination. This ascetic tendency, which grew out of Kant's Christian background, was unnatural for Buber because, as he wrote many times, God in His infinite goodness created nature as well as the human senses and, therefore, all of creation is good. To create a moral being through the suppression of the senses, as Kant argued, was not an act of free human choice but a coercive measure that denied the human being the chance to act morally in accordance with his or her intrinsic morality. In Kant, the will was not creative energy as it was in God and would be in Nietzsche but was viewed rather as the censor that suppressed the senses. Buber could not follow Kant's path, for in his view, even the evil inclination is in the service of the Divine and can be transformed into good.

The subject of the sublime became of the utmost importance during the neoclassical period, 1730 to 1830, especially for Friedrich Schiller (1759–1805), who, together with Johann Wolfgang von Goethe (1749–1832), created a neoclassicism that captured the imagination of the literary elite of the period. Schiller was Buber's childhood idol. Although a student of Kant's, Schiller did not ascribe the same negative function to the will as Kant did, and though Schiller retained Kant's negative attitude toward the senses, asserting that we feel the sublime as a result of overcoming our sensuality, the very overcoming of our sensuality is tied to the autonomy of our will—our freedom to choose this path. Schiller's theory of the sublime, though ascetic, was not coercive but voluntary.[38]

According to Schiller, "All other creatures *must*, the human is the only being who can will." That is, only the human being has the capacity to make choices. Nothing offends human dignity as much as force, for force negates our humanity. But the Nietzschean superman had not yet come along, and Schiller could not conceive of the human being who was strong enough to ward off outside force. This inability to reconcile capacity with need created an unhappy contradiction. In Schiller's conception, culture stepped in to help the human being assert his will. Culture forms the moral being, and only the morally educated person is completely free. "Either he is superior to nature as a power or he is in agreement with it. No act of nature can become force, for before the action reaches him, it has already become his action as well, and dynamic nature can never get to him and harm him." The sublime transforms an act of nature into the human will. It allows humanity to act freely, completely unaffected by the senses, "as if the spirit obeyed only its own laws."[39]

Schiller focused primarily on the positive aspects of the individual personality, which was helpful to Buber in constructing his own theory of personality. Schiller asserted that "we tremble before a terrible power" but that we are left with the sure thought that the rationality and indestructibility of our being will prevail. This certainty "constitutes a triumph which lifts us beyond all the defeats of our sensuality." It allows us to feel sublime because we become aware that we, "even as victims of this terrible power, do not have to fear for our independent selfhood, for the autonomy of the will."[40]

Although Buber pointed out that Arthur Schopenhauer (1788–1860) retained Kant's and Schiller's basic conception as well as their systematic methodology, Buber did not like the passive character Schopenhauer created. He asked, "Does not character develop necessarily from the relationship of one human being to another?" He questioned whether we can still speak of character when the dynamics of this relationship no longer exist.[41] Such an individual, whom Buber perceived to be apathetic toward his fellow human beings, did not possess the strong personality that Buber desired for community building, but rather resembled the slave personality against which Nietzsche railed.[42] Despite Nietzsche's high praise for Schopenhauer, the latter's negation of the will dismissed him altogether from Buber's intellectual universe.

The Beautiful

In his essay "Schopenhauers Lehre vom Erhabenen" (On Schopenhauer's theory of the sublime), Buber no more than pointed to the distinction between the two concepts of the monistic sublime (the Beautiful) and the dualistic sublime (the philosophical sublime).[43] But he did single out Moses Mendelssohn, Kant's contemporary and counterpart,[44] who "discussed another side of this very same subject," the Infinite, at the same time that Burke and Kant were developing their theory of the philosophical sublime. According to Buber, Mendelssohn thought that "*the Infinite which we consider a whole* [emphasis added], but cannot encompass, causes a mixed feeling of pleasure and of discomfort. The magnitude of the subject creates pleasure, but our inability to grasp its [the Infinite's] limits mixes this pleasure with some bitterness which enhances it." Two thousand years earlier, Longinus had noted, "When we follow these flights of fancy, we forget that we are human beings, that is, weak, limited human beings, and retain only that in our nature which elevates [*erheben*] us to the dignity of the gods."[45] Mendelssohn also blamed human limitation for the inability to comprehend, for if the Infinite acts upon the human soul, there can only be unity, no essential dualism or separation, merely inadequacy. The imagination is therefore not limited to activation by the philosophical sublime; it can also be activated by the monistic sublime, or Beautiful.

Buber was very interested in the ideal of the Beautiful, which he developed in his association with Die Neue Gemeinschaft, in his dissertation, and in his Hasidic studies. In contrast to the philosophical sublime, the Beautiful that Buber envisioned is the result of Divine bounty, which lavishes its treasures on humanity; there is no struggle involved. The Beautiful, represented in Moses Mendelssohn's concept of harmony and Johann Wolfgang von Goethe's idea of the beautiful soul, overflows.[46] Jakob Böhme's theosophy also expressed unity between humanity and God as the most important quality of life.

Because of his ultimate dissatisfaction with aesthetics as a foundation for life, and despite his continued admiration for Nietzsche, Buber decided to take another look at two earlier thinkers, Nicolas of Cusa and Jakob Böhme. Having agonized over philosophical issues throughout his student years, Buber was so intent on resolving this particular philosophical issue, the foundation of individuation, that he chose to write his dissertation on the problem of individuation.[47] Buber's focus on two theologians indicates a resolution of his struggle with aesthetics and, in a sense, a liberation from Nietzsche's spell.

Even though God as the source of human individuation was not a popular conception in Buber's time, Buber decided that he wanted to give individualism a metaphysical foundation. To be sure, art continued to have a prominent place in Buber's theological basis of life. After all, God is the greatest artist of all. His is the ultimate concept of beauty, as it is realized in creation, and humanity ever after strives to approximate this Divine norm. The difference between a theological conception and one that is rooted in a philosophical-aesthetic basis is that in the latter there are many different conceptions of the nature of the source, whereas in the former God and only God can be the source of our ideals.

The manuscript, which was completed in 1904, was intended as part of a larger work on "the history of the question of individuation from Aristotle to Leibniz and beyond,"[48] but this systematic history was never written.

Buber's knowledge of Nicolas of Cusa and Jakob Böhme was mediated for him by Wilhelm Dilthey, his teacher.[49] Both stood at the threshold of respective new eras. Cusa was a theologian, philosopher, and mathematician, who loved science and mathematics as much as he did classical antiquity.[50] Jakob Böhme was not the educated scholar that Cusa was. In fact, Böhme, a cobbler by profession, was not formally educated. He was born near Görlitz in Silesia, and his contribution to mystical literature consisted of rapt ecstasies. The Catholic church did not view his ecstatic confessions kindly and forbade his writing. Buber looked to Cusa and Böhme as models for a communion with God because for Buber the experience of the soul was the very basis of life. His interest in their thought was very specific. In the preface to his dissertation, Buber pointed out that Cusa and Böhme were

> two of the founders of the more recent metaphysical individualism. They were authentic philosophical representatives of their [respective] epochs, whose desire for personality was described so convincingly by Wilhelm Dilthey.[51] They were two of the first thinkers who formed the transcendental foundation of the very personality ethics which found its most ideally harmonious expression in [Friedrich] Schleiermacher [1768–1834] and its most convincing literary expression with [Ralph Waldo] Emerson [1803–82].[52]

The "desire for personality" in Cusa and Böhme interested Buber. But it was just an idea, not a reality. Individuation was the prototype of individualization, which was first realized only during the romantic period. Hence Cusa and Böhme were able to provide merely the very basic building blocks, the idea, for a transcendental foundation of community.

Buber complained that contemporary scholarship showed interest only in "Cusa, the theoretician of knowledge" (*Erkenntnistheoretiker*) and in "Böhme, the theologian." But *Erkenntnis* (knowledge) was on the wrong side of the Cusa phenomenon that Buber was interested in, namely, the spirit; and systematic theology, as seen in Ernst Tröltsch and others, was the core of rational theology and of dogma and was not the part of Böhme that interested Buber. With his dissertation, Buber intended to rescue Cusa and Böhme from the "commonly accepted perception" that these two thinkers were not among the founders of the more recent metaphysical individualism.[53] In fact, Buber considered Cusa and Böhme to be *the* founders of the idea of metaphysical individualism and two strong personalities who deserved to be studied, though not imitated, because they represented models of original thought. He found the two to be daring individuals who expressed opinions that were contrary to those expressed by the major thinkers of their own day. This made them "activists of the word," a term he attributed to himself as well.[54]

Buber shared with Cusa and Böhme an interest in the "development of the multiplicity and manifoldness of the sensory world from the unity and simplicity of the idea,"[55] though this development found a different expression in Cusa than in Böhme. In Cusa, it consisted of "the birth of relative realities from absolute reality," whereas in Böhme the idea meant "realization of the absolute possibility."[56] What mattered to Buber was the organic process and the centrality of God in the scheme.

Nicolas of Cusa

Buber saw Nicolas of Cusa as *ein Ahnender* (one who anticipates), like Böhme and Nietzsche.[57] Cusa had also been part of a renewal, the European Renaissance, and Buber perceived him as a model in the shaping of new ideas. Although Cusa did not have to deal with the human being's alienation from God and from self as Buber did, his task consisted of mediating between mysticism and Scholasticism.[58] In Buber's view, Scholastic philosophy, in contrast to Nietzsche's existential philosophy, was primarily theoretical; it merely progressed to the formulation of a concept, which it placed in the context of other, general concepts, and was not an imperative for action. In Buber's opinion, medieval Scholasticism remained decidedly on the far side of "the revolution of ideas" ushered in by Nicolas of Cusa.[59]

Buber pointed out that although there had been brief glimpses of personality and individuality during the Middle Ages, these were not conscious, sustained efforts to realize oneself. In fact, Buber argued that, in accordance with the leveling tendencies of the period, the issue of fundamental distinctiveness was neglected throughout the Middle Ages. Cusa once more revived the idea of the individual in his uniqueness and the absolute and irreplaceable value of the individual *as* individual. With his formulation of the problem of individuation, meaning "the process of individual differentiation and uniqueness," Cusa established himself as the first modern thinker. Yet all the possibilities he entertained were constrained by "the narrow, lifeless, foreign-to-reality schemes of the just completed epoch [Scholasticism]," while the new was still in the making and therefore resisted clear expression.[60] This was a symptom of changing times, also visible in Buber's own first theoretical efforts, "Alte und Neue Gemeinschaft" and "Kultur und Civilisation."

Buber pondered what the significance of individual differentiation might be. According to Cusa, the purpose of creation is the employment of Divine energy for differentiation. "God Himself is the most perfect artist." In accordance with the Divine plan, individual development reveals God Almighty in His infinite variety and beauty. Buber saw diversity as an intrinsic quality of beauty: "Infinite beauty can shine forth only in infinite manifoldness." Although diverse eternal elements manifest themselves in a limited and finite way in the individual, every person develops his or her unique potential and preserves his or her uniqueness. "All things progress toward completion individually."[61]

Buber saw in Cusa an opportunity to recover the key to the Divine that was lost and to start anew in an effort to reestablish contact with the Creator of all life. If the multiplicity of fundamentally different, even contradictory, things in the world is contrasted with the absolute unity and uniformity of the Divine, the question arises, How are these two spheres of absolute unity and of relative multiplicity related? Buber asked, How does the world evolve from eternity?[62]

According to Cusa, God reveals Himself in individual things in such a way that He is fully present in each, but "in a different degree of realization and potential, of consciousness and unconsciousness." From this, Buber concluded, "If the purpose of Divine self-revelation is realized most completely in fundamental differentiation, then the distinction between beings cannot be of a basic, qualitative nature, because everything is contained in everything." Rather, their function is complementary, with the soul being the unifying principle of the individual, its enfolding, as the body is the diversifying principle, or unfolding.[63]

Cusa's observation that the soul has the same relationship to the body that God has to the world was immensely useful to Buber because it meant that the world is the body of God. Such a perception allowed Buber to see God as transcending the universe and also being simultaneously immanent in it. Most important, creation reflects the essence of God, for "every created thing is . . . a finite Infinity, it is God created."[64] To assert, as Cusa did, that we have knowledge of the essence of God was a bold step in itself, for throughout the Middle Ages, God had been knowable only in what He was not. No one had dared to assert that the created world reflected God's essence. By his reading of Cusa, Buber totally negated the predominant dualistic worldview that had taken on renewed currency during the Enlightenment and lasted into his own time.

According to Buber, Cusa based individuation on the principle of noncontradiction, which "unites totality and particularity, infinity and temporality, unity and differentiation." Cusa derived this principle from the concept of potentiality. In Buber's reading, potentiality for Cusa was not nonbeing but "minimal being, from which an infinite range of degrees leads to Divine perfection."[65]

Although in Cusa the possibility of transformation from potential to actual exists in everything, "no being can ascend to a higher rung" because "reality and potential were distributed in different ways and degrees within the particular level of creation: the degree initially was no more than the form which was gradually realized, as more and more potential became actuality." This process parallels that of God's emanation (*Auswicklung*) or becoming.[66] He, too, unfolds. According to Buber, "this process of actualization constantly brings the individual closer to his own perfection," which means to God. Cusa's view was indeed enlightened, for he suggested that "the God-proximity for the individual consists of his meeting his own needs"; when these are met, then the individual has achieved his form (*Urbild*) as well as his goal, and he comes to complete rest.[67] Thus human completion is also the perfection of God.

In Buber's reading, Divine energy plays an important role in individual realization. God Himself advances creation toward realization of its potential. "God does not want to abolish the particularity of things, in which He has revealed Himself, but He wants to complete the thing within Himself—*perfection of personality, not depersonalization* leads creation back to God" (emphasis added). The human being contains all things, as does God, but while "in God things exist as forms, in the human being they emerge as relationships and as values."[68] This transformation of Divine essence into ethical imperatives in humanity was of great interest to Buber. In his own philosophy, the individual's capacity for decision was of the utmost importance.

Jakob Böhme

In 1901, three years before he completed his dissertation, Martin Buber published an article on Jakob Böhme in the Vienna newspaper *Wiener Rundschau*.[69] Böhme's theory primarily expanded and elaborated on Cusa's thought, providing a bridge from the Renaissance to the romantics.

Böhme's interest centered on the relationship of the individual to the world as one of individual striving, a new idea since the time of Cusa. Buber considered Böhme to be "the individualist of German mysticism" because, "for him, the problem of individuation was the problem of the real essence of creation." In his dissertation, Buber pointed out that Böhme perpetuated Cusa's thoughts of organic unity and the microcosm via the works of two other mystics—Paracelsus and Valentin Weigel.[70] By adopting Paracelsus's "pan-organic philosophy of nature," Böhme attempted to explain the contradiction between the all-inclusive character of the individual and the complete distinctiveness of all individualities. Like Cusa, Böhme argued that if all elements are present in every creation, each must operate via "a creative principle that singles out certain elements and qualities to form an individual." Nature is the helpmate of God in this process of selection, choosing from the multitude of possibilities that exist potentially. Yet in contrast to Cusa, who apprehended the universe only intellectually—"all *ideas* are contained in every individual, only in different *degrees of consciousness*," Böhme conceived of the world existentially. He understood "the inclusiveness of the individual" to mean "realization of the absolute potential," that is, "all *qualities* are contained in every individual, only in different *degrees of development*" (emphases added).[71]

Buber admired Valentin Weigel, a somewhat older contemporary of Böhme's, who contributed to Böhme's deeper understanding of the problem of individuation, particularly his "creativity of thought," a quality Buber did not ascribe to Cusa or Paracelsus. Buber thought that Weigel actually superseded Böhme in stating that "God becomes God only through creation." "All creatures in their particularity are *different stages of development* of Divine life." The creative process is God's way of getting to know Himself. Buber noted that Weigel's 1615 book, *Erkenne Dich Selbst* (Know thyself), "exerted the greatest influence on Böhme," whose *Mysterium Magnum* was published eight years later, in 1623.[72]

Buber attributed to Weigel the organic conception of creation. This idea stood in contrast to the prevailing Aristotelian mechanistic and atomistic conception of the universe still visible in Cusa. Thus the concept of the *Urpflanze*,[73] later popularized by Goethe, was already expressed by Weigel, who held that "God is the concept of all creation; He carries creation within as the seed contains all parts of the tree."[74] According to Weigel, the human being is the small world, a microcosm, and contains all there is to be found in the heavens and on earth as well as above them.[75] Although individuals cannot yet ascend to higher levels as they do during the romantic period, every life fits into a vertical chain, an idea Weigel appropriated from Cusa. All of these lives together complete Divine development (see Figure 3).[76] In German thought, the idea of personality stages of development within the individual asserted itself only during the romantic period, whose synthetic thought processes celebrated the possibility of individual human ascent to the universe.

The question of the purpose of a multitude of different, separate lives moved more and more into the center of Böhme's observations and culminated in his *Mysterium Magnum*, in which he applied the theory of the microcosm to the problem of individuation. If everything is contained in the human being, then everything unfolds from within, organically. We recognize the world because it is contained within us. According to Buber, this idea of the microcosm was merely indicated in antiquity and flitted around Scholasticism in a schematic but lifeless form.[77] After Cusa, Agrippa (1486–1535), Paracelsus, and Weigel, it was Böhme who developed the concept most beautifully and in accordance with our feelings: "God is not differentiated, but everywhere whole, and where He reveals Himself,

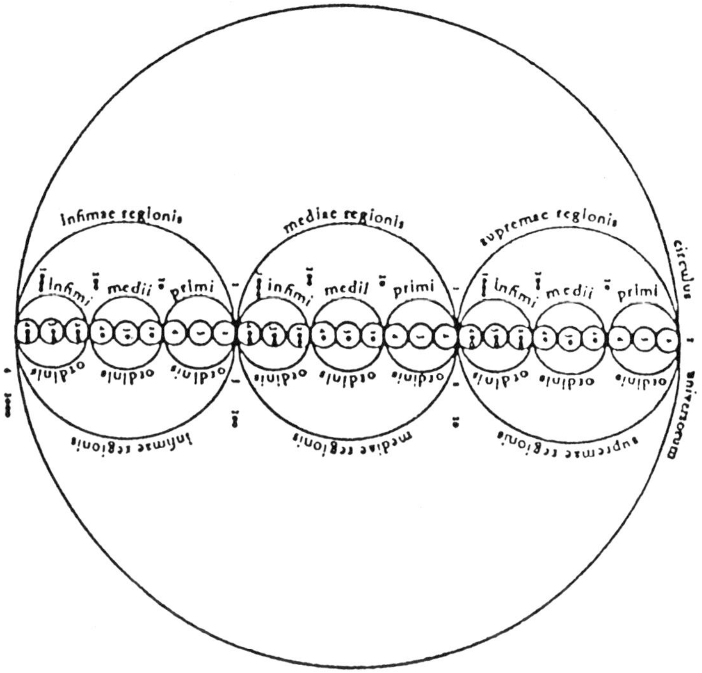

Figure 3. Diagram of Nicolas of Cusa's *Figura Universi* from Ronald Levao, *Renaissance Minds and Their Fictions: Cusanus, Sidney, Shakespeare* (Berkeley and Los Angeles: University of California Press, 1985), 52.

He reveals Himself in His totality."[78] Every single entity contains within it "*the qualities of all things*, and that which we call the particular individual is merely a higher degree of development of this or that quality" in that specific person. In Böhme's *Mysterium Magnum* we read, "Every star . . . has the qualities of all stars within, yet hidden, and we see only one (major) quality."[79] Thus every star displays different qualities which we perceive as unique, thereby creating the celestial stages of Valentin Weigel mentioned earlier.

Most important, because creation emanates from God and is an ongoing endeavor, in Böhme's view, human beings cannot perfect or fulfill themselves apart from God, for God holds the key to human creativity. For humanity to be able to produce, God has to "unlock our spirit with His spirit." Here Böhme intimated an idea that Friedrich Schleiermacher later developed prominently, that of the human being's "ultimate dependence" on God.

Böhme was in awe of the Divine creative process, considering the creation of diversity from unity as a miracle, an expression of God's "inscrutable manifoldness." Incapable of explaining how the form of creation was contained in God, he pondered: "We realize that God is no being as such, but merely the energy or the reason [*Verstand*] of the being in the form of an unfathomable, eternal Will." Divine energy was the unity of "an irrational, dynamic potential, not that of an absolute substance."[80] And yet Böhme maintained that "God and nature are one, like body and soul or rather, like energy and organism." Here Buber found what he was searching for—the certainty of unity between God and creation. "You can see . . . how nature cannot be differentiated from God's energies, all is one body.[81]

Energy as such is not visible. It becomes visible only through the activity of energies in nature—"God becomes God only through the creation of the world—for that reason the world is not in a state of being, but of becoming." This also means that "we don't have to accept the world as it is," but can change it. "Every morning reality offers itself anew to our creative hands," for "we are not the slaves [of our world], but the beloved," and "still today all possibilities are contained in the human creative act."[82] Such a positive attitude toward human productivity did much to bolster the sense of human purpose.

In Böhme's scheme, all things are moved by two basic energies: the yearning to play or struggle and the yearning to love. Struggle and love emanate from the same Divine source: "the yearning of things toward each other, which takes on different forms," depending on the origin. "The motion of struggle," by which he means play, "leads from God to the individual, the motion of love from the individual to God." All of creation comes into being through the tension that exists between different energies. Böhme wrote, "If this did not occur, there would be no nature, only eternal silence and no Will."[83]

To God in His greatness, creation is a voluntary giving of His resources and His energies. "All of God's creative activity is play for Him. Since play and creation are related in essence, both are an emanation of organic energy surplus freed from any utilitarian purpose." Just as "the sun gives of its strength without distinction, loving every fruit and plant, not withholding itself from anything; not wanting anything but to give a good fruit to a good plant, accepting all, good or bad, helping them to fulfill themselves, for she cannot help it," so God gives of Himself selflessly in creation. The overflowing that results from this activity between different elements within energy occurs in harmonious reciprocity according to the laws of the Divine Will. For Böhme, this creative play is the world's only meaning and purpose: "It [all the world] is the stage for the Divine energies 'to play their love games.' "[84]

The other activity, love, leads the individual in the opposite direction, toward a new unity of energies: "Every being yearns for the other, the upper for the lower and the lower for the upper, for they are different from each other, and in their yearning they meet."[85] Divine love, which is comparable to fire, attracts and consumes creation in a desire to return the essence to its origin.

For Böhme, play and love bridged the gap between the self and the world. In play, one self unfolds (*entfaltet*) the other and reveals its beauty, and in love, beings unite in God. From the mutual interaction of both, life derives; things are neither rigidly separate nor solidly fused, but they condition each other reciprocally. Thus, Böhme's conception of the relationship between play and love provided a non-narcissistic paradigm for self-fulfillment which provided Buber with a model of selfhood ideally suited to the formation of community. Böhme's process of completion was still lateral like Cusa's, however; his process of creation intimated "improvement" by changing stations. Such thoughts were, no doubt, connected to the newly emerging physical and social mobility at the dawn of the Enlightenment.

Cusa and Böhme provided Buber with the historical continuity of the idea that individuation is compatible with a belief in God. In fact, they provided Buber with a model of selfhood in God. Their "transcendental personality ethics" emanated from a conception of unity that superseded all Western duality and hence indeed superseded modernity. Their ethics allowed Buber to envision the achievement of a new kind of beautiful soul with God at the center. The approach of these thinkers was dialectical without being dualistic, for their philosophy was one of unity. Yet Buber did not find their philosophies to be totally satisfactory. They did not allow for a dynamic growth of the personality both physiologically and psychologically, but rather merely for an unfolding of the potential in the sense of Goethe's organic plant. Böhme's suggestion of stages was later taken up enthusiastically by the German romantics, for whom Böhme became the prophet, and whose vivid imagination developed his intimations to full bloom.

Schleiermacher and Emerson: Toward Transcendental Idealism

If we take a look at the reasons Buber thought that metaphysical individualism found "its most ideally harmonious expression in Schleiermacher" and "its most convincing literary expression with Emerson," we discover that Schleiermacher and Emerson effected a transformation of the metaphysical individualism which existed only schematically in Böhme. Schelling's formulation of transcendental idealism allowed these two thinkers to press their ideas into the service of social activism within their respective societies.[86]

In his famous *On Religion: Speeches to Its Cultured Despisers,* Schleiermacher wrote: "I speak to you, as a human being, from my point of view, of the sacred mysteries of humanity, of that which was in me when I, still in my youthful freethinking, searched for the unknown, and of that which . . . is the innermost catalyst of my being and which will forever remain the most important, no matter how the tendencies of time and humanity may move me."[87] Schleiermacher, who had lived and studied with the Pietists in Herrnhut, understood that the private communion with God must become a public celebration of the spirit because only in this public affirmation of private feelings can human individuation occur. In his fourth speech, Schleiermacher stated categorically, "When one has religion, it is of necessity social: this is not only intrinsic to the nature of the human being, but also most assuredly to the nature of religion. You have to admit that it is quite contrary to nature if the human being wants to shut away within himself what he has thought out by himself."[88] These private feelings which derive from man's *unio mystica* with God translate into "personality ethics" that coincide with God's Will. Yet the individual can only realize God's Will and thereby him or herself in activity within the human community. This is an idea Buber later developed in *Ich und Du* (I and thou) (1923).

For Schleiermacher, contemplation of the universe was the basis of all spiritual life, for "the universe is mirrored in humanity's inner life." This thought echoed Cusa and Böhme. Schleiermacher asserted that "the human being is finite and religion is infinite," therefore "no human being can fully comprehend religion." This idea had already been voiced by Moses Mendelssohn, who pointed to human limitation as the stumbling block to unity. Echoing Böhme, Schleiermacher lectured to his audience that there are different "kinds or degrees" of religion, therefore religion must contain within itself "a principle of individuation."[89]

Like Cusa and Böhme before him and Nietzsche and Buber later on, Schleiermacher considered himself a mediator for his contemporaries. He tried to show the "cultured despisers" among them that religion is not merely a dry system of dogmas but a personal concern for every person—an ethical imperative. Religion is "only another name for all higher feelings and aspirations; religion is the poetry of the soul."[90] But the audience he was addressing did not know anything of religion, let alone poetry of the soul, only aesthetics. Hence, after the long reign of rationalism, Schleiermacher, who saw contemporary culture to be the greatest impediment to true religion, tried once again to awaken the spirit of the German people.

Ralph Waldo Emerson, like Schleiermacher, sought to root the process of individuation within a communal framework. His unique approach, which consisted of a healthy dose of idealism mixed with a spiritual foundation for a God-fearing society, inspired Buber to push ahead with his own effort to realize the transformation of German Jewry. Emerson's significance lay in his perception of nature, much as Böhme had done, as a Divine and human helpmate in the perfection of the world. Emerson's conception of nature differed significantly from that of other post-Enlightenment thinkers and touched on Jean Jacques Rousseau, in that nature was benevolent.

> We must trust the perfection of the creation so far as to believe that whatever curiosity the order of things has awakened in our minds, the order of things can satisfy. Every man's condition is a solution in hieroglyphic to those inquiries he would put. He acts it as life, before he apprehends it as truth. In like manner, nature is already, in its forms and tendencies, describing its own design. Let us interrogate the great apparition that shines so peacefully around us. Let us inquire, to what end nature?

Nature for Emerson illumined the dark contours of the Divine plan. "It is the organ through which the universal spirit speaks to the individual, and strives to lead the individual back to it."[91]

Buber was able to point to Emerson in his assertion that the duality of nature and spirit was not unbridgeable and not a deterrent to unity. According to Emerson, the transcendentalist believes "in miracle, in the perpetual openness of the human mind to new influxes of light and power; he believes in inspiration, and in ecstasy." In Edward L. Ericson's view, Emerson, "the chief celebrant of individuality and self-reliance," possessed the key to the Divine. He "is . . . the foremost teacher of the eternal unity and of the essential identity of the individual self with the oversoul, the universal self. This dual aspect poses no problem or contradiction for transcendentalism, which sees a complementarity, a harmony, of the individual and the universal."[92]

Buber considered Emerson to be a courageous man, like Nietzsche. Emerson boldly asked: "Why should not we also enjoy an original relation to the universe? Why should not we have a poetry and philosophy of insight and not of tradition, and a religion by revelation to us, and not the history of theirs? . . . There are new lands, new men, new thoughts. Let us demand our own works and laws and worship."[93]

These were powerful words for a man like Buber, who was himself looking for a new way to bring about a revival of the spirit. Yet for Buber there were no new lands, only an ancient homeland, rediscovered, but there certainly were new people and new thoughts. According to Emerson, it was no longer necessary to be satisfied with telling the story of how things had been done. Rather, it was once again possible to be the creator, who knew how to perform the task at hand. Emerson's approach tore asunder the cobwebs of tradition that stifled human creativity, but without destroying the religious foundation Buber considered essential as a basis for life. Buber was forever looking for original thinkers and doers, and Emerson combined both aspects in a more perfect way than did anyone in Europe. Emerson's transcendentalism provided a more satisfactory harmony between nature (the created world) and spirit (God) than Cusa and Böhme had been capable of providing.

And yet if one asks where Buber found his heroes for the powerful and effective Zionist work he undertook from 1897 to 1904, one has to come back to the Dyonisian dynamics of Friedrich Nietzsche, for Nietzsche provided the model for Buber's own behavior. In studying the earlier thinkers, Buber saw the significance of their concepts for the Jewish people. Self-preservation and self-esteem were ideas of great importance to an ethnic group whose self was in the process of emancipation and whose liberation was overturning the traditional basis of communal life. Buber's interest in the problem and nature of individuation, therefore, was an *Antwortspruch* to a problem not yet articulated. His own application of this later theory had begun around the time when Theodor Herzl convened the First Zionist Congress in 1897, seven years before the completion of his dissertation. From then on, Buber addressed himself consistently to Jewish attainment of dignity in preparation for, and in anticipation of, full participation in a new Jewish community, and not only a human community.

3

KADIMA!
Apprenticeship in Jewish Culture, 1898–1905

The emancipation of German Jewry proceeded in fits and starts over the course of the nineteenth century. Throughout the century, advocates of religious reform had been stressing the need to modernize the meaning of Judaism and the nature of the liturgical service for the people. This new way of thought was nowhere more apparent than in the Jewish communities of central Europe, especially in the German states, where Abraham Geiger (1810–74), Gabriel Riesser (1806–63), and Samson Raphael Hirsch (1808–88) worked diligently to bring about major religious reforms. German Jews wanted Judaism to be seen as a respectable sister religion within contemporary society. Emancipation served as the framework for the completion of this modernization effort.

The Jewish community in Germany reorganized itself substantially in response to the demands of Emancipation. The power of the communal government, which had hitherto organized the life of ghettoized Jewry, diminished considerably. Instead, the *kehilla* became primarily a communal body with which one could choose to affiliate or not. The completion of Emancipation in 1871, however, proved to be less than fully satisfactory. To be sure, German Jews attained legal equality and gained economic and educational opportunity, but they were still barred from civil service jobs, the military, and full social acceptance. The last perhaps stung the most because it meant that even if the traditional German Jew was willing to take the step toward acculturation—a very big step—German society was to a great extent still closed to complete Jewish integration. In addition, a political version of anti-Jewish sentiment emerged in the form of anti-Semitism.

Nevertheless, with the freedom to choose a domicile, to choose one's occupation, and to choose one's course of study, the need to remain within the protective walls of the ghetto practically disappeared. Hence many—especially younger people, like Buber, eager to take advantage of the new opportunities—chose to turn their backs on their communities and often also on their tradition. Individuals who had clung to the Jewish community structure for support and protection in a hostile world could now leave the group and be assured of the right of citizenship, at least on paper. Thus, whatever Jewish community continued to exist operated under a changed mandate: the free choice of its members to belong to the existing community, to reform it along new lines, or to abandon it altogether.

Perhaps most important of all, people were free to choose their conception of Judaism and to live it. Religion was no longer the binding link among Jews that it had been traditionally. People now joined together because of a variety of interests or convictions or, less joyfully, for self-defense. This fragmentation of the group for the purpose of individual fulfillment seriously threatened the chances of survival for a people that had persisted for nearly two thousand years in a variety of cultural and social diaspora contexts. Now there was the danger that they might disappear among the nations like grains of sand at the seashore.

The affirmation of Jewish peoplehood began to emerge within one decade of German Jewry's political Emancipation. Expressions of Jewish nationhood were first identified with the nonpolitical Hibbat Zion (Love of Zion) movement and emanated from eastern Europe. Following the 1881 pogroms in Russia, a new Jewish interest in settling Palestine emerged. In 1884, Leo Pinsker founded Hibbat Zion, which represented an amalgamation of groups committed to Jewish resettlement in the ancient homeland.[1] For these Russian Jewish nationalists, a direct tie between the regeneration of the people and its settlement on the land was clear.[2] For some, the settlement idea possessed a mystical quality. According to Samuel Hayyim Landau, "the divine spark can influence our people only in its own land," and even more compellingly, "to dwell in the Holy Land is a mitzvah [holy commandment]."[3]

Zionism, a term coined by Nathan Birnbaum (1864–1937), came to mean different things to different people. The World Zionist Organization, founded by Theodor Herzl in 1897, became much more of an umbrella organization for diverse points of view and organizations than a unified political body. For example, Herzl stood for political or territorial Zionism, Ahad Ha-Am for spiritual or cultural Zionism, Rabbi Isaac Jacob Reines and the Mizrachi movement for religious Zionism, Aaron David Gordon for socialist mystical Zionism, and Chaim Weizmann for what later became known as synthetic Zionism.

Just as there were many different orientations within Zionism, Zionism was not the totality of Jewish worldviews. On the contrary, only a small percentage of German Jewry joined the Zionist cause, although the percentage in the East was larger. In addition to the continuation of traditional Judaism, which rejected the notion of a Jewishly initiated return to the ancient homeland, the liberal accommodationist position called for Jewish integration into Western life and supported the process of reform and expressions of acculturation. Furthermore, a decidedly anti-Zionist identity crystallized, which became known as diaspora Jewish nationalism. Jewish socialism flourished widely, and the Bund, the foremost exponent of the effort to harmonize Marxism with Jewish cultural nationalism, repudiated the Zionist idea. Some sought to weld together the secular Zionist initiative with traditional religious behavior.[4] A few Jewish individuals even favored a closer interaction between Zionism and the traditional Yiddish culture of eastern Europe. For instance, among Buber's papers was the protocol of a meeting held in Vienna in September of 1903 by a group that represented the interests of a segment of Galician Jewry.[5]

In this large sea of opinions, Martin Buber occupied a position between the Eastern thinker Ahad Ha-Am, associated with the Hibbat Zion movement, and Theodor Herzl. Buber supported Ahad Ha-Am on the issues of spiritual renewal and unification of flesh and spirit and, after initially supporting his ideas, fought Theodor Herzl because of his narrow political conception of Zionism. It was Buber's contention that the Jews in the diaspora had to be prepared for a Jewish way of life in the land of Israel. To that end, the specific task of the Zionist movement was to awaken the exilic Jew to his Jewishness. Buber saw it as his particular task to further the Jewish education of his fellow Jews. Although his focus within German culture and in his university studies was on philosophy and the philosophy of art, his Zionist interest focused on artistic production, not the critique thereof. This art took the form of literature, poetry, visual art, and new ways of Jewish life, indicated theoretically in Buber's 1901 essay on old and new community.

Buber's View of the Jewish Movement

Buber saw the Zionist movement as a propaganda organization and hence as the conscious member of a large organism.[6] This organism he called the Jewish movement.[7] Buber pointed out that the Jewish process of renewal contained the same elements that had been present in the great European Renaissance of the fourteenth and fifteenth centuries: the mystical-emotional element appeared as Divine wisdom, and the linguistic-idealistic element was called humanism. Both components, therefore, were not new but merely a renewal of submerged greatness.

Buber saw the Jewish movement as differing sharply from other nationalistic movements because it included all of modern Jewry, reaching beyond the national boundaries of a particular host country. The sole purpose of other nations was racial, based on blood and soil. Because the Jews were a mixture of many different races and did not own a homeland, their notion of peoplehood clearly differed from the other European efforts at nationhood. Buber considered the Jewish movement to be the umbrella for all that was consciously Jewish, a concept that stood in contrast to simply being born a Jew.[8] According to Buber, to understand the phenomenon of Jewish renaissance, one must comprehend it "as of one piece," or organic, a crucial term in Buber's language. Modern German culture was no longer of one piece.[9]

Buber placed the origins of the Jewish renaissance in the second half of the eighteenth century, when "the petrified existence of Juda ism was rejuvenated by two powerful streams from within and from without—Hasidism and Haskalah." These two movements reestablished the connection to the classical period of Judaism—the Hasidim via their piety (*Gottgefühl*) and the *maskilim* in their interest in the Hebrew language. The Hasidim renewed the Jewish *Uridee* of God-connectedness, while the *maskilim* renewed the interest of the people in their ancient language. In both cases, renewal rather than repetition or imitation was the key to their importance for Martin Buber. The Jewish renaissance was "not a return but a rebirth of the entire human being." From this stage, "slowly and gradually, a new type of Jew was developing."[10]

According to Buber's view of Jewish renewal, until the middle of the eighteenth century "the energy of Judaism was . . . held down by external forces," that is, "by suppression in the host nations, by fear and suffering, by dire need and crowded living conditions," as well as by internal conditions, "mainly the imprisonment of the 'Law,' " by which he meant "a misunderstood, obtuse, caricatured religious tradition." Buber accused the "foreign-to-reality imperative" of the tradition of destroying "all that was instinctively light and joyous, everything that thirsted for beauty and freedom. It caricatured feeling and handcuffed thought." By the eighteenth century "the Law [in Judaism] had reached a power it had not known in any people and in any period." Everything became subordinated to the Law. In contrast to the Jew of earlier times, the Jew of the Law era became "a passive hero," who "accepted all stages of martyrdom without sound, with a dead heart and dead lips, motionless." As far as Buber was concerned, only one Jew, Baruch Spinoza (1632–77), had broken through the self-imposed wall of defense, and his reward was excommunication.[11]

As we can see, Buber did not consider the time of the exile conducive to unity, but rather "a period of unproductive intellectualism [*Geistigkeit*] . . . far from all living and from active striving for unity. . . . [It] nourished itself on words in books, and from the interpretations of interpretations, and eked out a wretched, caricatured, sick existence in the atmosphere of idea-less abstraction." And then the momentum was lost. "The productive struggle within the community . . . the creative struggle of the prophets and redeemers against the godless and self-satisfied had ended." Although Buber admitted that "the unproductive struggle" was once necessary to preserve the particularity of Judaism against the influence of the world, he decried the unimaginative nature of the struggle, which "increasingly criticized the creative expression" and was against all "that was free, new and fluid, for [all of these sorts of things] seemed to threaten the remnant." Although this struggle initially arose from a basic impulse of self-preservation, Buber saw it as ending "in blind self-destruction." He did not hold back his criticism of Rabbinism, which he perceived to be "Jewish Scholasticism." "In this cruel, heretical, hard-hearted, thoughtless struggle of official Judaism against submerged Judaism, the great ideas of unity disappeared in a tradition that was more and more emptied of spirit. Wherever the striving for unity fought for new ideas and new form, it was forcibly suppressed."[12]

As a result of this suppression, any "striving for unity" waned. The "idea of redemption" continued merely "in the imagination of a great poet" and "in the continuously glowing inner embers of the Jewish heretics and mystics." They were the ones who fashioned "a subterranean continuity, passing the torch from hand to hand, always readying Judaism for the moment of redemption." Only the mystics were in a position to affect the community; the heretics who operated outside of the communal structure could not accomplish anything against the Law. In Buber's view, the struggle finally broke through "in a double rush against both the philosophy and the dogma of the Law."[13]

The struggle first expressed itself in the Jewish community in the East, in the Hasidic movement, as an expression of a higher rule of life. In Buber's view, Hasidism embodied the latest phase of Jewish mysticism and "culminated in the liberation of the emotions." Although Buber saw the Hasid to be a pious person, he stressed that Hasidism is not Pietism. While the Hasidic worldview is "strong and deeply felt mysticism which brings the beyond [*das Jenseits*] into this world [*das Diesseits*] and allows this life to be formed by the other," he cautioned that Hasidism is not sentimental. Hasidism taught "the productive feeling which is a bond between the human being and God." Furthermore, Buber understood Hasidism's goal as enabling the human being to become a law unto him or herself. Buber pointed out that "the founders of Hasidism were not negators." Rather, "they liberated the old forms by giving them new meaning." In fact, the inner liberation of Judaism in the form of Hasidism chronologically preceded outer liberation, namely Emancipation. Hasidism created a Jew who was "regenerated in feeling."[14] Tragically, no one had passed the torch from the Hasidim to twentieth-century Jewry. It was Buber's intent to do so.

The Haskalah (Jewish Enlightenment), on the other hand, achieved the freeing of the intellect. As far as Buber was concerned, "the Haskalah emerged in the name of knowledge, civilization, and Europe. It wanted to enlighten." As we saw in his 1901 essay on culture and civilization, Buber considered civilization to be superficial and utilitarian. The *maskilim* fought Hasidism as well as Rabbinism because in their view "both rested on faith and not on knowledge."

But the Haskalah's butterfly-like agility came to its aid against the "frozen and hardened orthodoxy," and Judaism benefited from its fresh approach and conviction that it was fighting "a holy war for self-determination." Not only did its unorthodox approach give it an advantage, but "it carried positively Jewish, futuristic elements" as well. The Haskalah, in Buber's view, "wanted to Europeanize the Jews . . . not denationalize them." This was evident in the Haskalah's revival of the Hebrew language and Jewish thought. Thus, even though the Haskalah aimed at negating tradition, "indirectly it served as the intellectual regeneration of Jewish thought."[15]

In the view of many, Buber included, two Jewish communities of vastly different character stood side by side in contemporary Europe: one in the West and one in the East. They represented two worlds, "a Judaism of community and a Judaism of dispersion." Curiously, the "inner liberation" associated with Hasidism and Haskalah had taken hold only in the eastern parts, while the "outer liberation," political and legal Emancipation associated with modernity, had affected only western and central European Jews. Thus, while "the eastern Jew lacked material wealth, the western Jew lacked access to the creative powers" emanating from the tradition.[16]

The origins of the Jewish renaissance were not lost mostly because eastern Jewry was less fragmented than was western Jewry. In Buber's view, eastern Jewry was a closed community and "possessed more of its own cultural elements." The unfolding of the Haskalah in eastern Europe was gradual and thus was able to substantiate itself within the community to a much greater degree than it did in Germany, where the Jewish Enlightenment swept away the obstacles that stood in the way of external integration into society at large. As a result, western Jews had no language of their own but were compelled "to accept foreign words together with foreign conceptions and thought processes." In the East, by contrast, the Yiddish language held the people together, and a newly revived Hebrew culture, which manifested itself in Hebrew literature, began to develop and grow within the community. Among the East European *maskilim*, "the language of the Hebrew Bible was becoming more and more an adequate tool of modern science and modern ideas" while preserving the original texts, which it continued to convey to the people. Buber concluded that western Jewish life was "breaking off piece by piece," while positive and creative developments were taking place in the eastern communities.[17] In his assessment of this East/West dichotomy, Buber followed in the footsteps of Ahad Ha-Am, who did not speak favorably of the slave mentality of his western brothers and sisters and called for a Jewish transvaluation of values based on the Nietzschean model.[18]

Both movements, Hasidism and the Haskalah, contributed to the Jewish renaissance of the modern era. Buber thought that "the Jew of the liberation era was walking in the footsteps of Spinoza, without his genius, yet with daimonic daring." This Jew was no longer passive, but acted freely; "he did not act [mechanically] according to the Law, but according to his own conscience and feeling." Even so, this new Jew was not yet complete, for "creativity still eluded him." Buber saw his free spirit as "surging into the infinite [*Uferlose*]," rather than being harnessed for a specific goal. The tragic nature of the Jewish rebirth had not yet ended. Although some "original personalities" felt at home in the cosmos, in the West "this cosmopolitanism often led to assimilation."[19]

The Jewish movement embodied the striving for free and total activity of the newly awakened powers of the people. Although the will appeared at first reflexive and compulsive (*triebhaft*), under the influence of the developing consciousness it became more differentiated and was more directed by the spirit. Now emergent Jewry needed to channel its energies toward specific goals. Buber saw the character of the Jewish people to be one of

> muscle-flexing, of upward-looking, of elevation. The word resurrection comes to mind: a reawakening that is a miracle. But history knows no miracles. It does, however, know streams of national life that seem to cease, but actually continue underground, only to emerge again after thousands of years, storing up their resuscitating energies. The Jewish people can look forward to a resurrection from half a life to a full one. That is the reason we may call our participation in the modern nationalinternational [one word!] cultural movement a renaissance.[20]

The Jewish renaissance was to be part of a renaissance of all humanity. Buber hoped that the self-reflection (*Selbstbesinnung*) of national groups would be the foundation of a new global federation of peoples and pointed out that "Goethe's dream of a world literature takes on new forms: only when every people speaks from its own essence does the common treasure increase."[21] The Jewish people was no exception. It, too, would contribute to this new development, on the basis of its own, Jewish character.

The Zionist movement, given form by Theodor Herzl in 1897, was able to give the Jewish people a direction: namely Jewish peoplehood. Buber saw his mission as helping the Jewish people in its self-discovery and formulation of a meaningful Judaism for a modern, liberated people. He pointed out that, previously, God had commanded the people to observe the festivals. Now, Buber called on the Jewish people to take this yoke upon themselves by initiating the observance of the ancient festivals in a new mode. He pointed out that in his time there were numerous individuals whom he considered to be *Johannesnaturen*, heralds, "who recognize in their own pain the formation of a new way of life for humanity." These "visionaries" were privileged "to behold the heralds of a new renaissance of humanity." They managed "to intuit future forms from the gestation of the moment":

> They suffer as the prophets once did: because they are knowing and lonely; and because they see in the future more beautiful, happier conditions for development than they themselves will reach. We have to trust their prophecy which is born from suffering. It points us to the nearing of a rebirth, in which every one and every people will participate, each in its kind and according to its values, a renaissance of humanity, a rule of "new lands."[22]

For this reason, Buber appealed to the productive nature of the Jewish people. *Geistige Hebung* or cultural Zionism could serve as the vehicle to realization. Buber saw cultural Zionism as a preparation in the diaspora for a return to the soil because he thought most Jews had no conception of what this thing was they called "Palestine." He believed that the Zionist movement should support these efforts at cultural regeneration and pleaded at every Zionist congress and in many publications for his cause.

Zionist Propaganda

From 1897 to 1901, every year the World Zionist Organization under the leadership of Theodor Herzl convened a congress which was attended by delegates from all Zionist organizations, East and West.[23] In 1899, while still a student in Leipzig, Buber became a member of the Agitations Comite, the propaganda arm of the Zionist organization, and from August 15 to 18 he attended the Third Zionist

Congress as a delegate. From the congressional minutes we learn that Herzl called on Buber to speak, as a member of the Agitations Comite, in a session of the Organisations Comite which Herzl himself chaired. In Buber's view, "organization and propaganda are two connected and complementary functions."[24] His request to be given "a little more time than other speakers" to make his case was granted, and Buber addressed some of the issues he considered important in the contemporary propaganda efforts of the Zionist movement.

In Buber's view, the function of the propaganda committee was twofold: "to publicize the work of the movement" to the outside world and "to maintain and strengthen the movement within." Here Buber asserted that "Zionism is not a matter of party, but a matter of worldview" and that it was "the responsibility of internal propaganda to develop this worldview within the movement." This statement became the primary bone of contention between him and Herzl. According to Buber, this undertaking should not be carried out in a nominal way but through total commitment, by being "a human being or an artist . . . through the perpetuation of Jewish culture, that is to say, the preservation of the common national heritage; the national spirit, national history, and national literature, through the education of the Jewish people."[25]

In presenting his views, Buber made it clear that his was a proposal to refashion modern Jewry via education. But the education he had in mind was not based on rabbinic Judaism: "We wish to be effective *through life*. We wish to create songbooks, literature, a youth library, because our youth is our life and our future. . . . Theater performances will dramatize the Zionist idea. But we want to act through life itself in many different ways."[26] Buber would express the same idea in his 1901 speech to Die Neue Gemeinschaft.

He suggested that one of the Jewish holidays, "perhaps Shabbat Hanukkah," might become the Zionist festival.[27] "On that day, all Jewish hearts shall beat joyfully. In uplifting solidarity with all earlier and later generations of our people we will say: It is us the Maccabees fought for, and we too shall behold the new redemption." Buber envisioned that Zionism would penetrate into "synagogue, school, and home down to the children." He wanted to demonstrate "in the East and in the West" what it is like "to feel the freedom and pride of the national spirit." Somewhat patronizingly, Buber addressed especially the Jews in the East, whose national spirit was "subdued and humbled" because of the everlasting persecution against them.[28]

The minutes note that all of Buber's suggestions were greeted with affirmation, even enthusiasm and wild applause. Carried by the spirit of the moment, Buber concluded his remarks with a vision few shared at the time: "And as the time has come when, once a year, the Jewish flag, our flag, flies on the roof of the Basel Congressional building, so the time will come when, on our own soil, from our own homes, the flag of national freedom will fly in our land and will once more convey to our children the eternally new message [of the Jewish nation]."[29] This was indeed an intimation of the future.

Although Buber devoted much of his time to the Zionist cause during these years, even to the point of complaining that he was ill and totally exhausted, his disillusionment with the workings of the World Zionist Organization came swiftly. Before the Fifth Zionist Congress, December 26–29, 1901, Buber wrote an article in *Die Welt* which he called a platform for the congress.[30] He did not sign the article with his own name, using a pen name, Baruch, instead. In this article, which supported the "creative struggle," he developed the theme of cultural Zionism in a visionary manner because the reality of the congress still looked different.

We hear about the events of the Fifth Zionist Congress from Buber in two consecutive issues of the *Jüdische Volksstimme*.[31] This report of his experiences sheds some light on the problems he and his friends encountered. Scheduled to give a lecture on Jewish art at the congress, Buber was preceded by Max Nordau (1849–1923), Herzl's lieutenant, who was supposed to address the assembled on the threefold meaning of Zionism, including cultural Zionism.[32] In the printed version of Buber's lecture, "On Jewish Art," we do not get his personal reaction to Nordau.[33] But in the manuscript version, we learn of Buber's and his friends' response to Nordau's speech. Referring to "the, as always, rhetorically spectacular speech of Max Nordau's," he complained that "we, who represent the young Zionist generation," were "painfully touched . . . by Nordau's way of speaking on the issue [of Zionism]" because, "since becoming Zionists, we have shown Max Nordau only love and admiration."[34] Pointing out that "we young ones" decided to work for the cause of Jewish culture first in the cultural subcommittee, then in the senate, because "we are of the belief that the yearning for a Jewish culture is the soul of Zionism and that *only that body is beautiful which is formed by the soul*" (emphasis added),[35] Buber and his friends felt that Nordau had intruded into an area they had identified as theirs, but without sharing their concern. More important, Buber voiced his concern that this speech would cause misunderstandings which would hurt the cause of cultural Zionism at a time when it was in need of support. Commenting at length on Nordau's misconception and "insensitivity," Buber charged that Nordau did not see the "wonderful gestation of a new Jewish culture of the people,"[36] only the narrow political objectives. Although Buber's attack focused on Nordau as the culprit, the underlying charge targeted Herzl, with whom Buber came to blows at this congress over the goals of the World Zionist Organization.

The *Jüdische Volksstimme* of January 15, 1902, reported that Buber's address was "received with great applause" and that the congress resumed the debate on important propositions made by Buber at 1:30 A.M. These included proposals for the formulation of a national educational program in the diaspora, studying the feasibility of a Jewish college, and a subsidy for the national library in Jerusalem. Other proposals by Buber that were received warmly included a suggestion for the development of a Jewish encyclopedia and the establishment of educational committees at the state level to continue developing Jewish-Zionist curricula.

After Buber had concluded his presentation on behalf of the cultural committee, Herzl ruled that discussion and vote on these matters would be postponed until new delegates for the coming year had been elected. At previous congresses, the debates and some of the decisions regarding cultural work had systematically been postponed. Even though the delegates had listened to the presentations, when it came time for debate and decision, the leadership suddenly remembered the order of business and pressed to move on.[37] This was also the case this time, even though the issue of cultural Zionism had been included in the program of the second day. Buber was indignant that everything was important to the delegates *except* the concerns of the cultural Zionists. Finally, at the very last session of the Fifth Congress, the speakers for the cultural committee, Chaim Weizmann (Geneva) and Martin Buber, were given the floor. Sixty speakers had indicated an interest in responding, but they never had a chance. Buber complained, "We got to listen [only] to the two Russian rabbis who were present."[38]

In his report on the congress in the *Jüdische Volksstimme*, Buber was particularly concerned with clarifying what he termed the "Secessio in Montem Sacrum," or the reason for the walkout of forty delegates when the propositions Buber had presented came up for a vote. In addition to voicing his unhappiness with the way the congress dispensed with the need for committees and pointing out that the delegates were not appointed for the sake of personal honor, but to serve the people, he took exception to the fact that his own committee, the Agitations Ausschuss, which had the most members of any committee, was not allowed to speak. He charged that "committees for the sake of holding honorary office are not conducive to the mission of the Zionist Congress."[39] He and his friends also objected to the high-handed manner in which the cultural debate was suppressed, seeing it as a "blind hostility and indifference to the formation of the people's soul." He argued that "the congress, the Zionist legislature, was supposed to recognize and bless the work of the soul, the work of the people." Buber and his friends were furious that their objections were overruled. "When this had happened, we left the room, without a sign, without prior agreement, all guided by the feeling that now we cannot participate in the work of the congress. We watched from the gallery as the propositions were accepted. We then returned to our seats." Because the favorable outcome meant a broadening of the platform from previous congresses, Buber and his friends' "agitation" had been effective. In fact, the acceptance of the resolutions proposed by Buber amounted to a sanctioning of the cultural activities through the congress. The text of the resolution read, "The Congress declares the cultural elevation, that is, the national education of the Jewish people, as one of the most essential elements of the Zionist program and obligates all like-minded persons to cooperate [in this endeavor]."[40]

The delegation's act of protest led to the secession of nearly 15 percent of the delegates and to the formation of the Democratic Fraction, a separatist branch within the World Zionist Organization. The Democratic Fraction was not a vehicle exclusively for the promotion of cultural Zionism; it also offered a critique of the leadership style as well as the structure of the World Zionist Organization. Buber thought that the Democratic Fraction furthered the development of the Jewish spirit, but Max Nordau disagreed and perceived the Democratic Fraction to contain the *galut*. In Nordau's view, Zionism created unity, whereas Buber argued that "this unity was achieved at the cost of individuality" and was "the enemy of the soul." Although Buber agreed that unity at all cost had been necessary in earlier times "against the penetration of the enemy," he felt that now, "in the *Neuland* of the spirit" which Zionism had created, it was out of place. Instead of stifling all the young shoots, "the daring creative energies," among whom he counted himself, Buber demanded that the World Zionist Organization should "let the individuals grow, become active, persevere, realize their perceptions and their given rights." Such an attitude would, in his view, also lead to unity, but to a unity "which arises as a harmony of free, full voices."[41] What the Democratic Fraction considered to be Herzl's narrow definition of Zionism emerged once more in Herzl's 1902 novel *Altneuland*. The ensuing clash between Ahad Ha-Am and Max Nordau once more underscored the serious nature and also the magnitude of the rift not only between two individuals but between the adherents of political and of cultural Zionism.[42]

Nevertheless, Buber praised the Fifth Congress overall as having been one of the best, convinced that the party was on the way to developing into a *Volkszionismus* (a Zionist people's movement).[43] But as we can see, during the early years, though Buber was wholly supportive of the Zionist cause, he was nevertheless critical of individuals and their actions. Because Zionism was a movement in progress, a movement that was evolving every day, there were many aspects that needed to be dealt with on a daily basis, some of which had major implications for the term *Zionism* and for the future of the Zionist movement.

Cultural Zionism

In his 1901 essay "Wege zum Zionismus" (Ways to Zionism), Buber argued that if one had a choice between comfortable happiness and a beautiful death after a final moment of full living, one ought to choose the latter. Such a human being "would create something Divine, even if for a moment, while the other sojourner would achieve something merely 'all too human [*Allzumenschliches*],' " an allusion to Nietzsche's 1878 work, *Menschliches, Allzumenschliches* (Human, All Too Human).[44] This perception is derived from the German romantics and from Nietzsche, both of whom abhorred mediocrity.

For Buber, the ideal Zionist was the Jew who lived life fully. "Creation! The Zionist who feels the whole holiness of this word and lives according to it seems to stand on the highest rung." Creation is godliness, and humans, who are created in God's image, are capable of godliness. Therefore, "to create new values and new works from the depths of her ancient uniqueness, from the particular, incredible power of her blood, so long hemmed in by the shackles of unproductivity—that is the ideal of the Jewish people." Although Buber had visions of all the miracles the Jewish people would achieve someday, the first step that had to be taken was "to discover oneself, to find oneself, to fight for oneself"—the awakening.[45]

Many were the avenues of Jewish self-discovery: a sense of Palestine,[46] the ability to express oneself in Jewish art, Jewish literature, Jewish theater, Jewish education, and the establishment of a Jewish college. Buber was aware of the ways, and he tirelessly organized, wrote, and spoke on the subject of Jewish self-discovery in an age when, as he put it, the self was subordinated to the cause, not realized in the cause as it should have been.

In his 1902 article "Ein geistiges Zentrum" (A spiritual center), we learn that some Zionists complained about Buber's and his friends' cultural activities. These Zionists assumed that "Jewish culture can develop only in a Jewish environment," therefore "the beginnings of a Jewish culture . . . here and now . . . are impossible." Buber countered that such an objection assumes that "there is no Jewish culture" here and now "and that we [now] are attempting to create one." But that was not so. In Buber's view, a Jewish culture existed then and had always existed. There was no such thing as "a cultureless diaspora." Buber pointed out that the continuing development of Jewish mysticism and the resurrection of the Hebrew language in the diaspora were manifestations of Jewish culture. All the expressions of the psychophysical particularity of a people belong to its culture. A folk song, a dance, a wedding custom, a poetic expression, a legend, a belief, a traditional prejudice, a shabbat candlestick, a set of tefillin, a philosophical system, a social act—"all this is culture." Rather than a high culture derived from the Talmud, however, Buber envisioned a folk culture of the kind once practiced by the Hasidim. The life of East European Jewry still possessed the forms of Jewish culture, although it was no longer considered to be healthy. Nevertheless, "even a sick culture is . . . culture." The recovery can occur "only on its own land." This article postdates by only one year Buber's nebulous essay on culture and civilization, in which he had spoken in general human terms, whereas he now spoke specifically of Jewish culture based on that earlier model. In Buber's view, the history of diaspora life was sporadic. He did not perceive anywhere "a continuous flowing of productivity" because, in his mind, there had been no continuity of the spirit. Since the inspiration had been interrupted, the Jewish *galut* community lacked a continuity of personalities and of production. The energies of the people glowed below the surface, like embers, for decades, even centuries, only to erupt suddenly in a great human being, such as the Baal Shem Tov, or a great work of art, such as Lesser Ury's *Jeremiah*. Gradually, the inner transformation occurred, growing stronger and stronger. This is "what I have called the Jewish renaissance."[47]

Yet for the people truly to go forth from Zion, settlements in Palestine were needed. In response to the criticism from those who would say that the cultural Zionists wanted to give the people "culture instead of bread," Buber argued that "we want to prepare the people and prepare it for the fight for bread, which, in reality, is the fight for national existence."[48] Buber was convinced that the only way for a great Jewish culture to exist was for there to be the actual production of culture, especially by Jewish youth.

Perhaps not totally unaffected by the contemporary German youth movement, Buber envisioned the Zionist congresses to be reincarnations of the mountaintop fires with which the ancient Israelites had signaled the arrival of the new moon to each other. "They shine into the world and speak with flaming tongues." He dreamed that "we look into the rich, flowing play of the flames, moved in our innermost soul. And the sweet dream of dawn finds an echo." The most important act of the new Jew was to signal to others and to the outside world that "here is life."[49] All activity was to stem from positive motivation. In his 1904 essay "Was ist zu tun?" (What to do?), Buber wrote, "When we labor to get rid of the *galut* in our soul and to build up Zion, to rid our spirit of the negative Judaism and to foster the positive one, we do not do that in order to be liked by those who do not like us, but because we yearn for rebirth in a very real sense." Likewise, "a healthy organism of the people, a Judaism which is regenerated in spirit and in deed, a transformed spirit" can result "only from the ingathering of our people on our soil, from the renewal of the historical continuity, from the power of the Palestinian farm."[50]

Buber was concerned that not many Jews could actually *visualize* Eretz Israel and what it would be like to live there to such a degree that it could become reality for them, "true, eternal, innermost reality." He inquired, "How many Jews carry Palestine in their soul?"[51] and demanded that "every one of us shall desire Palestine for himself with all our soul, then we shall gain Palestine."[52] Yet the article also revealed Buber's own ambiguous attitude toward Palestine. Despite his fiery commitment to Zionism, Buber's Zionism was, very much like Herzl's, diaspora-inspired. He was still very much estranged from a lived Zionism in Eretz Israel, signaled perhaps in no small way by his preferred use of the word *Palaestina* rather than Zion or Eretz Israel, words preferred by Ahad Ha-Am and other cultural Zionists.

Buber's imperative was of a radical nature. The Zionist was not interested in "the improvement of our situation" but in "the redemption of the [Jewish] nation." Hence "true love for our people" as in Hibbat Zion was not the same as philanthropy; it was not that "which one feels for the innocently persecuted and suffering," but that which one feels "for one's blood and one's being, for one's fathers and one's sons, for the generations that were and for the generations that will be, the feeling of unity of our self with all from which we sprung and that will grow from us." The renewal of the spirit which Buber here advocated erupted within the individual who had been awakened. With determination one could achieve anything one desired. "Every one of us shall feel with our entire soul: I am the people. Then the people will arise."[53]

Jewish Education

Jewish education was for Buber the very heart of Jewish cultural renewal. He was convinced that the first efforts of Jewish educational reform had to take place in the diaspora in preparation for living in Zion. "The education of human beings is connected most closely with national education; in true cultural activity the two [education of the human being and national education] always appear together."

Absolutely opposed to *cheder* education, Buber argued that every reform of the traditional Jewish *cheder* "brings us closer to a strong and ripe generation of people capable of settlement, and we cannot found one agrarian school that will not be a source of national rejuvenation."[54] That the human being would work the soil instead of spending all of his time reading books would be progress.

The most pressing issue was that of youth education. Although adults can be reeducated, young and impressionable souls are more amenable to the great work of transformation, albeit in steps. In Buber's mind, the success of this work depended on convincing the parents because a thorough reform of Jewish education was pointless without parental involvement. Otherwise, there would be tension between the curriculum and the home. Buber advocated for that purpose "the creation of a great educational institution for the people."[55]

Buber envisioned the eventual "great and radical education of the people." He thought that this idea was only in the gestation stages and needed to be fleshed out into a program of applied Zionism. For the moment, it seemed to him enough to coordinate the loosely connected efforts of consciousness raising among the people, to strengthen and guide these efforts. The first step was "to educate the educators and the uncertain ones" and "to bring home those who had fallen by the wayside because they were not fulfilled." The program, he hoped, would make room for all "national-Jewish movements within the Zionist movement" and pave the way to a broader Zionism. "The program will expand [the concept of] Zionism by combining all spiritual aspects of rebirth and deepen it by freeing it from the stiff and superficial schemata of propaganda, raising it to a truly living conception of peoplehood and productive activity." In Buber's view, "only a program of intensive activity could exercise the awakening and inspiring power which at all times sprang from manifestations of triumphant life and transformed worlds."[56]

The high point of Buber's commitment to Jewish education was his devotion to the idea of creating a Jewish college. Alas, in Europe the college was also one of the aspects of his work which eluded fulfillment. Until the establishment of the Hebrew University on Mount Scopus in 1925, Buber carried out Zionist education on many different levels in Europe.[57]

The idea of a Jewish college was in part a response to the considerable problems Russian students experienced because of the restrictions of the *numerus clausus* and the awareness that in the West it was getting harder and harder for Jews to attend technical colleges and universities. Buber's first efforts in the direction of a college can be traced to 1902. In that year, he published a brochure about a meeting that he, Berthold Feiwel, and Chaim Weizmann had convened in Geneva-Leysin.[58] The three men thought that a Jewish college would be the solution to the problem. Buber made it very clear that he did not want to begin with a traditional Jewish course of study because he disapproved so much of the result produced by *cheder* education. He stressed instead that they wanted to work from the center outward, to start with the highest goal, the college, and then develop the lower institutions. The proposal, which included a budget down to the last detail, was modeled upon colleges then operating in several European countries.

There would be a bureau for the Jewish college located in Switzerland, but the location of the Jewish college as such was not designated; it could be in either England or Switzerland, although Palestine would be the ideal place. Buber stressed that the Jewish college would be "a cultural center, whose spirit will radiate in all directions."[59] It must be stressed that this idea of a college in the diaspora was not meant to be a substitute for Ahad Ha-Am's cultural center in Zion, but rather was a more realistic goal, a reason for Buber's hesitation to locate the facility squarely and exclusively in Eretz Israel.

In Buber's view, the Jewish situation was unique. He explained that "we have to build at the same time from top to bottom and from bottom to top. This may not be natural, but it is necessary." Buber was astute in perceiving the need for Jewish education from the top and from the bottom. He was sure that those Jews who were still rooted in the Jewish people understood this paradox without further explanation, and he thought it would be held up in vain to the assimilated who were moving away from a traditional Jewish way of life. Buber wanted to reach only those who were interested in the productive nature of the Jewish *Volk* and the unfolding of the soul of the people. He was not interested in those who were filled with "social feeling," which he considered a kind of pity, and for whom "the Jewish question was primarily a question of *Judenheit*" (Jewry) rather than "*Judentum*" (Judaism). Sadly, "even those," like Theodor Herzl, "for whom the rebirth of the Jewish spirit was something absolutely valuable," did not accept "*Kulturarbeit* [cultural Zionism] as being of equal value to the economic and political work."[60]

Buber protested that one cannot simply "load a people onto a ship like dead freight, send them to Eretz Israel, and then expect that the soil can perform a miracle: namely to restore the sickest people of all to true life." Rather, building on Ahad Ha-Am, Buber argued, "we must transvaluate the Jewish spirit, not through theories, but through deeds: through the development of ever new groups of human beings who are capable of colonization. We must design a plan on the basis of which these most developed circles can become the nucleus of settlements once colonization begins on a large scale."[61] Buber here actually argued that the people would not be ready to settle the land until they had divested themselves of their *galut* mentality. Yet at this very same time, the First Aliyah was well under way and serious, large-scale settlement efforts in the *yishuv* had already begun. Despite his Zionist activism, Buber apparently did not comprehend the positive impact of these settlements on the renewal of the spirit.

Jewish Literature

In addition to his propaganda work, Buber wrote a profusion of poems dealing with the awakening of Jewish consciousness which were published in diverse journals.[62] Three of these poems especially merit our attention because they address those Jews who might become victims of assimilation out of sheer apathy.

In one poem, "Gebet" (Prayer),[63] published in 1901 and dedicated to Josef Marcou-Barouch, a Zionist artist, Buber appealed to the Almighty to shake up His people, angrily or gently, and to kindle the flame of enthusiasm that would then lead to inner liberation and healing. His impassioned plea called for God to send a fever, for only such a drastic measure could unleash the wild overabundance slumbering within and provide the people with the creativity necessary for a return "to the river Jordan."

Another poem, published by "Martin Buber, philosophical student in Berlin," was titled "Unseres Volkes Erwachen" (The awakening of our people).[64] It was based on Psalm 44:24 and asked, "Oreh, lama tishan?" (Wake up, why are you sleeping?), which was printed in Hebrew across the top of the poem. But while the psalmist appealed to

God to awaken to the plight of His people, in this poem, Buber appealed to his fellow Jews, "Wake up, my people, the night has ended! Get up and stride forward, for now you will live." In its tenor, the poem resembles the story of the Exodus, and Buber took on the role of Moses. It is written in dialogue form, and the people responded that they were wounded too seriously to see the light of which the herald spoke. But the herald kept encouraging them, assuring them that they would recover, for "we shall wash the blood from your wounds."[65]

Buber published his poem "An Narcissus"[66] in the 1901 annual report of the *Lese- und Redehalle jüdischer Hochschüler in Wien*, a student publication. The dedication, "to some young Jews," was omitted from the printed version. Here he identified the narcissistic personality, the model available from secular German culture, as the major impediment to the formation of the type of personality and community he envisioned. The poem brought to light that Judaism and Western individualism were mutually exclusive. Buber was not against individualism. On the contrary, he went to much trouble to show that the Jew could not exist in relation to the world unless he was an autonomous human being. But one of the pitfalls on the road to selfhood was a self-interest that was nauseating because it bore no consideration for anything but one's own concerns, with no thought for the needs of the community. The self-centered person was an island unto him- or herself, without any desire for socializing or any sense of self-criticism. The classical image of Narcissus was part of the German cultural heritage on which Buber was weaned. During the romantic era, Heinrich von Kleist (1777–1811), an influential and precocious romantic poet, had written a famous essay on the narcissistic personality.[67] Buber took his cue from the past, cleverly appropriating Kleist's idea, transforming it, and presenting it as a warning to young Jews who might be tempted to follow the misguided Narcissus.

Buber's poem, written as a series of eight-liners, addressed the young Narcissus, who lived in a fantasy world as if a Greek god, totally oblivious to his fellow human beings and their plight. He spent the days feeding new riches to his soul and the nights weaving sweet and colorful fairy tales about himself. Buber reprimanded him: "You never struggle to rejoin the world." This is a criticism Buber had already voiced in his assessment of the twentieth-century Viennese poet Hugo von Hofmannsthal. Although Narcissus often recalled the fire and yearning of the Jewish people, a people that had shriveled up and become distorted in an effort to sustain itself, he merely became faint. Regretfully, his response was not fueled by the *agon*; he did not respond with a raised fist, in fierce terror and in tears, or with passionate promises.[68] Rather, his sorrowful dreams dissipated in a whimper, like the tired autumn sunsets of the Young Vienna literary circle. Narcissus withdrew into his own self and played his love games with himself, as did von Hofmannsthal. He was a blossom on a weak stem that was hardly well-grounded. So he floated away, freely and effortlessly, focusing on his magic world, unaffected by the wind gusts and thunderstorms of life, barely touched by the troubles of the Jews in the modern world—a thoroughly detached modern individual.

But Buber warned that the day would come when Narcissus would experience the gray light of autumn. On that day, his spirit would not be spared the quiet nagging of untold pain, and he would be handed worries in a sparkling goblet. No amount of either riches or self-pride would spare him a creeping and horrible fear. And then, Buber predicted, Narcissus would thirst for the smell of the soil; he would desire anger and hope, sorrow and joy, but instead he would despair as the days went by, for he would have access only to his dream world. In the end he would yearn for Divine commandments and the moral imperative. He would yearn for direction from a God who would command him thunderingly, "Thou shalt!"[69] In other words, Narcissus would yearn for a center more powerful than his weak, misguided person to give him true direction.

This stark yet beautiful poem revealed a Buber who was not afraid to antagonize his still uncommitted and uncaring contemporaries. He attempted to summon them to accept the responsibility for their role in their own renewal and that of their people. If they did not, he predicted, the gates of repentance in the form of Zionist activism would close for them, and their hour would pass. He implored them to awaken, to take stock, and to participate in the business of the day, which to him meant Jewish renewal via the Zionist movement. Ironically, Buber himself tarried in leaving Germany, barely escaping to Palestine in 1938.

In Buber's mind, the Jew of the twentieth century had no choice but to develop his or her personality so as to participate in contemporary life. He accused Theodor Herzl, no less than the old *kehilla* elders, of denying the development of the individual; he charged that both sought to channel a person's energies into predetermined structural forms. Buber and his friends from the Democratic Fraction sought to rectify this situation by stressing individual development to its fullest. But rather than leading to unbridled individualism, the developed personality was to put himself or herself into the service of some higher purpose, which, in this case, was Zionism. This is what Buber did himself, and he expected the same commitment from his fellow Jews.

For Buber, the problem was that the people had not yet achieved a level of physical and spiritual unity at which they were capable of creation. He thought that most Zionists produced propaganda, but that was not yet "true productivity," but rather a precursor to it. True productivity would express the personality of the creative individual in a formidable deed. Zionist activism for Buber was not a formula but a commitment. He pleaded, "Let every one commit his own life, his vocation, his productivity, to the life of the people." It is important to understand that, in Buber's eyes, for a Jew to be fully human he had to be fully Jewish. And to be fully Jewish from his perspective meant being a committed Zionist. Rather than arguing European cosmopolitanism, as he had a few years earlier, Buber now argued the opposite. The person who was a strong Jew would also be a strong human being. One had to "realize his particularity from his innermost soul," in the place where one stands, everyone in his or her way and yet together. "Then," Buber concluded, "soul and work will become one and Zion, our Zion, will arise."[70]

Buber undertook the translation of a story by David Pinski titled "Das Erwachen" (The awakening) from the Yiddish, which he published in *Der Jüdische Almanach* of 1902.[71] This story symbolized the dilemma Buber perceived between the "old" and the "new" Jew. The old Jew was a good Talmud student who did not know life. He knew only his books and the world of those books but was alienated from real life. He also did not perceive women as human beings but merely as servants. One year, at Passover (and not at Hanukkah as of old), a great miracle happened to the "yeshiva bocher." He discovered love and therewith real life as well as love of the world. "All of his thoughts had vanished, but he was no poorer for it." The conclusion Pinski drew, which Buber agreed with, was that "the heavens are for

God and the earth for humanity." Because God created the earth, it is our obligation to enjoy its treasures, not ignore them as the young man had done. Furthermore, Divine love is the model for all human love. Again the young man stands corrected. Although the philosophical wisdom can be found in the books of the tradition, the application of the teaching can be found only in life. Buber had already found these two ideals, of life and of love, in Jakob Böhme, and he would once again encounter them in his study of Hasidism. Both concepts became pillars in his philosophy of life.

Isaac Leib Peretz (1852–1915), a Polish Jew from Zamosc, was Buber's ideal of the new Jewish poet. Peretz, a lawyer by profession, began as a Yiddish writer. After the 1881 pogroms, his writings turned toward nationalism; from then on Peretz wrote in Hebrew. On the occasion of his twenty-fifth anniversary as a writer, Buber commented that "the life of the Jewish people is the Worpswede of the nations." Worpswede was an obscure mining town in Germany which no one had ever heard of. It was "gray, heavy, and dull."[72] One day some artists came to town and painted scenes from it. When the world saw those scenes, people suddenly realized the beauty of the town. Such was also the case with Jewish life. No one knew of its beauty. Those who lived it had been robbed of the power of vision by the cares of everyday life, and those who were outside saw only the surface, which appeared drab. Only "one . . . had the eye and the hand of the artist." His name was Isaac Leib Peretz. "His eye beheld the deeply hidden, glowing light and his hand awakened that which was slumbering to bright, visible life, so that all should see the life of the Jewish people, how beautiful it is in its misery and in its wild, yearning struggle."[73] Such words of praise from Buber were reserved for unusually gifted individuals such as Shmuel Agnon, Aaron David Gordon, and Peretz.

One may ask why Buber did not also write this way about Schalom Aleichem, surely one of the greatest of the Yiddish storytellers. In his assessment of art, Buber's emphasis was on *jungjüdisch*, on the newly Judaic, a regeneration of the ancient Hebraic culture, now called also the young Hebrew culture. The idea of *jungjüdisch* is an adaptation of the term *jungdeutsch* from the German artistic reform movement under the leadership of Heinrich Heine in the 1830s, called *Jungdeutschland*, which promised death to the old guard and its ways and looked forward to a new dawn. Likewise, the Viennese poets who belonged to the Young Vienna group also prided themselves on their avant-garde status. Schalom Aleichem, however, was not an avant-garde writer but a chronicler of traditional Jewish life. Though not disparaging Schalom Aleichem, Buber appreciated Peretz more because of his novel way of viewing Jewish life. Although Peretz was not considered a Zionist but a national Jew, for which he was criticized by what Buber called "the hard-liners [of Zionism]," Buber thought that German Jews were in his debt. "Others have given us ideas and programs, but he gave us beauty, and the beauty of our own world. Those who give us this gift are Zion's most faithful fighters; for Zion is for us the kingdom of future Jewish beauty." What was important for Buber was not the ideological but the clear vision Peretz brought to his perception of Jewish life, the purity of his soul, which in turn presented to his readers a purity that cut through all the layers of diaspora life which ordinarily obscured the essence. Buber concluded the laudation with the words, "We young people love each one who looks into the Jewish soul with a pure eye and a pure heart and gives voice to its yearning. Thus we love you, poet of our people, and honor you on your anniversary."[74] Buber wished to uncover more Jews who viewed Jewish life positively. Because the *galut* mentality was often tied to Jewish self-hatred, low self-esteem, and a negative self-image, Buber wished to hold up as a model for the Zionist personality such positive and original thinkers as Peretz.

Jewish Art

One of the most serious debates in early Zionism revolved around the question of Jewish art. Buber not only spoke on Jewish art at the Fifth Zionist Congress in 1901 and published an entire volume on Jewish art in 1903, but when he published the second edition of his 1916 collection of essays on Zionism in 1920, he included the preface to his 1903 book as the postscript to the edition.[75] Why focus so much attention on this particular topic?

In his 1903 book *Jüdische Künstler*, published via the Jüdische Verlag, which Buber and two friends had founded in Berlin, he objected to the contemporary opinion that Judaism had no plastic arts, explaining that "the Jew of antiquity" lived in a world defined by time and impressions, rather than a world of space and experiences. This meant that "he was filled to the brim with feeling, a feeling that was so wild that the senses could not bridge the gap from this fullness of the innermost soul to an art form that created visible 'objects.' " He either "had to become a prophet, or he had to explode from the fullness of his passion." The true prophet could only act out, not produce a representation, of his feelings.[76]

Largely as a result of Christian influences which the Jewish person picked up during his forced wanderings in the diaspora, over time just the opposite developed. "The human body became despicable, beauty was no longer a treasured value; looking [at the body] was sin, [even] art was sin." As a result, "religious Law achieved a power that was never before known by any people and at any time. Education occurred exclusively as a tool of the Law; all creative impulses were stifled as they emerged."[77]

Somehow, in the eyes of non-Jews, the Jewish religious injunction against representational art, which Buber attributed to the tragedy of the diaspora, translated into the viewpoint that Judaism had no art. Richard Wagner went so far as "to deny Jews the capability to become plastic [*bildende*] artists." Although Buber was anxious to explain "the sources of that infertility," one notes with alarm that he did not deny the existence of such infertility.[78] In his 1904 essay "Was ist zu tun?" Buber challenged his fellow Jews to "become Jewish human beings" again. Jewry could not assume to be such because "the fetters of the *galut* wounded and devastated our soul." He implored his fellow Jews to understand that "we are very ill."[79] In Buber's view, the diaspora Jew suffered from "narrowness and desperation of life" and, echoing Ahad Ha-Am, from "separation of the body and the spirit," which produced a *Luftmensch,* all of which suppressed his creative impulses. "His sense of being separated more and more from reality, fleeing further and further into a petrified tradition and into a completely foreign-to-life intellectualization."[80] It was therefore everyone's challenge to begin the work toward recovery "here and now" because today's Jewish youth does not know "how to live, to see, to produce."[81] Dualism, the obstacle to unity, yet at the same time the impetus for striving toward perfection, could also be discerned in the life and the vision of the ghetto Jew. It hampered his creative activity, not only because of his physical isolation but because of the general and continuous focus on the dualism of body and soul.

Buber, at this time, was deeply steeped in the study and contemplation of aesthetics. He believed that resuming production of Jewish art, which he considered broken off, would be a real achievement for Jewish renewal as well as Judaism's reputation in the world. It appears, though, that in the process of exploring these issues, he came to realize that creativity was not restricted to the production of art. Every human being who produces "something whole and independent from his soul" is a creator: "All true work of the people is creation."[82] Buber had already made this point in a different context, in the article on old and new community, in which community was acclaimed as an "original creation."

Ultimately, Buber's appeal was addressed to a Jewish elite, for he believed that the Jewish movement could mediate between the productive Jews and the masses. In Buber's view, the land would once more heal the dualism between body and soul, as it had done in ancient times. To be sure, "only the soil of Palestine would give us new life," but "in order to regain this soil, we have to educate ourselves, straighten that which is crooked, fill the empty void, subdue our inability to live."[83] He was convinced that "our will first has to change us before it can change circumstances." The new Jews would then indeed create new worlds. In Buber's view, the tragedy was that most modern Jews did not follow the call to develop their potential. They did not see the danger; "they continue to vegetate." He felt that by having entered into an epoch of continuity, "Zion, too, would arise from an inner development of the people." For this to happen, it was especially crucial to develop one relationship: that "between the thought and the deed."[84] He and his contemporaries were chosen to guard this development and to further it.

It was Buber's view that the original fire of the prophets had broken forth once more in eighteenth-century Hasidism. "Hasidism was the birth of a new Judaism," most miraculously so because the human body once more became "the miracle of the world," beauty became "an emanation of God," and vision once more became "a unification with God." In Buber's interpretation of Hasidism, "the law is not the purpose of life," rather, "the purpose of life is love." According to Hasidic teachings, the human being is to become a law unto himself. Buber counseled that "there is no sin which separates us from God. Everything physical that occurs with pure intent is service to God [*avodah*]. . . . [And] all joy of life is revelation of Divine love."[85]

Buber explained that "with the onset of Emancipation, the Jew had a chance to develop from *a human being in relation* [*Beziehungs-*

mensch] to a *complete human being* [*Vollmenschen*]." The danger of narcissism lurked in the wings, but if an individual was able to develop in a healthy way to completeness, as Buber put it, he or she once more needed to go beyond the self and live in relation, but in a higher sense, in a freely chosen type of community. Nevertheless, "the plastic arts were the last to develop," even though one way to achieve an unfolding of the soul is through the production of art. The true artist harnesses fire into productivity. Only occasionally did one encounter artists such as the ones identified by Buber in *Jüdische Künstler*, in whose creations "the energies [earlier] expressed in the religious acts of the Hasidim burn brightly, inspiring the productivity of the artists of our time." As we saw in his essay on the four Viennese poets of the Young Vienna group, Buber perceived most contemporary artists to be decadent. It was Buber's goal "to present the artists in this volume through their works" rather than write analytically about them. The secondary aim of the volume was "to create a Jewish public which would know and appreciate Jewish artists and their art."[86]

In his essay "Ein geistiges Zentrum," Buber pointed out that it is one of the great historical miracles that Jewish art exists, even though it is different from "Dutch art." The important thing is that in the vision and in the art of these new Jewish artists something of Jewishness comes to life. This is crucial, for it signals that "the continuity of production has been restored." The artistic energies rose from the soil. Buber considered early Zionism to be "the youthful year of an ancient people." Unfortunately, along with the resurrection of creativity there came "that murderous pair of the eons," Jewish culture's arch enemy, "the narrowness of life and the narrowness of the mind." Buber perceived these to represent the inner and the outer ghetto, powers that were so far still subdued. He advocated fighting "a holy war" against those two counter powers, "to protect the young energies of the people so that they can unfold."[87]

Buber attempted to delineate the relationship between "the productive Jews, the people [*Volk*] and the movement." In 1902, he wrote that "the productive Jews can be intellectuals as well as artists."[88] They are able to combine human activity so that it "can achieve new developments in spirit and in deed." We hear echoes of a theme he had already developed in the essay on old and new community, namely that a people is "not bound together by secondary elements: usefulness and faith (as in economic or religious groups)." Rather, in

Buber's view, "a people is a human *Gemeinschaft* whose purpose is *beyond* all usefulness and *before* all usefulness." The individual who joins the cause of the people is freed from the wheel of utilitarianism. Once freed, he or she will proceed "from the wheel of utilitarianism [*Nutzgetriebe*] to the original powers, from the external to the internal, from the preservation in a specific moment to the preservation between generations."[89]

The problem of Jewish productivity occupied Buber endlessly. In analyzing the commitment to Zionism by a group of young Galician Jews, he concluded that their answers, though "beautiful and sublime," offered slogans such as "total dedication, development of character, self-education, concentration of the spirit," which did not answer the question of how to be a productive Zionist. Buber agreed that the study of the Hebrew language and Jewish history was important, as was the study of Jewish philosophy, but it was not enough just to study. Applied Zionism, or a fully developed program of action, was called for.[90]

As we know, Buber perceived contemporary religion to have lost the power "to take souls into its arms and place them at the bosom of the world." He saw contemporary religion to be a lie to the living, coercing the free-flowing spirit. Therefore, an alternative had to be found, for "he who has lost his God is deeply orphaned." In Goethean imagery, Buber then pointed out that this individual "descends to the mothers," living with a dark and powerful sculptor "who hews him or her out of a formless mass, as the artist then will create himself." This realm of pristine energy lies beyond and before all confessionalism. On the path back from the mothers, the *Volk* becomes a first way station.[91]

In the third part of his 1902 essay on productivity, Buber isolated two key words, "rootedness" and "form-controlled tragedy." In discussing rootedness, Buber lamented that in his age, Satan did not take the productive Jew to the top of the mountain and show him all the kingdoms of the world so he would have to choose. Rather, Satan told him that it made no difference in which kingdom he dwelled, and the contemporary Jew believed him. This apathetic attitude needed to be overcome. In Buber's estimation, rootlessness (*das Wesenlose*) is not conducive to production because meaningful production grows out of rootedness. Hence he who has his own little piece of soil to dwell on, he who sits under his own fig tree, is the most blessed. But even for one who is banned from his homeland, as the Jew was, this yearning, though altogether inadequate, is nevertheless inspiring.[92] It is the vision that may lead to realization. And this certainly was true of Theodor Herzl and of Martin Buber.

The power of the tragic is most obvious in the creative Jew. We see in him or her "a deep despair" and "a being torn asunder," which—miraculously—turns into harmony. He has seen the lowest and accepted it. Individuals who can harness tragedy and allow form to control its passion are "the secret kings of the people." Like the ancient prophets, "they rule the subterranean fate of the people, of which the outer is only the visible reflection."[93] Buber cited as an example the artist Hermann Struck (1876–1944), whose sketches and drawings were published in a 1904 book by Adolf Friedemann, *Reisebilder aus Palaestina* (Travel pictures from Palestine). According to Buber, in contrast to most artists, who did not paint a Jewish Palestine because they were rich in color and poor in mood, Struck presented truly Jewish art, from a lonely palm tree in Jaffa to the young [Zionist] settlements. The drawing *Jerusalem*, Buber wrote, is not in Struck's book but in the studio, and one gets the feeling that it is waiting for the Jew who will come "to see the land."[94]

Buber was always rather dramatic in his presentation of a point that touched his heart. It did not matter what branch of the arts he discussed, he always sought out images of great emotional impact, betraying his Nietzschean flair for the dramatic. In 1901, Buber reviewed the opening of a Jewish art exhibit featuring specifically the artist Lesser Ury (1861–1931). Ury, like Struck, was an artist who, Buber thought, "took historical material and developed great visions," as seen in his painting *Jeremiah*. Wrote Buber, "In Ury there lives the old, sacred flame of the Orient, the hot breath which caresses the rough earth, the gigantic figures of elemental creatures before the grandiose background of an immeasurable desolation." Buber contrasted Ury's *Jeremiah* to the "theatrical hero of old Düsseldorf," with whom he has nothing in common, for *Jeremiah* is a piece of this wretched earth. "A cancer of the earth, he cowers on the ground, continuing only as a dark line, a massive piece of misery, shattered, bent, crushed." He thought that to the civilized Western individual, whether Jew or not, who is used to the sublimity of Western art, this must be a terrible image—"a great, deep, and heartfelt old Jewish curse."[95] Yet to Buber it was a refreshingly honest portrayal of the human condition.

In a sick people, such as the Jewish people, the productive ones are remote from the life of the *Gemeinschaft*. "They speak a different language than the masses who spawned them. And they have a completely different willpower." As in the time of the prophets, "there is no bridge which leads from them to the dark and fertile masses, nor do they want one." Buber considered this to be the tragic result of two thousand years of pathological Jewish existence. There are those, however, "who want a bridge, but don't really know how to build it." In Buber's view, for them, "the Jewish movement is a strong helper which grows daily." The movement pointed to the people "as a living and forward-looking being, and vice versa, the movement awakened in the people a constantly growing understanding of the productive ones." Therefore, it was the movement that mediated between the people and the creators.[96] In Buber's conception of diaspora Jewry, whose development he considered volcanic, the restoration of productivity was crucial, for it meant that diaspora Jewry could wage a creative struggle not only against *galut* existence but also against the duality that keeps human beings, and the Jew in particular, from reuniting with God.

Jewish Theater

If one has Jewish literature and Jewish art, one cannot stop short of a Jewish theater.[97] Buber's criticism of the Jewish theater may be hard to understand, for it is well-known that there existed a lively Yiddish theater in Europe, and especially central and eastern Europe. With the minor exception of Pinski and Peretz, mentioned under Jewish literature, Buber chose to leap over two thousand years of Jewish history, including the culture this period of the Exile produced.

In a 1901 article, Buber responded to a suggestion that encouraged the founding of a young Judaic stage, partly for Jewish drama in German and partly for the "dramatic products of a blossoming original Hebrew literature." Buber addressed the primary concern of most people who would perceive the creation of young Judaic drama as "a fantastic idea" that should be dismissed because the obstacles to its realization would be too great. After all, there would be no public, no repertoire, and no resources. That would be the end of it. Buber conceded that for the regular theater the lack of these three components would be deadly. But he noted that he was "not speaking of such a theater," but rather of "theatrical productions of a young Judaic laboratory theater [*Jungjüdische Freie Bühne*] that could take place either at regular or random intervals."[98]

What exactly did he mean by *Freie Bühne*? By Buber's definition, such is "the theater of a society which from time to time produces dramatic performances of an artistic repertoire for its members that for some reason is not at all or only rarely performed in the public theater." There is a particular public for such fare, it does not need to be a large repertoire, and the subscriptions would make it a self-sustaining undertaking.[99]

If one wonders where Buber got his ideas, one must remember that this was a time of great cultural experimentation within European society. The spirit of freedom from the American and French revolutions did not stop with the Emancipation of European Jewry. Rather, there subsequently was an awakening global women's movement and various artistic movements, such as Andre Breton's surrealism in France and expressionism in the form of Wassily Kandinsky's Blaue Reiter group in Germany. The theater also went through a period of renewal, anticipating the methods of the laboratory theater of Erwin Piscator in the 1920s. Thus Buber's vision of Jewish renewal in the arts was not an isolated notion but fit into the overall excitement of a new dawn for all of humanity.

Buber and Theodor Herzl

It has been emphasized again and again that the young man who made Zionism the watchword of the modern Jewish renaissance, Theodor Herzl, had done so without having heard contemporary voices in the East. His interest in his people grew out of his awareness of anti-Semitism, and he was reborn with the awakening of this awareness. In the aftermath of his witnessing of the infamous Dreyfus case (1894), Herzl took a new approach to the contemporary problems of European Jewry. He concluded that, despite Emancipation, Jews everywhere would continue to be subjected to suspicion and discriminatory practices and therefore desperately required their own homeland, where they could live as a majority in their own state. In an 1895 diary entry, he wrote:

> For some time now I have been engaged in a work of indescribable greatness. . . . It has assumed the aspect of some powerful dream. But days and weeks have passed since it has filled me utterly, it has overflown into my unconscious self, it accompanies me wherever I go, it broods above all prosaic conversation . . . it disturbs and intoxicates me. What it will lead to is impossible to surmise as yet. But my experience tells me that it is something marvelous, even as a dream, and that I should write it down—its title: The Promised Land.[100]

Budapest-born and Vienna-educated, Herzl was a sophisticated and cosmopolitan journalist who served as the Paris correspondent for the distinguished liberal Viennese newspaper *Die Neue Freie Presse*. Buber saw Herzl as a *litterateur*, one of those modern, alienated, fragmented individuals whom he had described in his essay on the four decadent Viennese poets. At the time of Herzl's death in 1904, Buber wrote:

> On July 3 of this year, Theodor Herzl died at the age of forty-four. He was known as a master of the feuilleton, who knew how to say with a melancholy grace the most delicate things about matters near and far, particularly about the souls of children and the Rococo period; [he was known] as the poet of philosophical tales, in which the world was observed from a not obvious vantage point and was seen new and in a special way; [he was known] as the author of dramas in which problems like the social question were solved in a manner too simple, but with much tact. He was also known as the leader of the Zionist party, that is to say, people knew about it from the newspapers which report about Zionism. For most of them, the concept Zionism was exhausted with Herzl and his business. Now that the life work of the early deceased can be overseen, the time seems right to correct this mistake and to show that Zionism is broader and greater [than Herzl's conception of it], but even broader and greater than Zionism is the Jewish movement. Through such an effort, to honor and measure the man on the basis of his story and the human nature in the entire tragedy of its limitation, the deceased may be honored in the purest fashion.[101]

In an article in the *Freistatt*, simply titled "Theodor Herzl," Buber attempted to illuminate what he considered to be Herzl's shortcomings by asserting that, in his youth, "Herzl was not weaned on emotional Judaism nor did he gain extensive knowledge of Judaism." In Buber's view, he was deprived of a Jewish education and upbringing, the rich and meaningful storehouse of symbols and imagery that "traditionally served Judaism's defensive battle on the inside and its mystical hope toward the outside."[102] Therefore, Buber disparagingly considered Herzl an outsider, not a true Jew like himself and others.

Buber criticized Herzl for starting from an external perspective, although a host of halachically observant Jews have viewed Buber in the same way. He complained that the Jewish state which Herzl envisioned did not possess one single Jewish institution and no cultural treasures that would arise from the peculiar nature of the new Hebraic personality. "Herzl was a Western Jew without Jewish tradition, without Jewish childhood memories, without Jewish education, without Jewish knowledge acquired in his youth; he had grown up in a non-Jewish environment and never met the Jewish masses; no human being was as foreign to him as a Jewish worker [*Proletarier*]." Buber thus drew the conclusion that Herzl "was a whole man, but not a whole Jew."[103] That translated into a pretty damning assessment of the leader of modern national Jewry.

Although Buber admitted that "in the seven years since the First Zionist Congress, I have come to admire the beauty and sublimity of his human figure, his noble dedication and strength of action, his unquestionable loyalty," he also complained about Herzl's "human mistakes."[104] Buber prefaced his 1904 essay on Herzl with an epigraph from Herzl's book *Das Palais Bourbon* (1897):

> There are in the life of a people . . . many, many individuals. Their shortcomings and outstanding characteristics belong to the unquestionable property of the nation which creates such figures. They have to live according to their nature, do harm, be useful, fascinate the people. . . . They have to spread mistakes like a terrible flood of the Nile over the entire land, for a distant purpose.[105]

It is obvious that this statement was not chosen to point to Herzl's many and considerable accomplishments. Buber further asserted that "as a Jew he always seemed to be half and incomplete. It is wrong to celebrate him as a Jewish personality. There was nothing basically Jewish in Herzl. He did not reveal the people's daimon."[106]

In Buber's view, the persecution of the Jews had for Herzl become the Jewish question—the common enemy that served as the basis of Jewish peoplehood. Such motivation was not a sufficient foundation upon which to regenerate the Jewish people. Herzl's impetus for acting Jewishly stemmed from self-defense because, as Herzl had himself stated in *Der Judenstaat*, "the enemy makes us into a people against our will,"[107] and not from a deep-seated love for Judaism. Although Buber had much more understanding for the individual who became a Zionist because he identified with the people that suffered and needed to be saved, he nevertheless found this practical point of view to be much too narrow and too utilitarian, corresponding to that of "the good British moralist for whom the greatest happiness of the greatest number was the highest ideal."[108] Buber did not think Herzl understood that the true Jewish question was an internal and individual one, that is, one that dealt with the attitude of each Jew to his inherited peculiarity within, to his inner Judaism. He was disappointed because for Herzl the Jewish question never became "a question of Judaism," as it had for both Ahad Ha-Am and himself, but "merely" a question of "the Jewish people."[109]

Buber criticized Herzl's inability to understand "that the Zionist party was only the conscious member of a large organism, that the Zionist activity is only the ordered part of a large evolution." In Buber's mind, Herzl considered Zionism something that had to be constructed, not something that was evolving and therefore had to be given form. Buber claimed that Herzl had never experienced the Jewish renaissance within his heart, but rather understood it as a form of propaganda for a cause. "His greatest mistake was that he never grasped the Jewish movement in its totality." Rather, Buber thought that Herzl identified the movement only with himself. Paradoxically, although Buber saw this as the basis of Herzl's greatest weakness, he also recognized it as the source of his greatest power. Herzl believed in himself not as a person but as a cause.[110] His book *Der Judenstaat* (1896) showed the way. In that book, Herzl provided his answer to the Jewish question. There Buber no longer saw him as the slick newspaper columnist; rather, "the ironic man was silent." The language was "serious and controlled, based on facts, and expressed in an intensified, objectifying manner."[111] Herzl followed a narrow path; even though "in the process he destroyed many a young seedling . . . his step nevertheless remained firm." Buber thought that Herzl did not allow the individual personality to develop. He was interested only in the Zionist party. Yet it was owing to Herzl's artistic genius that the Zionist organization even developed, for he channeled the movement into a party. Thus Herzl became the hero of a transitional period. He was the master of a sick people, whose great deed consisted of giving his people a vision.[112]

With the convening of the First Zionist Congress in 1897 in Basel, "Herzl's second life began." Buber perceived his tenure as "seven years of strange transmigration of the soul," or rather, "revelation of the soul." Until then, Herzl's material had been words, but now it became people. Although the movement was structured according to a committee system, Buber thought that Herzl had the power of a dictator. Still remembering the 1901 confrontation over cultural Zionism, Buber also attributed to Herzl "the soul of a dictator." For Buber, Herzl's limitation lay in the fact that he saw all spiritual and artistic production which arose from the unique rejuvenation of the people merely as a means of propaganda and that it never took on a purpose of its own.[113]

Buber perceived three paradoxes in Herzl's circumstances. First, he paid only lip service to Hebrew. "He stood, totally as a son of the West, at the top of a movement that had its roots in the East." Second, Buber pointed to the contrast between Herzl's original intentions, which were political, and his ensuing work with which he could not always go public. Through his actions, Herzl had negated parliamentarism, yet he had nevertheless founded a Jewish parliament, the Zionist Congress. He had fought against distinct programs because they impeded the actions of the professional politician. Yet he fashioned the most distinctive program of all, the so-called Basel Program. And finally, Herzl presented himself as a statesman, yet he was without a state.[114]

In spite of all the weaknesses, Buber had to admit that Herzl affected his environment incredibly. In his remark that "popular imagination wove a tender legend around him [Herzl]," one detects a touch of reluctant admiration for this modern folk hero. Not even the East Africa project, which undercut the official Basel Program, could shake Herzl's popularity among the masses. Buber recognized Herzl as "a poet whom fate had led to his people" and concluded that "he died, warmed by the rays of his sun at its zenith."[115] Therefore, in spite of Buber's criticism of Herzl, there is no doubt that he greatly admired Herzl as a man of action and as one who possessed a brilliant mind. The differences between the two men came from their different perceptions of what Zionism and ultimately Judaism consisted of.

Not until six years after Herzl's death (1910) would Buber acknowledge the great contribution Herzl had made to the preservation and rejuvenation of the Jewish people. In 1910, on the occasion of Herzl's fiftieth birthday, Buber wrote a *Gedenkschrift* about him under the title "Er und Wir" (He and we).[116] The essay was to show what Herzl meant to the Jewish people. In the quiet of memory, Buber acknowledged what he was not willing to grant to Herzl in 1904, that he was "a servant of the light," of progress in the form of Zionism, and that that was a good thing to be.

The first part of the essay was written in a vein not often seen in Buber, one of humility, even regret. In looking back, he perceived himself and his friends as doctrinaires, albeit "lyrical doctrinaires." "We felt the greatness and the beauty in the storm of history which surrounded us . . . in the flood of deeds, which carried us . . . in the flames of the Jewish experience, which made our soul burst . . . but we felt them not, not enough in the individual human figures whom we encountered."[117]

In essence, Buber affirmed that he and his friends, too, were carried away by the enthusiasm of the moment, a charge he had previously leveled against Herzl. He truly spoke in a different voice from that of the early years, realizing that he and his friends in the Democratic Fraction had had a particular agenda to the exclusion of all else. "We . . . asked above all about the contents of the human spirit. What do you think about the essence of Judaism? What do you think about Jewish culture? What do you think about the work in Palestine? That was the measure." With the gravity of the seasoned earth dweller, the thirty-two-year-old Buber concluded that "the decisive years of life on earth have since passed, and we have changed." In reflection, Buber acknowledged that "Herzl thought differently about the matter of Judaism than we did, he saw it differently." Buber still stood by what he had written in 1904, and Herzl would remain forever impenetrable to him because his stature was "naive, primary, elemental," and Buber's was not, but he now also saw "the essential," which he had not seen before, namely Herzl's greatness, his "exemplary stature."[118]

By 1910, Buber perceived two types of Jews among the early Zionists. He belonged to one group and Herzl to the other. Buber theorized that all greatness stemmed from "an elemental lack." This was, however, not a deficiency but a plus. The individual who becomes active because of this "elemental lack" becomes conscious of his Judaism. This realization, in turn, awakens in him the will to help the Jews to whose group he now feels he belongs, and he will do what his will tells him to do. "The elemental active one walks in the light even if he is wrong." Buber acknowledged that this was Herzl's greatness. He was "pure and strong" and as such saw the task before him: to reach unity within. Therefore, in Buber's opinion, "Herzl set the example for the active life."[119]

Buber considered Jews who saw everything as problematic as the counterpart to the "elemental" Herzl. He counted himself among those individuals. "We know all the problems of Judaism, because we also perceive our inwardness as a problem, even our existence is a problem." He saw the "*galut* form of inner duality" as the biggest problem and thought that "all great unification efforts of Judaism" stem from the yearning "to free ourselves from this duality." The problem child, for example, "knows his interiority merely as a host of questions." Likewise, "existence is a mass of contradictions which has to be solved, but which allows for a solution only in the metaphysical realm, never in the empirical." Furthermore, the problem child is aware of his Judaism, but only in the incredible paradox of his existence as a Jew. "He sees everything, all degeneration, all guilt, all inner hesitation." Buber explained that such an individual has to overcome a thousand desperations before he can act. Yet the problem child can go beyond the duality within to that "unity of soul powers which are capable of receiving enlightenment that teaches work and deed."[120] To know that this is his goal, he has to look to someone, like Herzl, as the model for the active life. Nowhere else did Buber come as close to exposing his own romantic inwardness and the danger this posed to his self than in this very honest assessment of his own complicated personality. The reader is justified in asking what changed, for it seems that the leader of modern Jewry who could not do anything right "Jewishly" for Buber during his lifetime was, at last, accorded his rightful place as a leader and a visionary of modern Jewry by him.

Buber and Ahad Ha-Am

Ahad Ha-Am was the pseudonym for Asher Hirsch Ginsberg, a Hasidic Jew who had embraced the Haskalah for the benefit of Judaism. Although his humility commanded him to write as one of the people (*ahad ha-am*), Ginsberg became the Socrates of modern Jewry, berating especially the young Western Jews for falling prey to German thought. One of these young men was Theodor Herzl. Ahad Ha-Am attended the First Zionist Congress in 1897. He commented that he felt like a mourner at a wedding feast and never returned to the fold of political Zionism, even though he cooperated with Buber and Weizmann in their efforts to achieve cultural Zionism.[121]

The message of the "secular Hasidic rebbe," as Arthur Hertzberg calls him, radiated to the West with the help of Martin Buber, whose keen sense comprehended the position of both political and spiritual Zionism.[122] Buber recognized the German Zionists' inability to grasp Ahad Ha-Am's message. Thus Buber mediated the message to make it accessible to German Jewry, much as he later mediated the spirit of Hasidism. Buber became the Jewish link who could communicate the new ideas being developed within this cultural movement to the near-assimilated German Jews in language and terminology that had meaning for them on the basis of their common German cultural background. Buber was one of the few at that time who could fulfill this mission by attempting to integrate the split realms of "external experience" and "inner substance." The result of the unification of these two spheres led to *Bejahung*. The essence of this affirmation was the imperative, "The past of his people is his personal memory, the future of his people his personal task."[123] Thus Buber not only translated Ahad Ha-Am's program into an idea acceptable to modern German Jewry, but he added his personal emphasis as well.

Ahad Ha-Am's focus was "the people, not the faith," and "the study hall, not the synagogue." Buber followed his mentor in the latter but not in the former. Although he steadfastly refused to submit to the yoke of the ritual, Buber was firmly rooted in prophetic biblical Judaism, and he considered faith as well as the people to be necessary for a Jewish life. Nor did Buber subscribe to Ahad Ha-Am's gradualism, seeing instead a volcanic transformation of the people. In retrospect, this turns out to be a problematic formulation, for Buber described the development of the Jewish movement as a gradual one, requiring two centuries at least.

It was Ahad Ha-Am who proposed the way to the "true" spirit in the form of cultural Zionism. Ahad Ha-Am was very unhappy with exilic Judaism, comparing it to a fossil, as did Buber, because the "people of the book" no longer used their conscience as an authority, but instead followed formulaic responses.[124] He thought further that the political asceticism of exilic Judaism was inappropriate because it reinforced a separation of the body and the spirit. Rather, he envisioned modern Pharisees who "represent the Prophetic conception of Judaism, with its unification of body and spirit." But not even Pharisaic Judaism was pure enough, for it created a "shadowy framework" within which "the Hebrew national spirit has lived its own distinctive life for two thousand years." Ahad Ha-Am desired to give the spirit once more a body through its restoration to Eretz Israel: "If there is to be a third [Jewish state], its fundamental principle, on the national as on the individual plane, will be neither the ascendancy of body over spirit, nor the suppression of the body for the sake of the spirit, but rather the uplifting of the body by the spirit."[125]

Ahad Ha-Am's primary concern was for the fate of Judaism, not the Jewish people. He realized that there could be no ingathering of all the exiles but that the "larger part of our people will [always] remain scattered on foreign soils." Yet he had a great vision:

> This Jewish settlement which will be gradual in growth will, in the course of time, become the center of the nation, wherein its spirit will find pure expression and develop in all its aspects to the highest degree of perfection of which it is capable. Then, from this center, the spirit of Judaism will radiate to the great circumference, to all the communities of the diaspora, to inspire them with new life and to preserve the over-all unity of our people.[126]

On the occasion of Ahad Ha-Am's sixtieth birthday, in 1916, Buber wrote an essay, "Der Wägende" (The one who weighs), which he published in his newly founded journal *Der Jude*.[127] He compared Ahad Ha-Am to the Rabbi of Apt, of whom it was said that he held golden scales between his teeth, for Ahad Ha-Am "weighs idea and reality faithfully, fairly, and reports the reliable results." Buber thought of Ahad Ha-Am as living "in his truth: a dual truth—the permanent one of his ideas and the changing one of his observations." The permanent truth he considered to be synthetic; the temporal one was critical. The former never changed, and he measured the other one by its standard. Ahad Ha-Am, in Buber's estimation, was a perfectionist who could not tolerate imperfection (*das Unzulängliche*).[128] The unfortunate venture of the B'nai Moshe society, founded by some of Ahad Ha-Am's followers in 1899 and disbanded a few years later, served as a reminder thereof. This organization hoped to realize Ahad Ha-Am's dreams of "raising the moral and cultural tone of the Jewish national revival" but failed to reach his expectations.[129] Buber suggested that his contemporaries, like Ahad Ha-Am, had to be prepared to act but that they "must first understand the purpose of our deed, not just be busy [*geschäftig*]."[130]

In this essay, Buber acknowledged that he and Ahad Ha-Am did not see things the same way, "not in the way we realize, not in the way we contemplate the meaning of the world, not in our conception of human history, not in the teachings of the essence and the task of Israel."[131] Already in 1909, Buber had expressed his views on Ahad Ha-Am. Ahad Ha-Am's writings were intellectual, like Buber's, yet Buber objected to his "talmudic problematic and Maimonidean abstraction."[132] Buber and Ahad Ha-Am also disagreed on the importance of the spiritual center for the diaspora. For Ahad Ha-Am, the spiritual center meant absolute renewal. Buber did not believe that this absolute renewal would occur without proper preparation beforehand, in the *galut*. The spiritual center was not the solution to Judaism's problems. Thus Buber ultimately disagreed substantially with Ahad Ha-Am, whom he admired in many ways. He nevertheless remained well disposed to the one "to whom I am devoted with my entire soul beyond all contradictions."[133] Whereas the differences between Buber and Ahad Ha-Am were mainly ones of focus, Buber's differences with Herzl were ideological and irreconcilable.

In these first few years, Buber put all of his energy into awakening his people. It was his first, consuming mission as a Zionist, a mission he would look back on years later with some disparagement. As early as 1901, in his essay titled "Gegenwartsarbeit" (Contemporary work), he almost mocked the enthusiasm of "the young ones," among whom he included himself, who joined the movement "with a burning heart and hands that were ready for action." He concluded somewhat sarcastically that this yearning and belief reflected a new enthusiasm, "a straw flame burning toward heaven, nothing more," for this belief was initially utopian and filled by the imagination, full of poetry and of mood; it was vague and without concrete contents.[134]

Although producing much empty rhetoric and slogans that fostered laziness in thinking, this propaganda work nevertheless produced a twofold educational effect. Positively, it introduced young idealists to reality and to facts, but negatively these individuals remained unsatisfied and needed to find another essential form of activity.[135] Buber was among these individuals. There is no doubt that the years 1900, 1901, and 1902 were Buber's most productive ones on behalf of the Zionist cause. This first phase of his Zionist activities came to an end with both the death of Theodor Herzl and the completion of his dissertation in 1904. In 1905, he withdrew from all propaganda work and devoted himself to studying Hasidism so as to infuse his political and cultural activism with substance. This work helped him to understand that the relative life, namely Zionism, was not enough.

4

HASIDISM

Apprenticeship in a Life of the Communal Spirit, 1905–1908

THIS CHAPTER explores primarily Buber's writings on spirituality. Buber studied the Hasidic sources and transmitted texts. In his view, because neither the Baal Shem Tov nor Rabbi Nachman (1772–1810) wrote down their teachings themselves, and we only have their stories transmitted by others, we must reconstruct their teaching from the stories or we must see the essence through the shell of the layers that accumulated over time. Buber took this task upon himself. He wrote that he collected these stories "from *Volksbücher* [popular literature], from notebooks and flyers, sometimes also through oral transmissions from individuals who had still witnessed" what he called "the stammering."[1]

Buber was disappointed with the truth value of the tales he discovered. He felt that they obscured the essence of the Hasidic message. He wrote that Rabbi Nachman liked to tell stories because he thought his teachings had no clothes. When he wanted to instill a mystical idea or a wisdom into the hearts of his students, the stories became the garments of the teachings. Unfortunately, his stories grew until they were no longer a teaching but a fairy tale or a legend.[2]

After some actual translating which he was unhappy with, Buber decided not to translate but "to tell the stories out of myself . . . as a true painter absorbs the contours of the model, and then creates the true image out of his creative mind."[3] He explained:

> I received and told it anew. I did not translate it, like a piece of literature, I did not adapt it as one might a fable, but I told it, as a *Nachgeborener* [one born later].[4] For I carry within me the blood and the spirit of those who created them, and also I created these stories anew from the same blood and spirit, which is also in me. I stand in the chain of storytellers, a link between links. Once more I tell the

> old story, and if it sounds new, that new element already was contained in it when it was told for the first time. My telling of Hasidic life neither aims at a real life situation nor at geographic specificity.[5]

Subsequently he produced two books, *Die Geschichten des Rabbi Nachman* (Tales of Rabbi Nachman) (1906) and *Die Legende des Baal-Schem* (The legend of the Baal Shem) (1908), parts of which were republished in his 1916 volume, *Vom Geist des Judentums*. He dedicated these efforts toward creating anew a traditional Jewish treasure "with devotion and love" to his grandfather, Salomon Buber, "the last master of the old Haskalah."[6]

Buber had a twofold agenda in his study of Hasidism. First, he wanted to counter Greek and Western rational thought with Eastern spirituality which would translate into deed. Buber considered the Jew to be Oriental, not Western. The Oriental person, according to Buber, is centrifugal, not centripedal.[7] Because he works from inside out, concepts are a beginning for the Jew, awaiting realization, whereas in Greek thought, and therefore in Western thought, they are the end point. Second, Buber wanted to renew the Jewish religion by recovering the mythical elements hitherto suppressed. He thought that ever since the Bible redaction, there had been a perception among Jews that there is no Jewish *Märchen* (fairy tale) because relatively little myth can be found in the Bible. This perception was fueled by the Gentiles, who disallowed the Jewish capability for myth on the ground that Jews are not creative. Buber disagreed with both and argued for the existence of a Jewish myth.

His work in Hasidism brought Buber into the contemporary debate of what should be the nature of twentieth-century Judaism. As Steven Aschheim has pointed out, both Neo-Orthodoxy and Zionism were marginal countermovements to the overwhelmingly large Reform movement among German Jewry at the turn of the century.[8] As we saw in Chapter 3, Buber had already spoken forcefully for Zionism with words and deeds. With his discussion of spirituality in the form of mysticism, religiosity, and myth, Buber joined this internal Jewish debate. He was not alone in his quest to return to Jewish spirituality (by which he did *not* mean Jewish religion),[9] but he was unique in his efforts to enrich national Jewish feelings with prophetic fervor by appropriating Hasidism for this purpose.[10]

There were many reasons why Buber thought Hasidism to be congenial to his purpose: it was a popular revivalist movement that had arisen from the masses very much the way Zionism did in his own day; Hasidism was an intensely pious movement, yet, in contrast to Christian piety, which was mostly otherworldly, it was rooted in life and in the world; Hasidism was often called an anti-intellectual movement because it opposed the intellectualism and casuistries of the Talmudic scholars and instead emphasized the importance of simple literary genres such as legends and songs. Hasidism also emphasized the importance of personal intervention with God; hence a rebbe or spiritual leader could become a hero among the people. One could say that Hasidism played the same antagonistic role in relation to the religious-political order within Judaism that Pietism played for the religious-political order of the church.

We saw in Chapter 2 that Buber had a serious interest in the human soul. He had earlier attempted to establish a mystical-ethical God-connectedness that would turn pathos into ethos. Now he again tried to understand how the personal experience of God is realized in the ethical deed of the individual. The importance of this reciprocal relationship between God and the human being became clear as early as his Bar Mitzvah in 1891. In his Bar Mitzvah speech, Buber addressed fundamental ethical issues that are important for leading a Jewish life.[11] In the intervening years, Buber might well have turned to Reform Judaism, which focused on ethical monotheism as well. But he did not do so. He likewise might have remained with the tenets of humanism, fusing Jewish and German Enlightenment values as he did in his Bar Mitzvah address.[12] Instead, he turned to a childhood memory, Hasidism, which addressed these very same principles, but in a mode more congenial to Buber's romantic temperament.

In the Hanukkah edition 5678 (1917) of the publication *Mitteilungen des Verbandes der Jüdischen Jugendvereine Deutschlands* (News organ of the organization of Jewish youth groups in Germany), Buber published an essay titled "Mein Weg zum Chassidismus" (My way to Hasidism).[13] It is an essay of great honesty, Buber's own "confession" of his travels to his roots. In this essay, he explained his earlier (childhood) and his later (adolescent) encounters with the Hasidic movement as well as his own spiritual homecoming during the years from 1905 on in which he studied and published many Hasidic tales. We learn of the agony Buber underwent after he left the roots of his childhood and the guidance and counsel of his grandfather. "As long as I lived with him, I was rooted, although some questions and doubts nagged me." As soon as he left his grandfather's home, however, "the confusion of the Age enveloped me."[14]

So he did not speak in the abstract of those who could not find the way to God, but rather from personal experience. He, too, was one of the modern, rootless souls, who needed to withdraw into seclusion, as he did for five years between 1904 and 1909, to determine what should be at the center for him and, if possible, to make contact with that center.

> Until my twentieth year, and somewhat also beyond that my mind was in constant and varied movement, in a change of tensions and resolutions which were influenced by varied sources and took on ever new form, but *without center* and without increasing substance: I truly lived in the "olam ha-tohu," the "world of confusion," the mythical habitation of the restless souls—in a fluid state of the spirit (mind), but *without Judaism* as well as *without humanity* and without the presence of the Divine.[15]

This rootlessness did not last very long. As early as 1898, Buber connected with the Zionist movement, and already in 1899 he was a delegate to the Third Zionist Congress. As we have seen, from then on, Buber was very active for the Zionist cause. Most important, however, in this essay Buber made an interesting observation, namely, that his connection to Zionism and his new link with his "context," Judaism, was "only a first step." It was his belief that the national commitment alone does not change the Jewish person; he or she can be just as spiritually poor, if not quite as rudderless, without it. This stabilizing image describes well Buber's conception of Zionism, not as the end point but as the point of departure for the Jew's spiritual quest. "If Zionism is not seen as a sense of satisfaction but as a catalyst, not as a homecoming to a port, but as the departure to the open seas, then it may well lead to transformation. This is what happened to me."[16] What was left to do now was to turn the spiritual poverty around.

Buber concluded that even though he had committed himself to Judaism by his rerooting in the *Gemeinschaft* through his Zionist activities, he did so "without really knowing Judaism." This led him to the second step—wanting to know Judaism (*Erkennenwollen*). Buber wrote, " 'Knowing'—which doesn't mean an accumulation of anthropological, historical, sociological knowledge, as important as this is—is . . . the unmediated knowledge, the eye-to-eye knowledge of peoplehood [*Volkstum*] in its creative origins [*Ur-kunden*]." This search for direct knowledge of the sources led him to resume his study of Hebrew, which he had been neglecting. He read and immersed himself in the nature of the language and in doing so, he claimed to discover the self.[17] Buber described how one day he found a little book, *Zewaath Ribesch*,[18] *Testament of Rabbi Israel Baalshem*—a book about the teachings of the founder of the Hasidic movement. The words, "which jumped out at me," were powerful and meaningful: "He shall grasp the quality of eagerness. He shall, in his eagerness, rise from his sleep, for he has been hallowed and has become a different person and he is worthy of creating and he has become as the Divine [has discovered his Divine attributes], blessed be He who created worlds."[19] This message brought about Buber's spiritual awakening, directing his productive genius into channels that allowed him to become one of the productive Jews he had written about in his essay on Jewish art in 1903 and on the productive ones in 1902. Following his thorough immersion in Jewish culture, Buber now understood that the missing dimension had been spiritual.

In this 1917 essay, Buber gave us an account of the crucial direct encounter with the Source, describing his response to the reading:

> It was at that time that I, immediately overwhelmed, experienced the Hasidic soul. I comprehended original Jewish knowledge [*Urjüdisches ging mir auf*], in the darkness of the exile it blossomed in renewed form: humanity's creation in the image of God as deed, as becoming, as task. And I comprehended this *original Jewish essence* as an *original human essence*, the contents of human religiosity. I understood Judaism *as religiosity*, as "piety," as *hasidut*. The picture from my childhood, the memories of the zaddik and his community returned and inspired me: I recognized the idea of the perfect human being. At the same time *I became aware of my calling* [*Beruf*] to proclaim this idea to the world.[20]

The encounter with the Divine allows the individual to discover his absolute self.[21] In Zionism he had discovered his relative self. Now this new and powerful revelation complemented Buber's untutored enthusiasm for Zionism, and the ensuing synthesis which he forged between the two became the basis for all of his future work. Buber hoped to be able to turn around what he perceived to be the godlessness of his time on the one hand and the petrified Jewish religion on the other. Instead of a religion of the rabbis, Buber desired a popular religion, as he described it in his platform for Zionism, but on the model of Hasidism,[22] which would prove that monotheism and myth were not mutually exclusive as the Reform movement and Christians asserted.

Jewish Mysticism

"Popular mysticism" or a "mysticism of the people" was not common in the history of Judaism. In his essay "Die jüdische Mystik" (Jewish mysticism), Buber presented what he considered a history of messianism which shows that until the sixteenth century Jewish mystical teachings were a closely guarded secret.

During Talmudic times, mysticism was a secret one would entrust only to "a master of arts able to whisper." Josephus reported that the Essenes closely guarded the mystery and the ancient sacred writings. According to Buber, only much later did the teachings reach beyond the sect and beyond personal transmission; the first preserved writings are found in the *Book of Creation* [*Sefer Yetzirah*], which he dates from the seventh to the ninth centuries. Between that period and the publication of the *Zohar* at the end of the thirteenth century lies the time of the actual development of the Kabbalah. But those who dealt with the Kabbalah were few in numbers and the teachings were removed from life.[23]

It must be pointed out here that Buber saw the Kabbalah through the eyes of Cusa and Böhme. He characterized it as a "theory in the neo-platonic sense, as a contemplation of God" that "did not demand that one walk in its footsteps, it did not depend on action, on choice, which . . . is so central to Hasidism; Kabbalah was outside the human realm and only in its perception of ecstasy did it coincide with the reality of the soul." In Buber's view, the Kabbalah was not an ethical imperative for life. Like Hasidism, the Kabbalah did oppose two other powers: one, "the rigid religion which was concerned for the Law and was against all personal life," and two, "the Aristotelian rationalism which was distant from all nature." But in Buber's view, it "did not counter the ethos of the two with its own [ethos], so that its meaning was not communicated to the people." Thus the Kabbalah truly remained a secret teaching for a few elitists and did not affect the spiritual life of the masses.[24]

In Buber's view, only in the last period of this epoch did new powers become visible. The expulsion of the Jews from Spain in 1492 gave messianic qualities to the Kabbalah.[25] He saw this as "the only concerted effort of the diaspora to create a community that would provide a home for the spirit," but, alas, "it ended in shambles and despair." Thereafter, "the old abyss once more opened and from it arose, as always, the old dream of redemption, mighty and imposing as it had not been since Roman times," and with it lived on the yearning that "the absolute had to become reality some day." Buber thought that "the messianism of the Jews had always been a desire for the impossible." The Kabbalah could not ignore messianism, calling God's kingdom on earth "the completed world."[26]

The Kabbalah harbored "the ecstasy of the people," and from there, the ecstasy "entered into the Jewish people as the messiah will some day enter into his city." This resulted in a new era of Jewish mysticism, around the middle of the sixteenth century, which "heralded *the ethical-ecstatic deed of the individual* [emphasis added] as a contribution to redemption." This new era began with Isaac Luria (1534–72). He was influenced almost entirely by the older Kabbalah, but "in his presentation of the indirect effect of the human soul, which purifies [*geläutert*] and completes itself, he gave new form to and created new followers for the old wisdoms." Luria believed that the perfection of a few people could bring about the messianic kingdom.[27]

That basic feeling found its expression one hundred years later in the great messianic movement associated with Shabbatai Zvi (1625–76). Buber called Shabbatianism "an issuance [*Entladung*] of unknown people powers and a revelation of the hidden reality of the national soul."[28] The seemingly absolute (*unmittelbar*) values of life and property became invalid, and "the masses left them behind like something superfluous and like a garment which glides from the hand of the running person, to reach the goal natural and free."[29] Thus "the tribe . . . became aflame for the sake of the message." But this movement also collapsed, more terribly than any earlier one.[30] Thereafter, messianism once more returned to the womb (*verinnerlicht*), and a period of true modification ensued. The people succumbed more and more to the belief that they would be able to force the upper worlds to cooperate through mystical exercises. Buber wrote that by 1700, fifteen hundred faithful went to Eretz Israel to await the Messiah, but most of them perished, some already on the way there.[31]

Hasidism, which Buber considered to be "the latest and highest development of Jewish mysticism," occurred around the middle of the eighteenth century. In Buber's view, a transformation had occurred. He claimed that "Hasidism at once continued and contrasted Jewish mysticism as it had existed." Until Hasidism, Jewish mysticism had been otherworldly, like Christian mysticism, secretive and enigmatic to the average person. But Hasidism changed all that. For in Hasidism, pathos, which had been the impetus to thought in the Kabbalah, had come home and become ethos.[32]

According to Buber, "Kabbalah become ethos" meant that "the life which the *hasid* teaches does not consist of asceticism, but of joy in God."[33] He was emphatic that, although "*hasid*" means "the pious one," Hasidism is *not* Pietism. Rather, Hasidism is "without all sentimentality and expressions of emotion," that is, without *Innerlichkeit* (inwardness), as it is known in German Pietism and romanticism. The *hasid* "lifts the beyond to the here and now and allows it to work and to form, as the soul molds the body. Its center is a God-filled and realistic guide to ecstasy as the meaning and pinnacle of life." But ecstasy is here not an unmaking of the soul, as in Christian mysticism,[34] but precisely the opposite, its unfolding; ecstasy is not "the limiting and ascetic soul, but the perfecting soul which unites with the Absolute." "In asceticism, the spiritual being, the *neshama* [soul] shrivels up, becomes listless, becomes empty and dull; in joy alone can it grow and perfect itself, until it ripens to godliness without any blemish." Buber thought that "at no time did any teachings connect the search for God to Jewish self-fulfillment with such strength and such clarity as in Hasidism."[35] With the exception of Jesus, Buber did not find the realized mystical experience in Christianity, only the theory *or* the individual ecstasy. Because he could not claim Jesus for Judaism without objection from fellow Jews, he did not find it in Judaism either, until the time of Hasidism.

In placing Hasidism in its historical context, Buber made two interesting points. It made sense to him that "this spiritual regeneration" should have happened in Poland because, first, "Poland had a strong Jewish community due to the alien, hostile surroundings and events, such as the Chmielnicki massacres in the Ukraine during the uprisings of the mid-seventeenth century"; and second, in Buber's romantic view of country life, the Jew in those areas had not become a city dweller who had shriveled up in narrow Rabbinic studies or become shallow (*verflacht*) in the mercantile atmosphere, but rather a villager, "lonely [*einsam*] and closer to his self, limited in [bookish] knowledge, but original in his belief and strong in his dream of God."[36]

In Buber's view, the people of that time were receptive to a message that praised the purity and sanctity of the soul over knowledge of the mind. Therefore, he believed that the Hasidic message was received "like a revelation," to which the established Orthodox world responded "with a declaration of war, banning them from the country . . . closing synagogues, burning books, imprisonment, and public mistreatment of the leaders [of the movement]." Unfortunately, the Jewish Orthodoxy "also did not shrink from denunciations to the [non-Jewish] government." But "the religious rigidity could not keep up with religious renewal."[37]

And yet Hasidism declined. Buber explained that "Hasidism wanted the impossible" from the people: it wanted "an intensity and concentration of the soul . . . which the people couldn't give." Hasidism offered redemption, but "the people couldn't pay the price." Hasidism offered "purity and clarity of vision, a tension and concentration of spiritual life . . . as the bridge to God." As any popular religious movement would, "it [Hasidism] addressed the many," but only a few were capable of comprehending. Buber saw "a dangerous opponent" to Hasidism in the Haskalah, the Jewish Enlightenment, whose adherents fought "the heresy [of Hasidism] in the name of knowledge, civilization, and Europe." But he keenly observed that it was only because of the splits that already existed within the Hasidic movement that the Haskalah was able to gain ground in the East.[38]

Referring to the continual efforts to refute the authenticity of Jewish mysticism, Buber conceded that, in comparison with Eckhart, Plotinus, and Laotse, or even the *Upanishads*, "Jewish mysticism may appear to be uneven, often unclear, at times trivial." Yet he celebrated Jewish mysticism as "the wonderful flower of an ancient tree, whose color is almost too bright, whose scent seems almost too strong, and yet is one of the few plants of inner soul wisdom and collected ecstasy." Buber insisted on the intrinsic nature of Jewish mysticism, defying those who claimed that the expression of mysticism was a reaction against the rational order. This was a very important step because Buber recognized an inner regenerative power in Judaism independent of external events. The fact that "extremes ignite each other, faster and more powerfully than in other people" was "a meaningful particularity of the Jew which hardly changed over the eons."[39] Such a spirit later emerged in the Zionist movement.

Most German Jews anticipated a new dawn in the wake of the French Revolution and adopted the stance of a Moses Mendelssohn, who looked forward to eventual freedom and full emancipation. Yet there were dangers connected with such total freedom, and Buber warned his emancipated fellow Jews not to fall into the trap of hedonism.[40] In the East, however, the most abject poverty and political oppression still continued after the Emancipation of western and central European Jewry. To Buber, it was therefore not surprising that mysticism should both arise and continue to influence Jewish life there. "Thus it happens that in the midst of an incredibly limited existence . . . suddenly, with a power which cannot be tamed, the unlimited breaks forth and then rules the unresisting soul." He thought that the vision of Elijah may be seen as a symbol of this power. Buber believed that one reason why the Jew's circumstances affected him so strongly was that he lived his life *"in relation,* not in essence." This expressed itself in one of two possible ways: "if he has a narrow soul, he becomes utilitarian," or, "if he has an expansive soul, he becomes an idealist." Buber thought that "almost never does the Jew live with things, nurturing them quietly, in tune with the world, and sure in his being."[41]

There is something, however, that "gives a core to the Jewish soul." Buber called this something *pathos,* "an intrinsic quality which once formed with all other qualities of the tribe from its location and its fate." Although "the demands of pathos are unfulfillable," pathos nevertheless "reaches out its arms to embrace the boundless," as can be seen in the examples of Moses and of the prophets, who demanded absolute justice; in Jesus and Paul, who demanded absolute love; or in the intention of Spinoza, who wished to formulate existence. Thus "the soul which cannot find grounding in reality is redeemed from its emptiness and barrenness by taking root in the impossible."[42]

Whether the Jews in Buber's day would be able to revive their mystical tradition, however, would depend on whether Jewish pathos (which is ethos gone underground) would again become Jewish ethos.[43] Thus, in Buber's interpretation, the mission of Hasidism was much different from that of the mysticism of other religions or even from earlier Jewish mysticism because the *inner* fate of Judaism was tied to the *external* realization of the spirit. Buber was under no circumstances looking for a return to traditional Judaism. Within Rabbinism, an independent course was not a desirable path to the sacred. Rather, Buber envisioned a new approach that would consist of individual yet communal seeking of spiritual communion in the world.

Jewish mysticism received its power from "an original quality of the people, which created it," and in which the destiny of the people is also centered. Thus the electrification is mutual. Again and again, "the wandering and the martyrdom of the Jews" put their souls into a state of utmost despair from which the flash of ecstasy can easily ignite. But at the same time, the wandering and martyrdom prevented them from developing "a pure expression of ecstasy," resulting in writings such as the *Zohar*, which Buber called "a pleasure and an abomination" because one finds at the same time "coarse anthropomorphisms and dull speculation," as well as "views of secret depths of the soul and revelations of ultimate secrets." Buber thought that the Jews were always in danger of "reducing pathos to rhetoric," a problem he perceived in the Zionist movement. Yet again and again "pathos is freed and becomes purer and greater than before."[44]

Jewish Religiosity

One of the first steps toward total communion with God is the spirit of religiosity. In his essay "Mein Weg zum Chassidismus," Buber confessed that he felt he had a calling not only to return to Jewish spirituality himself but also to teach the world how to do the same. So he apprenticed himself anew to the God of Abraham, Isaac, and Jacob. "First came a period of study. [In 1904] I retreated at the age of twenty-six for five years from the activities of the Zionist movement, from writing articles and giving speeches, and collected, not without trouble, the dispersed, partly lost writings [*Schrifttum*] [of the Hasidim], and I immersed myself in them, discovering mysterious world upon mysterious world."[45] The two Hasidic masters whose work and life he was most impressed by were Israel ben Eliezer, the Baal Shem Tov, and Rabbi Nachman of Brazlav.

The Baal Shem Tov

Israel ben Eliezer was the inadvertent founder of Hasidism. In 1908, two years after Buber wrote the story of his great-grandson, Rabbi Nachman, he published the legend of the Baal Shem. The book, according to Buber's introduction, consists of "a message and twenty-one stories." The message tells about the life of the Hasidim, "an eastern European sect that was formed around the middle of the eighteenth century and still exists today, but in degenerate form." He was not reporting the historical development and the decay of the sect, or its customs, but rather "the twofold relationship to the Absolute and to the world which these people thought, desired, and attempted to live."[46]

The Legend of the Baal Shem tells about the life of the founder of this sect, Rabbi Israel ben Eliezer, who lived from 1700 to 1760, primarily in Podolia and Wolhynia. Buber explained that "the life being told is not what we call 'the real life.' " He was not recounting the dates and facts whose compilation one could call the biography of the Baal Shem, although he was quick to add that this would be a worthwhile project for someone else.[47] Rather, Buber constructed the Baal Shem's biography "from his legend," in which are contained "the dream and the yearning of the people."[48] Orphaned at a very young age, Israel was raised by the community until he was old enough to care for himself. Thereafter he became a teacher who wandered from community to community until the time of his marriage, when he settled down. But Israel did not become a productive member of his community; rather, he lived in the mountains, helped by his wife, and they both experienced extreme hardship. This period ended in a revelation of his self to the people, whereafter Israel ben Eliezer became known as Israel Baal Shem and eventually, in recognition of his outstanding leadership, as Israel Baal Shem Tov. Baal Shem Tov means "master of the good name," and Buber characterized him as "untiring in *hitlahavut* [ecstasy] and leadership capability."[49] To Buber, the Baal Shem Tov was an authentic Jew.

Although the teachings of the Baal Shem Tov were preserved only very imperfectly from notes written by his disciples, Buber believed that their real meaning was recognizable.

> The Baal Shem teaches that God is the essence of everything. He who . . . beholds the essence of creation beholds God. God does not

> speak out of things, but he thinks inside of things; thus, he can be received only with the innermost strength of the soul. If this energy is set free, then the human being can in any place and at any time unite with God. Every deed which is hallowed, no matter how base or senseless it may appear to the outsider, is the way to the heart of the world.[50]

Buber explained that in all things, even the inanimate, there live sparks of life, which fall into the soul that is ready to receive them. "What we call evil is not an evil being, but a lack; it is 'God in exile,' the lowest rung of the good, the throne of the good; it is, in the language of the old Kabbalah, the shell [*klipah*] which surrounds and hides the essence of things."[51]

Hasidic teachings were the great antidote to the guilt feelings that Christian and also some Jewish teachings imposed on their adherents, challenging and reversing such doctrines. Buber knew the importance of such a message to Jews and non-Jews alike and stressed these qualities in Hasidism. For instance, Hasidism taught that there is nothing that is evil and unworthy of love. The desires of people are also not evil; "the greater a human being, the greater his drive"; but "the pure and hallowed person transforms his drives into 'a chariot for God,' " he separates it from all of the shell and allows his soul to perfect itself therein. "The human being must feel his desires in their roots and conquer them," learning pride and not being proud; knowing anger and not being angry. The Hasidic human being does flagellate himself; the difference is that he will do it "full of joy." While his glance looks far away, his vision concentrates on his immediate surroundings; while he listens to jokes, he may well be sad. Buber's uncritical stance marveled that "he sits here and his heart is in the Above; he eats here and enjoys this world and *simultaneously* partakes in the world of spiritual bliss."[52] This ability to have a foot in each world at the same time became the hallmark of Hasidism's unique character.

Buber postulated that "the fate of man is only the expression of his soul." So, for instance, if a person's thoughts ponder the unclean, he experiences the unclean, whereas the person who delves into the sacred experiences the sacred. "The human being's thoughts are his Being: he who thinks of the upper world is in it." As Buber had already pointed out in his dissertation, all outer law is merely a step to that within; and it is the final purpose of the individual to "become a law unto himself."[53] The model for a community of the spirit can be found in Hasidism.

Buber inserted an explanation of four terms which he considered central to the life of the Hasidim: *hitlahavut* (ecstasy), *avodah* (service), *kavanah* (intent), and *shiflut* (humility). The language he used in his discussion of these terms was mystical, but the meaning of each of these terms is existential, that is, ethical.

Hitlahavut (Ecstasy)

Through *hitlahavut*, Buber expressed the fire of ecstasy which he considered "the goblet of mercy and the eternal key." To find God means "to find the way which is without limits." And ecstasy is such a way because all the past and the future are telescoped into the present. This ecstasy was "not a sudden disappearance in eternity, but an ascending to the infinite from rung to rung."[54] Buber pointed out that the actual life of the ecstatic is not among the people. There, he would feel like a stranger[55] because everyone else lives only on the surface. The mystic who desires God, on the other hand, is capable of seeing Him in all of creation, while those who do not live on this rung "see things apart from God."[56] In further explaining the conception of *hitlahavut*, Buber used an example from a Hasidic master: "It [*hitlahavut*] expands the soul to [the dimension of] the universe. It narrows the universe to Nothing." Thus,

> the creation of heaven and earth is the unfolding of something from Nothing, the descent of the above to the below. But the saints [*zaddikim*] who separate from being and adhere to God always, they truly behold and grasp Him, as if the Nothing were the same that it was before creation. They again transform the something to the Nothing. And that is the nobler of the two: to lift up that which is below. We read in the Gemara that "the later miracle is greater than the former."[57]

Avodah (service, worship)

The second Hasidic term is *avodah*. The concept of *avodah* became well known through the reflections of one of the most revered early settlers in the new yishuv, Aaron David Gordon,[58] who was a nature mystic but not a Hasid.[59] The word may indicate anything from work to worship and means service with the right intent in all instances. If one hallows one's life, realizing that it is a gift from God which the human being is to use to perfect creation, then one serves God with the same devotion as in worship, for service with the proper devotion *is* worship.

Buber compared *avodah* to *hitlahavut*. He noted that *hitlahavut* is "the embracing of God beyond time and space," while *avodah* is "service to God in time and space." As "*hitlahavut* is a mystical meal," so "*avodah* is a mystical sacrifice." They are two poles "between which the life of the sacred moves back and forth." *Hitlahavut* is silent because the individual is embraced by God, but *avodah* speaks. According to Buber, "the mysterious which we leave when we speak of it," namely *hitlahavut*, "becomes visibly manifest in the rhythm of our deeds, in the form of *avodah*." Buber pointed out that *hitlahavut* is as far from *avodah* as fulfillment from desire. And yet, "*hitlahavut* goes forth from *avodah* like God-finding from God-seeking." Although we can today not even imagine how long since God created the world, Buber asserted that God actually today "works in the human being as he worked in the chaos at the time of the creation of the world." When the human being collects his thoughts and unites himself, "he moves closer to the unity of God and serves his master. That is *avodah*."[60]

Kavanah (Devotion)

"*Kavanah* is the mystery of the goal-oriented soul." Buber explained that *kavanah* is "a beam of the Divine glory that lives in each human being and means redemption." The Divine glory in the world is protected or hidden by shells [*klipot*], and in *kavanah* the shells fall away so that the kernel, which is the Divine Shechinah, is momentarily completely reunited with the Almighty. According to Hasidic teachings, "all human beings are the homes of wandering souls." As in Hinduism, the souls live in many beings and move from person to person until completion. Not only souls are trapped but Divine sparks as well. "They live in everything that exists." It is the purpose of *kavanah* "to allow the human being to uplift the fallen and to free the prisoners."[61]

The idea of the imprisoned Divine sparks bears dwelling on for a moment. This was a point of the utmost importance for Buber, who had suffered through the agony of dualism in its many dimensions throughout his young life. Dualism, a philosophical concept, was of Aristotelian origin.[62] In religion, it made itself felt most explicitly in the Christian heresy known as Gnosticism. Yet it not only plagued Christianity for many centuries, but also Judaism.[63] As I discussed in Chapter 2, the idea of dualism was reintroduced through the renewed focus on classical thought in the eighteenth century. Hasidism, which originated in the East at the same time that neoclassicism came to life in the West, contained the redemptive spiritual mechanism of unity in its teachings. In his attempt at a solution to the dilemma of modern alienation, Buber found a solution to Gnostic dualism as well as to individual alienation in this form of Jewish mysticism.

For the human being in the middle of the eighteenth century to participate actively in the redemption of the world was a revolutionary, even heretical, idea. Yet Buber insisted that the individual cannot only wait and watch, "the individual can contribute to the redemption of the world." He cautioned, however, that "in reality, everyone can only act in his sphere. Every human being has . . . an extended sphere of being for which he is responsible." This redemption does not occur through a miracle but through *avodah* with *kavanah*. "The human being can work on the form of the Divine glory through *any* deed." It is not the nature of the deed that matters but the intent with which one performs it. Buber argued that one can pray, sing, eat, speak, think, and transact business with devotion. Such an individual is capable of lifting the fallen sparks and of redeeming and renewing the fallen worlds. Every human being is surrounded by a "natural circle" of things he is destined to redeem above all else. These are the beings and things that belong to him: animals, garden, walls, anger, tools, food. "If he takes care of them and enjoys them with *kavanah*, he frees their souls." But even within his own soul there are sparks that need to be freed. These occur often in the form of "alien, disturbing thoughts" during prayer.[64] The goal orientation of *kavanah* will turn such alien thoughts into hymns of glory.

Shiflut (Humility)

Just as it is not necessary for the individual to do something unusual to redeem the Divine sparks, so it is also not necessary for the Jew to be someone unusual. Every human being is special because he or she is unique. Uniqueness of the individual is assured by the different combinations of human qualities and traits, and conversely, the individual's uniqueness assures his eternal being. Buber admonished that "uniqueness is the essential wealth of the human being and it is his task to unfold it."[65] Nothing is repeatable, not a flower, not an animal, and not a human being. Every act of creation is a onetime miracle. This is also an idea Buber had discussed in his dissertation.

According to Buber, the more special one is, "the more he or she has to contribute to others." The recipient might be limited in how much he can accept and use. The unique person redeems the fallen worlds so long as he remembers that he is no island but only a part of the whole. And Buber concluded, "the purer and more perfect he is, the better he knows that he is a part. . . . That is the mystery of humility."[66]

Thus humility is the ideal preparation for community, a process of give-and-take that works to redeem creation and thereby helps to redeem God. Buber stressed that one of the basic words of community is "love."[67] Here we hear echoes of Buber's Bar Mitzvah address and of his 1901 essay on old and new community. He thought that the person who understood this understands Judaism in a new way.

If the life of a human being is open to the Absolute in every thing and in every activity, then he or she shall live a hallowed life. Every morning the Hasid receives his vocation anew. "May he rise hurriedly and eagerly from his bed, for he is holy and a different human being and is worthy of creation, and he is *like God* who creates worlds." The human being finds God on all paths, and all paths lead to unity.[68] This is a much different conception of mysticism from that found in the ecstatic confessions Buber published in 1909.

Although all activities contribute equally to the redemption of the world, the purest and most perfect path is that of prayer, for God Himself speaks the inner word in the throat of the one who prays with *kavanah* (concentration). It is the inner experience that matters; the outer word is merely its garment. "As the smoke rises from burning embers, but the heavy parts stick to the floor and turn to ashes, so from prayer only the will and the ecstasy arise, but the outer words turn to ashes."[69]

In Hasidism, prayer occurs in great joy. "Joy alone is true worship." This idea is certainly different from the experience of the *Klosterekstase* in Christianity. In the *Klosterekstase* there is pain and regret at having sinned, and the joylessness of asceticism is considered an appropriate vehicle to a communion with God. But the spontaneous joy of prayer had also disappeared from the worship service in Judaism, at least so Buber thought, and his reminder of Hasidism was to call attention to this fact and to try to revive the spirit according to the mystical model. Thus the greater the ecstasy, the stronger the *kavanah*, and the more inevitable the union between the Creator and the created. As Buber stated, "It is a very great grace from God that the human being remains alive after prayer for, according to nature, he would have to die, because he buried his strength and put it in his prayer, because of the *kavanah* in him. . . . Before prayer he shall think that he is prepared to die for the sake of *kavanah*."[70]

Rabbi Nachman of Bratzlav

Buber's first intimation of the Hasidic treasures came in a booklet that he considered to be different from all the others. *Sipurei Maaseiot*[71] (Stories of deeds) was composed from memory by the students and followers of Rabbi Nachman of Bratzlav, the great-grandson of the Baal Shem, whom Buber called "perhaps the last Jewish mystic." Buber considered Rabbi Nachman's period to be "one of deepest tragedy" because it was the time of the untimely demise of the Hasidic movement. Although some men, such as Rabbi Nachman and Schneor Zalman, tried to restore pure thought by combining the pantheistic elements of the Hasidic idea into a system of great power and unity, others tried to replace the empty and deceiving miracle maker through the hallowed and dedicated mediator, but they "failed because of human small-mindedness."[72]

Rabbi Nachman did not suffer from such inadequacy. He was different in every respect from the zaddikim of the time. While they lived in fame, riches, and arrogance, he transmitted the Hasidic teachings in a small room. Although Buber mentioned Rabbi Nachman's struggle with temptation, which "also came close to him," Rabbi Nachman resisted. Buber considered Zalman and Nachman to be radicals, like the prophets of Israel, who did nothing halfheartedly but everything with full commitment. Hence these Hasidic zaddikim were not reformers but revolutionaries; they did not want to improve but to bring about absolute change; they did not want to educate but to redeem.[73] Buber considered reformers who wished to affect the world piecemeal as symptomatic of the modern, fragmented spirit, and therefore ineffective.

In Buber's opinion, Rabbi Nachman of Bratzlav was "the greatest, purest, and most tragic" of the late zaddikim. He "wanted to return the old glow to the crown," and he was angry at those who desecrated the Temple. He harbored the great dream of the zaddik, who is the soul of the people, and in his personal life he "sacrificed happiness and hope . . . to this dream," investing in it all his struggling and all his strength.[74] Nachman lost his dearest ones because of this commitment (though Buber did not tell us how).

According to the legend, Nachman was poor and surrounded by enemies to the end—enemies who were envious of his success and who disputed the truth of his teachings. Nachman's views on the matter were unusual, to be sure. When the local rabbis fought against him, he responded, "Why shouldn't they fight against us. We are not of this world, that's why they are against us."[75] To illustrate his point, Rabbi Nachman was fond of telling one of the Baal Shem Tov's stories, which Buber related. A deaf man came upon a group of musicians who were playing on their instruments while people danced to the music. Because he could not hear, the people's behavior was nonsensical to him. Rabbi Nachman thus justified his enemies, seeing their anger as a blessing. "All words of abomination and all enmity against the genuine and silent one are like stones that are hurled against him, yet he builds his house from them."[76] Thus the person being attacked transforms bad to good, an intrinsically Hasidic quality.

The concept of vocation (*Berufung*) was an important aspect of Buber's philosophy. To Buber, Rabbi Nachman's life was an example of one who follows his call. In his description, Buber focused on the different stages of development of Nachman's soul.[77] Buber pointed out that even as a boy, Nachman was "seeking and struggling." Like the mystics of other religions, especially Christian mystics, Nachman at first tried to bring on visions through suffering, fasting, and avoiding rest; at night he would run to a deserted place and speak to God "in the vernacular," meaning Yiddish, but to no avail. God would not answer. Once, Nachman wanted to welcome Shabbat in the proper fashion and began his preparations by going to the ritual bath as early as midnight on Thursday to purify himself. He then put on his Shabbat clothes and went to the synagogue, concentrating all his senses on experiencing a vision, but nothing happened. As Buber told it, the boy crawled under a prayer book stand, with tears flowing from his eyes, and he wept and wept for hours, until his eyes swelled shut and it was evening. When he opened his eyes, the light from the Shabbat candles greeted him like a flood and his soul became calm.[78] Even though deepest despair overcame him because he thought he was cast out, his fellow Jews did not know of his anguish. Nachman had a happy, strong nature and a fresh sense for the beauty of the world. In public, he carried on with silliness, jokes, and pranks so that no one knew what he was yearning for.

At age fourteen, Nachman was married according to the Jewish customs of that time and place, and he settled in the village of his father-in-law. Here, for the first time, he came close to nature. This had a profound effect on him, and Nachman developed a pantheistic notion of God in nature, which he later repeatedly conveyed to his students. He taught that "if man is privileged to hear the songs of the plants . . . how beautiful it is to hear their singing. It is good to serve God in their midst. . . . All of nature's speech fuses with your speech and increases its power. With every breath you drink the air of paradise, and when you return, the world is renewed in your eyes." According to Buber, "love for living and growing things was strong in him [Nachman],"[79] an idea that Spinoza had already held dear well before the eighteenth century.

It was Buber's opinion that this encounter with nature effected the turning Nachman had hoped for. He explained that

> the [ghetto] Jew who has spent his youth in the narrowness of the city is gripped by an incredible power, not known to the non-Jew. A thousand years of estrangement from nature kept his soul in fetters. And now that he is surrounded by . . . the green of the forest and the wild flowers, suddenly the walls of his spiritual ghetto come tumbling down. . . . The tendency to asceticism leaves him, the inner struggle ends, he no longer needs to strain for a revelation, he easily and joyfully finds God in all things. The boat, in which he rows onto the river, full of trust, although not knowing how to row, leads to God, whose voice he hears from the reed grass; and the horse, which . . . carries him to the forest, brings him closer to God, Who looks at him from all of the trees, and with Whom every plant is intimate. He is present in all the mountains and in all the valleys, each is a different way to get to God.[80]

In Buber's eyes, Nachman's persistence in pursuing an unpopular course made him a great man. As we remember from Buber's study of *Zarathustra*, to live dangerously was what life was all about.[81]

Fearfulness and cowardice were two terms that Buber connected to contemporary galut *Judentum*, and he hoped to show, by the example of these newly discovered courageous individuals, that it did not have to be so.

Rabbi Nachman was overcome by a desire to rekindle the flame of the tradition that had died in idle hands and to make it into a thing that would last, an idea that clearly influenced Buber as well. Hasidism was to become what the Kabbalah had never become: a living, growing tradition that would go from mouth to ear, "turning the wilderness of the hearts into a home for God." But Rabbi Nachman realized that the strength for such teachings could come only from life, not from books. He therefore went to live among the people, becoming one with them, so he could learn of their sorrow and their hopes. "In the beginning I requested of God that I might suffer the pain and anguish of Israel. At that time, if one came to me and told me his sorrow, I did not feel it. And I prayed that I should suffer the pain of Israel. Now, however, if one tells me of his pain, I feel it more than he does." Thus Rabbi Nachman lived with the people, as the Baal Shem Tov and his disciples had previously done, and not above the people, as contemporary rebbes were doing, and he found satisfaction and sanctification in this simple way of life. When he had gone through all of these preparatory stages for a righteous life, he made a pilgrimage to Eretz Israel, which marked the beginning of his real life.[82]

Despite all of this dedication, Buber concluded that Rabbi Nachman did not fulfill his destiny. Although he became "the soul of the people," he could not redeem the people Israel. He could not stop the decline and turn them around; thus with his death, and with the death of Rabbi Schneor Zalman, Jewish mysticism was also buried. It was Buber's contention that although Jewish mysticism "was the blossom of the exile, the exile also killed it." The Jews of the period were "not strong and not pure enough to preserve it," a problem Buber also recognized in his own time.[83]

The Jewish Myth

Buber wrote to the editor of the *Generalanzeiger* in 1905, complaining about an essay that claimed that "there is no Jewish Märchen [Jewish fairy tale]."[84] One might ask why he would make such a fuss over *das jüdische Märchen*. The underlying polemic is not apparent from Buber's work because he seldom addressed directly the point that caused him to respond. He simply responded. Here Buber took issue with the historical assumption that the Jewish people is "incapable of producing myth," a misconception again pronounced in his time "by the racial-psychological analysis of Judaism."[85] Here Buber referred to contemporary anti-Semitic outbursts that tried to show the inferiority of the Jews against the peoples of the West. This was the real issue—the Jews were denied the ability to be creative by non-Jews, a view that then was often endorsed by Jews themselves. This attitude had even more serious implications, for it meant that Jews were denied having a spirit and finally a soul, which is the source of all creativity. Buber argued that it would be futile to want to "produce" something cultural from an external source: "If we did not [already] possess the Jewish *Märchen* [within], no effort of the world could create it. . . . We would only produce artificial things that would have a fake effect."[86]

He further argued that "the *Kunstmärchen* can emerge only out of a tradition, whose beginning is the *Volksmärchen*." As the classical instance he cited Goethe's *Faust*, which evolved from the legend of Faust in the *Volksbuch*. Buber also referred to Goethe's "Märchen,"[87] which preceded that of the romantics,[88] and which arose from the depths of the tradition, no matter the authorial creativity, no matter the high degree of form. He thought that the very existence of a Jewish *Märchen*—which he did not doubt—allowed the Jewish artist to develop it further, an idea that can be applied to Jewish culture in general.[89]

Likewise, Buber did not agree that monotheism and myth are mutually exclusive, arguing instead that "the history of the development of the Jewish religion is in truth the history of the struggles between the natural order of the mythical-monotheistic popular religion and the intellectual order of the rational-monotheistic religion of the rabbis." In other words, the struggle was between the biblical redactor and the existing folk religion. Buber voiced his disappointment with the role of the redactor, who had tried to stifle the legendary traditions. For the spirit of the official, Jewish priestly redactor saw "the nourishing source of all true religiosity, the myth," as "the arch enemy of religion" and eliminated all myth as best as possible from the writings. Hence the Bible appears largely "free of anything mythical." In reality, though, the priestly redactors missed quite a bit. Along with antimythical elements that emphasized "the rigor of the Law and Rabbinic dialectics," one can still find "random veins of precious metal" in the books of the Bible.[90]

When it was no longer possible to deny the existence of a Jewish myth, "the rationalistic Jewish apologetics" supported the fight of Rabbinic Judaism against the myth. They considered other Oriental peoples' mythical motifs to be the original and the Jewish version merely an imitation. "In its blind effort to 'delimit' Judaism," Rabbinic Judaism attempted to create a faith cleansed of all myth. Thus the effort to build a fence around the Torah became oppressive: "Under the tyranny of the Exilarch, the living power of the Jewish God experience, namely the myth, had to hide away in the tower of the Kabbalah or behind the spinning wheels of the women or flee from the ghetto into the world; myth was either tolerated as a secret doctrine or despised as heresy or outcast as blasphemy." Neither did the rabbis recognize "the postbiblical literature . . . in its essence." They considered "the Aggadah as empty fantasy or flat parables; the Midrash as casuistic and fruitless commentary; the Kabbalah as a senseless and grotesque play with numbers," and Hasidism was "known only in name or was discounted as sick freethinking [*Schwärmerei*]." Fortunately, "new ways of scholarship" eventually showed that material which had been considered "willful commentary on biblical passages" was indeed "a recreation and reformulation of a people's ancient treasure [*Volksgut*]" and therefore worthy of preservation and exploration.[91]

In Buber's opinion, only Hasidism set myth briefly "on the throne of a short day," only to be purged and "to inhabit our melancholy dreams in the shape of a beggar." He defiantly asserted that "not Josef Karo, but Isaac Luria in the sixteenth century, not the Gaon of Vilna, but the Baal Shem in the eighteenth century, truly strengthened and protected Judaism since they raised popular religion to a power in Israel and renewed the personality of the people from the roots of the myth." Although Buber thought that myth was crucial to a regeneration of Judaism, he was convinced that it would not happen with the help of established religion. He admonished that if it is difficult for the emancipated Jews to reconcile their human religiosity with their Judaism into one unity, then "Rabbinic Judaism which has castrated the Jewish ideal—is at fault." He expected autonomous Jews "to complete ourselves and at the same time gain our peoplehood" because of the noble power of their myth.[92] And Buber was going to guide them. In the very first sentence of *Die Geschichten des Rabbi Nachman*—which he completed during a stay in Florence in 1906—Buber stated that his purpose for writing the book was not philological.[93]

As a revolutionary, Buber needed to be highly innovative, although within the tradition. He therefore chose an established form of communication, the legend, to bring his people back to a personal way of life. With his study of the Hasidic tales, Buber did not simply pick up material that was beloved and assemble it into a collection, but he actually chose material from a community that was initially despised within Judaism. Buber made the outrageous suggestion that the essence of that alien community ought to become the very life spirit of a rejuvenated German Judaism. Yet this impossible idea worked because of Buber's expertise in adapting the material to the needs of the community by using the conciliatory tools at his disposal—the form of the legend and the German language.

Of course, any mention of folklore in the German context brings to mind the German masters, Jakob and Wilhelm Grimm. They had pioneered the collecting and editing of folklore in the early nineteenth century—a hundred years before Buber—and Buber, who was a student of German literature, was well aware of their work and its impact. His choice of the legend for the Hasidic tales, which, he wrote, had hitherto remained formless, revealed the clever psychology of his plan: to smooth the way through form and language, lowering resistance to the contents, which might have been problematic if presented in an unfamiliar form. Buber pointed out that the Hasidic legends were not as far-reaching and elaborate as those of the Grimm brothers. They were, in fact, different from their German counterparts because in their shortness and simplicity "something big is intimated, but not yet articulated."[94] They were, in Buber's view, messengers of the future, who supplied the answers before the questions had been asked. The Hasidic legends played the same role as did so many of Buber's heroes—they heralded a new age.

Buber therefore used what the system had taught him to subvert the effectiveness of the system, as well as to reintroduce what he considered to be the authentic Jewish spirit. It was Buber's challenge to choose carefully the material he presented and the form in which to clothe it. It was Buber's brilliance and his humanity—Aschheim speaks of his elegance—which allowed him to find the right combination so that Hasidism could become "a respectable, even admired, part of 'higher' German culture."[95] In this way, Buber achieved communication of what he believed to be the essence of Judaism, even though it clashed with the values of German culture, because his method of presentation was acceptable and understandable to all.

Although the Hasidic legend fit into the general category of *Heiligenlegenden* (lives of religious people), it had its own character which distinguished it from the Buddha legend and the legend of St. Francis of Assisi. Neither did it grow out of the ancient meadows (*Haine*) of the Greeks or the silver-green olive groves of German literature, but it developed rather "in narrow alleyways and dark rooms, told by clumsy lips to fearful ears—it was born out of a stammering and passed on by a stammering—from generation to generation."[96]

The legend is spontaneous, unrefined, direct, alive—from one human being to another or others—dealing with practical life issues rather than with lofty philosophical speculation. The legend is tentative in that it is not as factually precise as history but also not as space- and timeless as the fairy tale. The legend is simple in style and simple in language and may deviate from the facts to varying degrees. This literary version of that most primeval expression, the spoken word, was intrinsic to Buber's goal, re-Judaization, because the Bible is one big string of legends about the founding fathers of the faith. The word has always been of great importance in Judaism.[97] God communicates with His people Israel through the word, and many biblical passages that transform God's message into teaching for the community are prefaced with "Vayomer Adonai" [and God said].

Buber explained that the Jewish myth actually had developed in two basic forms, the *Sage* (saga) and the *Legende* (legend). The *Sage*, also of biblical origin, deals with the deeds of the Almighty, constructing the eternal context of things, teaching us about redemption as well as God's role in the preservation of the universe.[98]

The legend deals with "the life of the central, completely actualized human being," beginning with some biblical personalities, "especially those mysterious figures which the canonical text neglected, such as Henoch, who was transformed from flesh to fire and from a mortal to Metatron, the prince of the Divine Countenance." The legend tells "in cosmic breadth of the lives of the holy men who ruled over the inner worlds, from Jesus of Nazareth to Israel ben Eliezer, the Baal Shem Tov." The legend portrays "eternal renewal" and "the possibility of becoming unconditioned [*unbedingt*]." It deals with the redemption of the world.[99] The legend, therefore, is the spoken form of the ethical-ecstatic experiences that relate to us how pathos became ethos, be it in Jesus or in the Baal Shem.

According to Buber, Rabbi Nachman of Brazlav also was in awe of the word. Like Buber, Rabbi Nachman believed that "teaching is first experience and only then thought." He did not utter a word of teaching that had not gone through much suffering; each word "was bathed in tears." As a result, the word developed late in Rabbi Nachman. "I have in me teachings without clothes, and it is very hard for me to clothe them." Nachman considered his own teachings a mystery because he was amazed at the way the words came out: "The word moves [a wave of] air and another one, until it reaches the human being who receives the word of the fellow human being and therewith receives his soul in it and is awakened by it." Although superficial words were frowned upon, Rabbi Nachman thought that the true word, the one that arises "from the bottom of the soul as the organic expression [*Ausformung*] of a rich and deep experience," is a great thing; in its living reality it is no longer "a product of the soul" but "the soul itself." Yet always "there was within him a fear of not being up to the task." He felt that "the word might close his throat, and before the first word of a teaching, it seemed to him that he had to die. Only the effectiveness of his words calmed him down."[100]

Nachman was fascinated with the process of communication. The decisive thing for him was not the effect on the speaker but on the listener, who is the recipient of the words. This effect culminates in the listener who becomes the speaker so that the final word comes from him: "At times my words enter the listener silently and lie there and act late, like slow medicine; other times my words don't act at all in the person who hears them, but when he repeats them, they enter his heart in depth and act there to perfection."[101]

Nachman experienced this in himself. "If one speaks to his companion, there is a simple light and a returning light." He thought that at times "his companion does not receive awakening from him via the simple light, but he receives awakening from his companion, when the returning words awaken him." The soul of the student shall be awakened in such a way that the word will be born from it and not from the master: "When I begin to speak with one, then I want to hear from him the most important words." Buber observed that the teaching method of Rabbi Nachman is a strange counterpart to the method of Socrates,[102] which was, of course, the dominant mode of discourse in Western thought. Thus Hasidism differed from Western, meaning classical Greek models of communication, a matter of the utmost importance to Buber in establishing Judaism's place as a culture that would provide revolutionary leadership.

By extracting the essence from the Hasidic tales and reconstructing the legends for his own time, Buber was, in fact, creating a new myth while at the same time transmitting the original myth of the prophets, of Jesus, and of the Hasidim. Gustav Landauer, in discussing Buber's *Legende des Baal Schem*, took the ultimate step when he wrote:

> Everywhere [in Martin Buber's *Legende des Baal Schem*] we are faced with the struggle of the soul to grasp the incomprehensible and ultimate, the experience beyond the life of the senses . . . the realization of God. . . . At the same time, however, this God is the Messiah who will raise the poor and persecuted Jews in the Diaspora out of their agony and oppression. Here more than anywhere else the legend, the fairy tale of God [*Gottesmärchen*], is steeped in a melancholy made of earthly depression and heavenly yearning.[103]

Buber considered all of his work to be an *Antwortspruch*, a series of responsive maxims to the existing situation, for in an *Antwortspruch*, "the question is contained in the answer."[104] Ernst Simon, in an article on Buber, quoted a Hasidic rabbi who experienced Buber's *Drei Reden über das Judentum* (Three speeches on Judaism) in this way: "I learned from them that my whole patrimony . . . had answers to general and Jewish questions which I did not know existed. In this way, I learned the essential character of my answers *qua* answers. This enabled me to use them in the future for whoever would ask me questions."[105]

"Works of the spirit" (*Werke des Geistes*), in Buber's view, should not be dissected, and one should not ask where they occurred "for the first time." Rather, he thought, "works of the spirit need to be venerated as a formed unity, as one image . . . as lived." The myth of the Jews is such a reality, which we can reconstruct "despite all Jewish and anti-Jewish attacks."[106] To get a sense of the atmosphere of the Hasidic "stiebl," the tenderness and awe, secretiveness and mystery, exuberance (*Ausgelassenes*) and paradise "of the Hasidic rebbe, the zaddik, the righteous one, the holy one, the mediator between God and humanity, who spins the mystery and the fairy tale wisely and with a smile," Buber recommended that one read I. L. Peretz, his hero of young Judaic literature.[107]

Causally, Buber supplanted the rational thought process of Western culture with an associative one. Individual thoughts or images are connected, though loosely, and each can stand on its own. Therefore, one example of a life experience is capable of illuminating an entire life. This thought pattern forms a mosaic rather than a linear chain and is a popular form of expression with revolutionary thinkers who wish to express themselves aphoristically as well as in oral traditions.

With his reconstruction of the Jewish myth via the examples of Hasidic legends, Buber turned the current order of things upside down, hoping once more to bring Jewish religiosity to the surface as the guiding principle for Jewish life. At the end of 1908, Buber had truly succeeded in appropriating material that was intrinsically Jewish but exotic for the cultural expectations of the German and central European Jews. The question was only whether German Jewry understood Buber's pointing of the way as meant for them.

EPILOGUE
Toward a Synthesis of All Syntheses

In an effort to create a composite picture of Buber's formative years, 1897–1909, we have looked at Buber's areas of involvement during this period. By Buber's own admission, he at times resembled the twisted image of Ury's Jeremiah and then again the primal Jew who raised his fist in joyous victory.

By 1909, Buber had moved beyond his teachers; his apprenticeship was over. He had explored the two poles of Jewish life that would hold his primary interest—the cultural and the spiritual. With the exception of his later efforts on behalf of Brit Shalom, a group committed to the reconciliation of Zionism and Arab nationalism,[1] Buber was not particularly interested in politics and so did not himself produce a body of literature on the topic, although he wrote occasionally on political matters.[2] He was now prepared to set his own course toward the implementation of his ideas regarding Jewish renewal via the course of education in the diaspora.

Despite his return to the Jewish community, Buber had no intention of leaving behind the German idealism of his upbringing. He loved German culture in all of its dimensions, whether language, literature, art, or the theater. The leadership position he attained among emancipated central European Jewry was not achieved primarily on a Jewish basis but rather on a German basis. Out of the different German as well as Jewish components at his disposal, Buber fashioned for himself his very own version of Judaism.

In his effort to escape from the superficial civilization that dominated his age, Buber at first resurrected heroes from German culture and the classics, not from Jewish culture—Goethe and Schiller, Cusa and Böhme, Schleiermacher and Novalis, Nietzsche and Plato provided the signposts to the future. They legitimized Spinoza and Mendelssohn, not the other way around. The norm for Buber continued to be provided by German culture, while he drew on Jewish sources for the contents to fill these forms.

Throughout his studies and reflections, Buber began with that which was familiar to him, which tended to be connected with German culture. Thus when exploring the concept of individuation, his first impulse was to examine the romantic personality he had long admired. A combination of factors, however, may well have influenced the decision not to publish his manuscript of five hundred romantic letters which he had prepared for publication in 1905. These probably included his study of individuation as seen in Cusa and Böhme, which projected a harmony and unity that he did not find in his romantic sources. His active involvement with Zionism surely must have made him aware again and again that the romantic instances he had collected portrayed the epitome of narcissistic individualism, not a personality conducive to community. In Zionism there was no room for "idle" introspection, just as there was no room for "idle" study as he perceived it in traditional Judaism. His conception of individuation as such therefore underwent a profound transformation. Even the romantic community which he so admired could not hold up under scrutiny as a model for a Jewish way of life. Yet Buber's very ideal of synthesis, not only of different Jewish perspectives but of all of the influences that he had thus far encountered, was taken directly from German romanticism.

Buber actively opposed the prevailing secular nature of twentieth-century life. He wished to help the individual reestablish the link to a metaphysical dimension. Yet he did not think that spirituality was directly accessible to the modern individual. The pathway had been blocked. As an alternative, Buber resorted to a cultural means, through adult education, to reconnect channels. He hoped to establish a Jewish college in the diaspora which would help guide European Jewry back to their culture, helping them to rediscover the Jewish spirit. Although the college did not materialize in that form in Europe, but in Eretz Israel, the formation of the Lehrhaus in Frankfurt provided a base for Jewish regeneration, and Buber's intensive efforts at educating the contemporary Jewish citizens of Germany left a deep impression on Jews and non-Jews alike.

In his adaptation of the Hasidic tales for German Jewish use, he resorted to the form of the German folktale, the *Märchen*, to clothe the unfamiliar Jewish content. Rabbi Nachman's tales as they had been handed down within the Hasidic community would not have been nearly as palatable to his German audience, Jewish and otherwise, if presented in what he perceived to be their original formlessness. Instead, Buber appropriated the Hasidic material and then transformed it into a literary genre his audience would feel comfortable with, thus "Germanizing" Hasidism. Furthermore, in his study of mysticism, Buber did not begin with Jewish mysticism, but rather with Christian mysticism, especially medieval Christian mysticism. Only after studying other forms of spirituality and writing about them was Buber ready to examine the merits of Hasidism for his concept of Jewish community. And here, too, he looked at the Jewish material through perspectives developed outside of that tradition.

Even the concept of dualism, which, according to Buber, came into being with creation, was not examined from a prophetic, and therefore Jewish, perspective, but rather from a philosophic point of view focused on aesthetic criteria. Body and soul were important concepts, but Buber approached the very topic of the soul from a cultural perspective by an examination of the sublime and the beautiful. His interest in aesthetics continued to inform the new German Jewish culture he envisioned. At the same time, however, he realized that aesthetics was not artistic production, but concepts. Yet he was interested in the making of art, not only its analysis. He therefore turned from a discussion of ideas to promotion of Jewish works of art and artists to revive the understanding that European Jews were capable of such productivity. Buber advocated Jewish art based on biblical motifs such as Moses and Jeremiah, yet the artistic execution of this art occurred in German studios such as that of Hermann Struck, for instance. Neither the poetry nor the plastic art that was created in this seminal period was produced in Eretz Israel, despite Ahad Ha-Am's call for a Jewish spiritual and creative revival centered in Zion. Rather than produce a brand-new Jewish art, Buber helped to effect a transformation of the art created by Jewish artists in the diaspora. He kindled the flame of conceiving art Jewishly in their hearts and helped to put ideas about Zion into their minds through his articles and speeches. Whereas Herzl had called for a modern Jewish state in Palestine based on Western models, Buber actively encouraged and supported a Jewish culture in Germany based on Eastern Jewish spirituality. Not only did he shift from the discussion of art to the production of art, but he postulated a totally new concept of art—life itself. In Buber's view, any original creative act was a work of art, so why not also the creation of community? After all, God created the world, and Buber accepted Him as the greatest artist of all. Buber encouraged deed over thought and action over theory, and he admired individuals such as Herzl who were able to apply themselves resolutely to the task at hand. Although Buber also began his Zionist career in organizational and propagandistic work, he never moved beyond that stage to political activism. He considered being what he termed an activist of the word sufficient.

Despite his admonitions that the Jews needed Eretz Israel and the Hebrew language, Buber's work in Zionism did not include living in the land of Israel in its evolving Hebrew-language-based culture. Rather, it was a German diaspora Zionism, a mixture of Ahad Ha-Am's Jewish culture and Nietzsche's new dawn culture, that seemed to satisfy Martin Buber. Although he justified his Zionist efforts under the category of Jewish awakening, Buber himself was hesitant to progress beyond that stage in order to emigrate to Palestine. He even admitted that it was very hard for him to use Hebrew actively because he thought in a foreign tongue, German. The realization of just how deeply he was steeped in the German culture, as well as his understanding of what he considered the superficial nature of Zionist propaganda work, may well have been the reason why he stopped his public work in 1905 and withdrew to study the Hasidic material and the origins of Hasidism at that time.

Buber's ideas during this period affected different contemporaries in different ways. Some of the young Jews, such as Hans Kohn, Hugo Bergmann, and Ernst Simon, elevated him almost to the level of prophet. At the same time, many traditional Jews were deeply offended by Buber's attempt to bring Jesus back into the Jewish fold and by his indifference or even hostility to traditional ritual and beliefs. Likewise, those Jews who were content to be German citizens and live within the German lands were not pleased with Buber's alienating ideas of Zion as the only true homeland for the Jewish spirit and Hebrew as the national language of the people.

In a clever transvaluation of values, Buber's Judaism differed from the other Jewish efforts at modernization by his effort at renewal. His emphasis focused on the Judaic content of his message while he adopted the form from secular models. During these years, Buber served more as a gadfly to his apathetic contemporaries than as the prophet of unity that he so much wanted to be.

After 1909, Buber pursued the problems he had first explored in

Zionism—Jewish culture—and then in Hasidism—Jewish spirituality—on a higher level, in an attempt at synthesizing the two within Judaism and extending the new synthesis to the world community. His time of apprenticeship was completed. Buber had achieved his personal goal, to become a teacher of Jewish thought and a leader of his people, and his voice hereafter was authoritative. No longer was he searching for the way, he was now pointing the way.

During these later years, Buber's sense of urgency manifested itself primarily in his continued call for a deepening of the active involvement of all Jews in the cause of the people through the study of the Hebrew language and Hebrew literature, which, in turn, was to prepare the community for the realization of the dream—the voluntary homecoming to the land.

Buber considered his *Drei Reden über das Judentum* (1911) to be the core of this phase of his work, with other essays as incidental or complementary to this basic work. His *Drei Reden*, delivered between 1909 and 1911, were his attempt to synthesize Zionism and Hasidism and to apply the results to contemporary human life. He dedicated this little booklet to his wife, Paula, his helpmate in all his endeavors.[3] Buber published the speeches at the request of his friends, although he was hesitant to put them into print because "they arose from the subjective experience of a particular time and place." In other words, they were a spontaneous response to a living situation. Although Buber's goal had been to publish a book on Judaism, these speeches originated "from Jew to Jew, primarily in a circle of young people, from the inspiration of subjective experience and in a sphere of unmediated [direct] action." Their language was "almost intimate," the contents fragmentary and without documentation, and he considered them to be merely "a forerunner to a book which had not yet arrived" and which he did not know "when it would arrive." At the same time, however, he was relieved to be publishing the speeches, "to escape their power," so he could go on with his life.[4]

The word *Zionism* does not appear in any of the speeches, although his audience, the Bar Kochba group in Prague, was especially committed to cultural Zionism. Rather, Buber supplanted the term *Zionism*, which had remained narrow in spite of the work and propaganda of the Democratic Fraction of the World Zionist Organization, and focused instead on the broader term, "A renewal of Judaism," the title of his third speech. Whereas his earlier work for the relative life from 1900 to 1905 had emphasized preparation via culture and education, the period from 1909 was devoted primarily to an integration of the absolute life into the relative life and the realization of this new concept.[5] Buber's work during this period shows an incredible seriousness and strength and was not ever surpassed in its effectiveness on the listening as well as the reading public.

Admitting that "we know that this is a great and difficult moment, when death and birth, decline and revival, end and beginning, despair and hope live side by side," Buber was certain that "ultimately it may depend on the deed alone which decides the future."[6] Buber foresaw a Jewish synthesis but wondered what it might be like. Perhaps, he suggested, it would be "a synthesis of all syntheses." He was confident that, whatever its form, "it will once more raise the demand of unity from humanity," and not just from Judaism, for "everything that you seek and do, that you desire and strive for, all your deeds and activities, all your sacrifices and enjoyments, they are all senseless without unity."[7] Buber projected these idealistic visions for all humanity on the basis of a spark of regeneration which he had seen in the Zionist movement. As a result of his diverse apprenticeships, Buber had attained a much clearer focus of his goal by this time. It may be noted, with satisfaction or annoyance, that he did not abandon his less popular efforts, doggedly berating Rabbinism and embracing spiritual trends and their originators in other religious traditions.

Although Buber actively worked for the Zionist cause after 1909, he was a Zionist of a peculiar kind. In contrast to Gershom Scholem and Ahad Ha-Am, he did not use his Hebrew name except in his personal library, nor did he make aliyah, but remained staunchly entrenched in Germany, almost too long. Many of his other interests were of a literary nature. One of his favorite projects was editing the journal *Der Jude* (1916–24), which could not get off the ground when he initially proposed it in 1903. His best-known book, *I and Thou,* begun in 1916, saw the light of day in 1923, and his journal *Die Kreatur* (1926–30) was perhaps his most creative literary venture.

Buber's most difficult period undoubtedly occurred during World War I, when he took a stance that alienated many of his followers and temporarily shattered the powerful friendship with Gustav Landauer which was such an important part of Buber's well of inspiration during these early years.[8] Though the personal crisis eventually passed, after Landauer's assassination in 1919 Buber determinedly cultivated his friendship with Franz Rosenzweig, which led to a decade of lively exchange until Rosenzweig's death in 1929, culminating in their creative and laudable Bible translation.[9] Only in the 1930s, with Hitler already on his doorstep, did Buber return to the problematic individual who had occupied so much of his time early on. His essay *Die Frage an den Einzelnen* (The question to the individual) (1936) finally put the two spheres—the individual and the communal—side by side. It was the swan song of the German idealist and the German Jew Martin Buber, whose imagination had untiringly searched for ways to create a beautiful soul that would satisfy the vision within. In 1938, at age sixty, Buber and his family left Heppenheim an der Bergstrasse, the Lehrhaus in Frankfurt, and his remaining friends to escape Nazi persecution and to realize for themselves in Eretz Israel the ideas he had so vigorously disseminated for so many years in central Europe for others to realize.

In retrospect, Buber's musings on the meaning of the moment in which a person lives were almost prophetic. "We know that the moment in which we live is a great and difficult one, that life and death are contained in its tensions, and that our deed may be decisive."[10] To be sure, the "organic progress of human qualities," which Peter Altenberg had once seen as the forerunner to the "progress of humanity," had occurred for Buber and his activist friends. The Zionist movement was without doubt a rebirth of the Jewish people. That there was a strong and viable remnant that remained physically untouched by the Holocaust and mustered all its energies and courage in the hour of Israel's need to proclaim the "third Jewish state," which Ahad Ha-Am had predicted, was the result of Buber's, Herzl's, Ahad Ha-Am's, Weizmann's, and all their friends' early, often frustrating, but also often rewarding, toil for the cause of Judaism. From the despair of the *galut* was born the hope for a strong and independent *Judenstaat,* from the end of the old *kehilla* arose the beginning of the new Zionist settlements in the *yishuv*; the decline of the host culture brought a revival of the Jewish spirit; and from the Nietzschean pronouncement of the death of God was born a new and powerful faith in the Jewish God who had carried His people with a mighty outstretched arm before and, many envisioned, would do so again, this time across the sea to Eretz Israel.

Buber's revolution of the word did not plug the holes in the damaged net of the European community, for the decline continued. The culture to which the ax had already been set at the turn of the century ended in incredible disaster. Yet in Eretz Israel a new culture along the lines of the new community Buber had wished for in his association with Die Neue Gemeinschaft arose among the people who had been considered incapable of culture. Buber and many of his friends progressed from Jewish self-preservation to Jewish self-realization, and in the process they graduated from German cultural heroes such as Goethe and Schiller, Cusa and Böhme, Nietzsche and Kant, to Jewish cultural heroes such as Moses and Jeremiah, Theodor Herzl and Ahad Ha-Am, Lesser Ury and Hermann Struck, and I. L. Peretz and Shmuel Agnon. After initially looking to German culture and especially German romanticism for models for the new Jew, by 1909 Buber understood the shortcomings of these models for the personality of the new Jew.

At this time, Buber began to display a different attitude toward the Jewish tradition, most notably his appreciation of the tradition for the renewal of the spirit. In the first of his *Drei Reden*, Buber questioned whether simply "to be a Jew because we inherited it" was enough. Those who possessed Judaism simply because they were born into it (*aus Erbgewohnheit*) Buber considered to be slaves to tradition. And yet he admitted that there was still something "which embedded in us the nature and the fate of the fathers and the mothers, their activities and their suffering, the great inheritance of the ages which we bring into the world that was valuable." Thus, being born a Jew, though not in itself a ticket to salvation, was a meaningful beginning. For Buber, this was an important admission. He now called these blood ties the "bone structure of the personality," very much in the way that Hebrew was the spine of the people, arguing that "all of this had helped to shape our being, and that we should be aware of it," just as "we should feel and know that within us there lives the disposition of the prophets, of the psalmists and the kings of Israel." He thought that "every one of us who reflects on this life will recognize traces of this power."[11]

After only about a decade of involvement with the Zionist movement, Buber had matured considerably in his conception of what mattered. He no longer considered *Bekenntnis* (to a cause) important, or belonging to a movement, but rather "living the truth which one knows to be redemption." Redemption, Buber was convinced, would result from unity. His dream of total unity "within the individual, between segments of a people, between peoples, between humanity and all that lives, between God and the world," was worth striving for. This notion of *Urjudentum* would help to free Judaism for its work in humanity, for in messianic times there will be unity, and we have to help bring it about.[12]

In Isaiah we learn of the voice of a herald in the wilderness, who admonished the people to prepare the way for the coming of the Lord. Buber warned that being ready for the Kingdom of God was our responsibility, "to educate oneself and others to the great self-consciousness of Judaism, to the self-consciousness which is informed by the spiritual process of Judaism in its greatness, in the fullness of its elements, in the manifold transformations of its historical revelation and in the nameless secret of its latent powers."[13] Considering himself the leader of the new era, Buber offered encouragement: "Let us raise the banner of hope and of desire for victory, and let us proudly carry it into the battle of life." With Nietzschean fervor he demanded: "Let our eyes look to the future, let our hand learn to guide weapons and plows. Let us leave behind the timidity of the slave, let us go forward without fetters and with courage." Redemption could come about only if "we turn our will into deed" and take an active role in the process.[14]

This might have been the end of Buber's odyssey. He had now achieved his goal—a purpose for himself and a new direction for German and central European Jewry. But was he not also a world citizen? Was he not also a microcosm within the macrocosm, and was humanity, at least in the West, not guided by German culture and Western values? Buber therefore had a responsibility beyond his own particular group. It was his desire that the two entities, the particularly Jewish and the universally human, should interact with each other reciprocally. Buber determinedly pursued the path of dialogue on a Jewish basis until his membership in the world community was rudely revoked by the host nation because he was a Jew.[15] While Buber took upon himself the responsibility for Jewish redemption, he ultimately could only point the way for humanity at large.

APPENDIX

In spite of Buber's formal entry into the University of Vienna, his registration booklet does not show any courses at Vienna.[1]

Rather, he went to Leipzig for the next year, where he registered for a total of ten courses for the winter semester 1897–98 as follows:[2]

History of the more recent philosophy with an introductory overview of the history of the older philosophy	Professor Dr. Wilhelm Wundt, Professor of Philosophy, Philosophical Faculty
Psychology of nations (psychology of language, mythology, and ethics)	Professor Dr. Wilhelm Wundt
Psychology	Professor Dr. Max Heinze, Professor of Philosophy, Philosophical Faculty
Philosophical seminar: Explanation of Kant's *Prolegomena*	Professor Dr. Max Heinze
Psychological lab: Introduction to experimental psychology	Professor Dr. Wilhelm Wundt
Aesthetics of the tragic and the comic	Professor Dr. Johann Volkert, Professor of Philosophy and Pedagogy
Psychiatric clinic	Professor Dr. Paul Flecksig, Professor of Psychiatry, Medical Faculty

Philosophical seminar: Introduction to philosophy starting from Schopenhauer's *World as Will and Idea*	Professor Dr. Paul Barth, Privat-Dozent, Philosophy and Pedagogy, Philosophical Faculty
Colloquium on David Hume's *Deliberations on the Human Mind*	Dr. Gustav Storring, Privat-Dozent, phil., Philosophical Faculty
Practicum: Spinoza's ethics	Professor Dr. Richard von Schubert-Soldern, Assistant Professor of Philosophy, Philosophical Faculty

The following year, winter semester 1898–99, Buber once more registered at Leipzig:[3]

Introduction to philosophy and logic	Professor Dr. Wilhelm Wundt
The philosophy of Kant and the Kantian schools	Professor Dr. Wilhelm Wundt
The cultural history of the Renaissance in Italy	Dr. Walther Wilhelm Gotz, Privat-Dozent, Modern History, Philosophical Faculty
On the problems of the science of history and the philosophy of history	Professor Dr. Paul Barth
German-Dutch art and cultural history in the age of the Renaissance	Professor Dr. August Schmarsow, Professor, Philosophical Faculty
Art history seminar: Exercises in Italian sculpture in the fourteenth and fifteenth centuries	Professor Dr. August Schmarsow

History of German economic, social and political science of the earlier and the most recent period	Professor Dr. Karl Lamprecht, Professor, Philosophical Faculty
Basics of German cultural history (introduction to the thought of contemporary cultural history)	Professor Dr. Karl Lamprecht
History of economic theory	Dr. Pohle

Although we know from Buber's registration papers at the University of Berlin, the Royal Friedrich Wilhelm University, that he previously attended the University of Zurich, I could not uncover any extant documents to that effect.[4] The Zurich period is shrouded in silence regarding academic work, even though it was an exciting and fruitful time in his personal life. It was in Zurich that Buber met Paula Winkler, a Catholic art student from Germany, who subsequently became his wife.

For the winter semester 1899–1900 in Berlin, Buber enrolled for the following courses:[5]

General history of philosophy	Professor Wilhelm Dilthey, Professor of Philosophy, Philosophical Faculty
Philosophical exercises	Professor Wilhelm Dilthey
Nineteenth-century philosophy	Georg Simmel, Privat-Dozent, Philosophy, Philosophical Faculty
Sociology	Georg Simmel
General national economics	Professor Adolf Wagner, Professor of Political Science, Philosophical Faculty

National economics	Professor Gustav Schmoller, Professor of Political Science, Philosophical Faculty

In the winter semester 1900–1901, there are but two entries:

Ethics and social philosophy	Georg Simmel
Aesthetic exercises	Georg Simmel

In 1901–2, Buber registered at the University of Vienna as follows:[6]

The philosophy of Aristotle	Professor Dr. Laurenz Muellner, Professor of Practical Philosophy, Philosophical Faculty
Practicum: On philosophy	Professor Dr. Friedrich Jodl, Professor of Practical Philosophy and History of Philosophy, Philosophical Faculty
Albrecht Dürer	Professor Dr. Franz Wickhoff, Professor of Art History, Philosophical Faculty
Spinoza and Spinozism	Professor Dr. Stohr

Although Buber's papers for 1901 indicate that the semester hours taken were not sufficient to fulfill university requirements, he seems to have made up the deficiency. Among his papers we find his *Matrikelschein* (registration form) of January 1902.[7]

NOTES

Prologue

1. Martin Buber, *Encounter*, trans. Maurice Friedman (La Salle, Ill.: Open Court, 1967), 49.

2. Martin Buber, "Zur Geschichte des Individuationsproblems (Nicolaus von Cues und Jakob Böhme)," Jerusalem, National Library, Buber Archives, Ms. Var. 350 A/2.

3. During these years, Buber also explored the German romantic personality and Christian as well as Sufi mysticism. See my dissertation, *From Turmoil to Unity: Martin Buber's Efforts towards a New Type of Jewish Community, 1897–1915* (Ann Arbor: UMI, 1991); also Buber's *Ekstatische Konfessionen, Gesammelt von Martin Buber* (1909), trans. Esther Cameron, ed. Paul Mendes-Flohr (Heidelberg: Verlag Lambert Schneider GmbH, 1985), and Buber's manuscript "Die Romantik in Briefen," 1905, Ms. Var. 350 B/1.

4. Martin Buber, *Die Erzählungen der Chassidim* (Zurich: Manesse Verlag, 1949), 5; translation mine.

5. Steven E. Aschheim, *Brothers and Strangers* (Madison: University of Wisconsin Press, 1982), 185–214.

1. A Time of Crisis: Contemporary Cultural Concerns, 1897–1901

1. Gotthard Wunberg, ed., *Die Wiener Moderne: Literatur, Kunst und Musik zwischen, 1890 und 1910* (Stuttgart: Philipp Reclam Jun., 1981).

2. For secondary literature on fin-de-siècle Vienna or accounts of this period and these developments, see John Neubauer, *The fin-de-siècle Culture of Adolescence* (New Haven: Yale University Press, 1992); Carl E. Schorske, *Fin-de-siècle Vienna* (New York: Knopf, 1980), Marsha L. Rozenblit, *The Jews of Vienna, 1867–1914* (Albany: State University of New York Press, 1983); and Allan Janik and Stephen Toulmin, *Wittgenstein's Vienna* (New York: Simon and Schuster, 1973).

3. Bahr wrote in an essay: "There is wild suffering in our time and the pain is unbearable. The cry for the redeemer is common and we can everywhere find crucified individuals. Has the great death enveloped the world? It is possible that we have reached the end, that this is the death of exhausted humanity, and that these are merely the final struggles. It is possible that we are at the beginning, the birth of a new humanity, and these are merely the avalanches of Spring. Either we climb up to the Di-

vine or we tumble, tumble into darkness and destruction—but there can be no continuation. Modernity believes . . . in this resurrection, glorious and blissful; [it believes] that salvation will result from suffering and that grace will follow despair, that the light of day will return after this terrible darkness and that art will return [to humanity]" (Wunberg, *Wiener Moderne,* 189; translation mine).

4. Ibid., 275.

5. Janik and Toulmin, *Wittgenstein's Vienna,* 45. Zweig joined the group after the period Buber is discussing.

6. Ibid.

7. Wunberg, *Wiener Moderne,* 226.

8. Karl Leberecht Immermann, "Wir sind Epigonen," in Walter Killy, ed., *Zeichen der Zeit,* vol. 3 (Darmstadt and Neuwied: Hermann Luchterhand Verlag GmbH, 1981), 30.

9. For an extensive analysis of Nietzsche's impact on Buber, see Chapter 2.

10. Friedrich Nietzsche, *The Birth of Tragedy* [1872] and *The Genealogy of Morals* [1887], trans. Francis Golffing (Garden City, N.Y.: Doubleday, Anchor Books, 1956), 9–11. In Wunberg's words, Nietzsche served as godfather to all of the young minds who hoped to bring about a new day (*Wiener Moderne,* 53).

11. Martin Buber, *Encounter,* reprinted from *Meetings* by Martin Buber, trans. Maurice Friedman, by permission of the publisher, Open Court Publishing Company, La Salle, Illinois, 49–51. This book is itself reprinted from The Library of Living Philosophers, Volume XII, *The Philosophy of Martin Buber,* edited by Paul Arthur Schilpp and Maurice Friedman (La Salle, Ill.: Open Court, 1967).

12. See Margot Cohn and Rafael Buber, *Martin Buber: A Bibliography of His Writings, 1897–1978* (Jerusalem: Magnes Press, 1980), item 1, p. 13. Also "On Viennese Literature" (typescript), trans. Robert A. Rothstein, ed. William M. Johnston, University of Massachusetts, Amherst, 1974, Jerusalem, National Library, Buber Archives, Ms. Var. 350 B/174. Published in William M. Johnston, "Martin Buber's Literary Debut: 'On Viennese Literature' (1897)," *German Quarterly* 47 (November 1974): 556–66. Reference courtesy of Margot Cohn.

13. Wunberg, *Wiener Moderne,* 142.

14. Buber, "On Viennese Literature," 2.

15. Ibid., 3. Bahr himself discussed this notion of the dilettante in an essay "Decadence and Dilettantism," in which he characterized the dilettante as someone who has style and form and finish but no feeling and life. The dilettante is an aesthete, who does not draw on nature for inspiration and thus has "a sense of art, but not the creative power of the artist" (Wunberg, *Wiener Moderne,* 238).

16. Buber, "On Viennese Literature," 2.

17. Ibid., 3.

18. Ibid. Compare also Wunberg, *Wiener Moderne,* 226, on Bahr's ro-

manticism of the nerves. For a good literary illustration of this idea, see Thomas Mann's "Tristan" (1898), in *Death in Venice and Other Stories*, trans. and intro. by David Luke (London: Secker & Warburg, 1990), 91–133.

19. Wunberg, *Wiener Moderne*, 232.

20. Buber, "On Viennese Literature," 5.

21. Ibid., 6.

22. Wunberg, *Wiener Moderne*, 425.

23. Buber, "On Viennese Literature," 8. Rudolf Strauss characterized Altenberg most incisively: "One has to have seen this pale, fine face with the pale gray eyes and the blond-reddish, drooping mustache; one has to have heard this tired and incredibly mild human being speak, in order to be able to totally assess him. Now he just sits, with a dull and disinterested face, the whole figure hunched over, every expression points to the sufferer, the poor soul—then suddenly he recalls a word which excites him—and now his head shoots up, this lifeless organism comes to life, his hands are busy, his eyes sparkle, and from his mouth come forth short, wild sentences full of deep, living wisdom" (Wunberg, *Wiener Moderne*, 428).

24. Buber, "On Viennese Literature," 8.

25. Ibid., 9.

26. William Blake, "To see a world in a grain of sand, and a heaven in a wildflower," in "Auguries of Innocence," in David V. Erdman, ed., *The Complete Poetry and Prose of William Blake* (Garden City, N.Y.: Anchor Books, 1982), 490.

27. Buber, "On Viennese Literature," 9.

28. Ibid., 11.

29. Ibid., 1.

30. Klaus Wagenbach, *Franz Kafka* (Reinbek bei Hamburg: Rowohlt Taschenbuch Verlag GmbH, 1964), 36; translation mine.

31. For additional discussion, see Paul Flohr and Bernard Susser, "*Alte und Neue Gemeinschaft*: An Unpublished Buber Manuscript," *Association for Jewish Studies Review* 1 (1976): 42. Reference furnished by Professor Alexander Orbach.

32. Martin Buber, "Alte und Neue Gemeinschaft," Jerusalem, National Library, Buber Archives, Ms. Var. 350 B/47. See also Flohr and Susser, "*Alte und Neue Gemeinschaft*." References in subsequent citations are to the printed version, with ms. pages in parentheses. Translations mine.

33. Flohr and Susser, "*Alte und Neue Gemeinschaft*," 51 (3, 4).

34. See Abraham H. Maslow, *Religions, Values, and Peak-Experiences* (New York: Viking Press, 1970), on self-actualization.

35. Flohr and Susser, "*Alte und Neue Gemeinschaft*," 52 (5).

36. See Buber's account in "Mein Weg zum Chassidismus," in *Martin Buber Werke*, Vol. 3, Schriften zum Chassidismus (Munich: Verlag Lambert Schneider, 1963), 960–73.

37. See poem in Chapter 3.

38. Other contemporaries also used this comparative method in their writing. Rudolf Eucken, whose writings influenced Buber during his student years, in 1909 published a most valuable book, *Geistige Strömungen der Gegenwart* (Contemporary spiritual currents), in which he discussed the many different polarities that served as current topics for intellectual debate. One can see here many of the dichotomies which Buber also addressed, although he did not always express himself that distinctly, e.g., subjective/objective, theoretical/practical, idealism/realism, mechanical/organic, monism/dualism, society/individual, and ethical/aesthetic. Likewise, Kurd Lasswitz (1848–1910), another writer whom Buber admired, wrote an assessment of objective/subjective and religion/feeling in an excellent study of contemporary issues (1908). Before all of them, Nietzsche had written in this way, contrasting different sets of assumptions in an effort to elucidate the nature of specific terms.

39. For an excellent source on socialism and the Jews, see Robert S. Wistrich, *Socialism and the Jews* (Rutherford, N.J.: Fairleigh Dickinson University Press, 1982).

40. Flohr and Susser, "*Alte und Neue Gemeinschaft*," 50–51 (1, 3).

41. Ibid., 50 (1–2). The last statement is reminiscent of Friedrich Schiller's *Wilhelm Tell*, where Tell and his friends declaim in the *Rütli-Schwur*, "We wish to be a united people of brothers, / who will not separate in any threat or danger. / We wish to be free, as of old the fathers," in *Schiller Dramen und Gedichte* (Stuttgart: E. Schreiber Graphische Kunstanstalten, 1955), 940.

42. Flohr and Susser, *Alte und Neue Gemeinschaft*," 51 (2, 3).

43. Ibid., 51 (3–4).

44. In *The Birth of Tragedy* (1872), Nietzsche asked, "How, then, are we to define the 'Dionysiac spirit'?" The definition is evident in Nietzsche's explanation of God's activity, which he described as Dionysiac: "God as the supreme artist, amoral, recklessly creating and destroying, realizing himself indifferently in whatever he does or undoes, ridding himself by his act of the embarrassment of his riches and the train of his internal contradiction. Thus the world was made to appear, at every instant, as a successful *solution* of God's own tensions, as an ever new vision projected by that sufferer for whom illusion is the only possible mode of redemption" (9–10). Contrasting this aesthetic conception to Christian ethics, he concluded, "In those days . . . my vital instincts turned against ethics and founded a radical counterdoctrine, slanted esthetically, to oppose the Christian libel on life. But it still wanted a name. Being a philologist, that is to say a man of *words*, I christened it rather arbitrarily—for who can tell the real name of the Antichrist?—with the name of a Greek god, Dionysos" (11).

45. Flohr and Susser, "*Alte und Neue Gemeinschaft*," 52 (5).

46. Ibid.

47. Ibid., 53 (5, 6).
48. Ibid., 54 (8).
49. Walter Benjamin, *Das Kunstwerk im Zeitalter seiner technischen Reproduzierbarkeit* (Frankfurt a.M.: Suhrkamp Verlag, 1963), 11–48.
50. Flohr and Susser, "*Alte und Neue Gemeinschaft*," 54–55 (8–9).
51. Ibid., 55 (9–10).
52. Ibid., 55 (9).
53. See Aschheim, *Brothers and Strangers*, 29. Buber was not the only one. Aschheim writes that, according to Emil Franzos, "those who sought *Kultur* and who were locked in struggle with their repressive orthodox elders" were considered " 'good' Jews."
54. Rudolf Eucken traced the term *Kultur* to Johann Gottfried Herder (1744–1803). He likewise defined civilization, coming to the conclusion that "culture is a formation from within and an elevation of the total human being, and is to be clearly separated from the sheer order of society. To designate order we look to civilization; thus, civilization and culture can be distinguished like the lower and the higher, like beginning and end." Eucken pointed out that *Bildung* is closely related to this elevation of culture, especially developed by the romantics. Eucken noted that the distinction between culture and civilization is not as clear as it used to be, referring the reader to Paul Barth's *Die Philosophie der Geschichte als Soziologie* (The philosophy of history as sociology) (1897). He likewise pointed out that different nations have different conceptions of civilization and culture. For instance, what the Germans call culture, the English and French call civilization. See Eucken, *Geistige Strömungen der Gegenwart* (Leipzig: Verlag von Veit & Co., 1909), 229–52.
55. Kurd Lasswitz seemed to see culture much more in terms of civilization than Eucken did. He also placed the beginnings of modern culture at the end of the eighteenth century in Europe. But according to Lasswitz, "freedom is order," whereas Eucken had said that order is to be categorized under civilization. In Lasswitz's scheme, freedom was the most important component of culture. He considered the development of the personality to be the highest expression of human freedom. Thus the freedom of the individual can be measured only by the degree of personality development achieved. Lasswitz saw personality development to be a moral function that necessitates community. Thanks to his personality, the individual is no longer at the mercy of the communal will, he is no longer just a cog in the machinery, but the free will of the *Gemeinschaft* realized in the individual will. Culture is tied to the dignity of the human being. The highest goal of culture is the ethical will to do good. Lasswitz did not think that "our definition of culture" could have been found among those people who allow dogma to stifle the autonomy of the individual: "Under the influence of a priestly rule there

can be no cultural state; there a temporary civilization is possible, but no culture as a development toward freedom." Here he, of course, echoes Nietzsche. See Lasswitz, *Seelen und Ziele* (Leipzig: Verlag von B. Elischer Nachf., 1908), 205–21.

56. Martin Buber, "Kultur und Civilisation, Einige Gedanken zu diesem Thema," Jerusalem, National Library, Buber Archives, Ms. Var. 350 B/171, 3. I have not seen the printed version.

57. Ibid.

58. Ibid.

59. Buber, "Kultur und Civilisation," 2.

60. See Nietzsche, *Birth of Tragedy and Genealogy of Morals*, trans. Golffing, 158–88.

61. Buber, "Kultur und Civilisation," 1.

62. For orientation on term *Bildung*, see *Der grosse Herder*, Reference Work for Knowledge and Life, 5th rev. ed. of the Herder Encyclopedia, Vol. 1 (Freiburg: Verlag Herder, 1952–56), 1462–64.

63. Buber, "Kultur und Civilisation," 2.

64. Ibid., 1, 2.

65. Ibid., 1.

66. Ibid.

67. Ibid., 1, 2.

68. Ibid., 2.

69. Ibid., 2. For Buber's view on culturally productive individuals in society, see his 1902 essay "Die Schaffenden, das Volk und die Bewegung," in *Die Jüdische Bewegung* (Berlin: Jüdische Verlag, 1916), 68–77.

70. Buber, "Kultur und Civilisation," 1, 2. In contrast to Gustav Landauer, Karl Marx, who considered religion to be the opium of the people, was interested in civilization. Buber sided with Landauer and opposed Marx as well as German socialism.

71. Poem, "Unseres Volkes Erwachen," *Die Welt* 3 (November 17, 1899): 14–15. See Chapter 3.

72. *Stenographisches Protokoll der Verhandlungen des III. Zionisten-Congresses* (Vienna: Verlag des Vereines "Erez Israel," 1899).

2. Academic Beginnings: Apprenticeship in Aesthetics, 1897–1904

1. Course registrations, Jerusalem, National Library, Buber Archives, Ms. Var. 350 A/5. For full course of study, see Appendix.

2. Buber, *Encounter*, 50.

3. Ibid., 50–51.

4. Ibid., 41.

5. Ibid., 42–44.

6. See Martin Buber, *Drei Reden über das Judentum* (Frankfurt a.M.: Rütten and Loening, 1911), 71–72, translated as follows in Nahum Glatzer, ed., *On Judaism* (New York: Schocken Books, 1967), 40:

The spiritual process of Judaism manifests itself in history as the striving for an ever more perfect realization of three interconnected ideas: the idea of unity, the idea of the deed, and the idea of the future. When I speak of ideas I do not, of course, mean abstract concepts; I mean innate predispositions of a people's ethos that manifest themselves with such great force and so enduringly that they produce a complex of spiritual deeds and values which can be called that people's absolute life. Every greatly and singularly gifted people possesses such unique predispositions and, created by them, a world of unique deeds and values. It therefore lives, as it were, two lives: one transitory and relative, lived in the sequence of earthly days, of generations that come and go; the other (lived simultaneously) permanent and absolute, a life lived in the world of the wandering and searching human spirit. Whereas in the first, the relative life, all seems chance, and often terrifyingly meaningless, in the other, the absolute life, great, luminous outlines of meaning and exigency are revealed, step by step. The relative life remains the possession of the unconsciousness of the people; the absolute life becomes, directly or indirectly, part of the consciousness of mankind.

7. Buber, *Encounter*, 44–45.

8. Ibid., 44.

9. Martin Buber, "Ein Wort über Nietzsche und die Lebenswerte," *Die Kunst im Leben* 1 (December 1900): 13. Courtesy of Margot Cohn, Buber Archives.

10. Buber, *Encounter*, 46. Simultaneously with Buber, a Polish author undertook the same task. When he informed Buber and offered to collaborate with him in the effort, Buber deferred to the Polish author.

11. In the opening of the book, Daniel descends from the mountain in the last light of the afternoon very much as does Nietzsche's Zarathustra. Among the manuscript fragments there was a dedication to Landauer that did not appear in the printed version. Buber wrote, "Among my friends you are the only one for whom Daniel has always existed. Thus it is more than the expression of a feeling, when I dedicate this first testimony of Daniel's life to you" ("Daniel," Jerusalem, National Library, Buber Archives, Ms. Var. 350 B/8).

12. Buber, "Ein Wort über Nietzsche," 13; translation mine.

13. Siegfried is the heroic character in the *Nibelungenlied* (ca. 1250), a Nordic saga which Wagner turned into an opera and which other German national poets such as Friedrich Hebbel (1813–63) had remythologized through the ages.

14. Buber, "Ein Wort über Nietzsche," 13.

15. Buber's critique of German culture stemmed in large part from his intoxication with Nietzsche. In the early years, he seemed to take Nietzsche's suggestions to heart, trying to follow in his footsteps. In *The Genealogy of Morals*, Nietzsche asks, "What accounts for our repugnance to man—not our fear of him, rather the fact that there is no longer anything to be feared from him; that the vermin 'man' occupies the entire stage; that, tame, hopelessly mediocre, and savorless, he considers himself the apex of historical evolution; and not entirely without justice,

since he is still somewhat removed from the mass of sickly and effete creatures whom Europe is beginning to stink of today" (Nietzsche, *Genealogy of Morals*, trans. Golffing, 176).

16. This was an effort that may have inspired Buber to write an essay titled "Das Ewige Drama" (The eternal drama), Jerusalem, National Library, Buber Archives, Ms. Var. 350 B/52.

17. Buber, "Ein Wort über Nietzsche," 13.

18. Martin Buber, "Zarathustra," Jerusalem, National Library, Buber Archives, Ms. Var. 350 B/7b, unpaginated.

19. Buber, "Zarathustra"; translation mine.

20. Ibid. Initiates are people who belong to a group that is closed to the general population. This concept was in vogue during the romantic period. Jakob Böhme, whose *Aurora* provided the bible for the romantics, was their prophet. German romanticism played an important role in Buber's cultural efforts at renewal and rebirth. Nietzsche reminds one of the dynamic romantic spirit and is considered a direct heir to romanticism.

21. There is considerable irony in Buber's use of this word. *Unart* means lack of discipline; someone who is *unartig* is ill-behaved, undisciplined. German institutes of education represented the epitome of discipline and rote learning (see Kafka in Wagenbach, *Franz Kafka*, 26). There is no doubt that Buber reveled in the knowledge that he, too, put a dent in the immaculate system of German letters.

22. Buber, "Zarathustra."

23. In the manuscript of his article "Über Jakob Boehme" (Jerusalem, National Library, Buber Archives, Ms. Var. 350 B/7), 2, published in *Wiener Rundschau* 12 (June 15, 1900): 251–53, Buber made a threefold distinction which he left out of the published version.

24. Buber, "Zarathustra."

25. Ibid.

26. Ibid. See also William Blake's poem "The Tyger" in Erdman, ed., *Complete Poetry and Prose of William Blake*, 24.

27. Buber, "Ein Wort über Nietzsche," 13.

28. Buber, *Encounter*, 41–42.

29. Martin Buber, "Zu Schopenhauers Lehre vom Erhabenen," Jerusalem, National Library, Buber Archives, Ms. Var. 350 B/7a, 2. For comparison, see Buber article on Böhme, 1900.

30. Buber, "Zu Schopenhauers Lehre vom Erhabenen," 2.

31. Beardsley, *Aesthetics*, 1. According to Beardsley, the work generally ascribed to Cassius Longinus, *Peri Hypsous* (*On the Sublime*), was probably not written by him (76). This work seems to have disappeared during the first century C.E. and, according to Beardsley, was not rediscovered and published until the sixteenth century.

32. Ibid., 77.

33. Buber, "Zu Schopenhauers Lehre vom Erhabenen," 3. See also Edmund Burke, *A Philosophical Inquiry into the Origin of Our Ideas of*

the Sublime and the Beautiful (1757), in *The Works of the Right Honourable Edmund Burke*, vol. 1 (1906; reprint, intro. by Judge Willis, London: Oxford University Press, 1925), 55–219. Burke's theory of the sublime was ambivalent. He emphasized that the sublime was produced by *ideas of* pain and danger, not by *actual* pain and danger, just the thought of them. For, "when pain and danger get too close to us, we are incapable of 'enjoying them.' " From a certain distance, however, and with certain limits, "they can delight." Buber quoted Burke, who wrote: "Whatever is fitted in any sort to excite the ideas of pain and danger" (Burke, section VII, 91) is especially suited to elicit the feeling of the sublime. But the delight that results from these collective feelings (of the sublime) is not "unmixed delight," rather, it is "blended with no small uneasiness" because "the sublime feeling acts on us at first in a depressing way, only to lift us [*erheben*] then over the depression through a strange turn of feelings." This "strange turn of feelings" is none other than antiquity's Dionysian thunderbolt.

34. Burke, *Philosophical Inquiry*, section VIII, "Of the Passions which belong to Society," 92–93, and section X, "Of Beauty," 94–95. This is what Buber wrote, but it is *not* what Burke meant. Buber is here appropriating Burke's framework but not his contents. From section VIII, 92: "The other head under which I class our passions is that of *society*, which may be divided into two sorts. l. The society of the *sexes*, which answers the purpose of propagation; and next, that more *general society* which we have with men and with other animals, and which we may in some sort be said to have even with the inanimate world." Under section X, 94–95, Burke wrote, "The passion which belongs to generation, merely as such, is lust only. This is evident in brutes, whose passions are more unmixed, and which pursue their purposes more directly than ours. . . . But man, who is a creature adapted to a greater variety and intricacy of relation, connects with the general passion the idea of some *social* qualities, which direct and heighten the appetite which he has in common with all other animals. . . . The object therefore of this mixed passion, which we call love, is the *beauty* of the *sex*. . . . I call beauty a social quality; for when women and men, and not only they, but when other animals give us a sense of joy and pleasure in beholding them . . . they inspire us with sentiments of tenderness and affection towards their persons."

35. Burke, *Philosophical Inquiry*, section VI, 90–91. Burke devoted this section to "the Passions which belong to self-preservation." He wrote, "Most of the ideas which are capable of making a powerful impression on the mind, whether simply of Pain or Pleasure, or of the modification of those, may be reduced very nearly to these two heads, *self-preservation* and *society*; to the ends of one or the other of which all our passions are calculated to answer. The passions which concern self-preservation turn mostly on *pain* or *danger*. The ideas of *pain*, *sickness*, and *death* fill the mind with strong emotions of horror; but *life* and *health*,

though they put us in a capacity of being affected with pleasure, make no such impression by the simple enjoyment. The passions therefore which are conversant about the preservation of the individual turn chiefly on *pain* and *danger,* and they are the most powerful of all the passions."

36. Buber, "Zu Schopenhauers Lehre vom Erhabenen," 3.

37. In this paper, Buber did not point to an essay Kant published in 1764, "Beobachtungen über das Gefühl des Schönen und Erhabenen" (Observations on the Feeling of the Beautiful and Sublime), but rather to Kant's *Critique of Judgment* (1790), which distinguishes between two branches of the sublime. See Immanuel Kant, *Observations on the Feeling of the Beautiful and Sublime,* trans. John T. Goldthwait (Berkeley and Los Angeles: University of California Press, 1960).

38. In his essay "On the Sublime," Schiller defined his feeling of the sublime. It is "a mixed feeling. It is a combination of pain which manifests itself in the extreme as awe, and of joy which can even appear as delight, a feeling which, although not gaiety, is preferred by gentle souls. . . . We learn from the feeling of the sublime that the state of our spirit does not necessarily follow from the state of our senses, that the laws of nature are not necessarily our own, and that we carry within ourselves an independent principle free from all sensuality." While for Schiller beauty consisted of a harmony between reason and sensuality, the sublime knew no such harmony, "and it is precisely the tension resulting from this contradiction which captures our imagination" (Friedrich Schiller, "Über das Erhabene," in Benno von Wiese, ed., *Schiller Werke,* definitive ed., Vol. 21, Philosophical Writings, part 2 [Weimar: Hermann Böhlaus Nachfolger, 1963], 38–54; translation mine).

39. Schiller, "Über das Erhabene," 38, 39, 42.

40. Buber, "Zu Schopenhauers Lehre vom Erhabenen," 8.

41. Ibid., 25.

42. See Nietzsche, *Genealogy of Morals.*

43. Buber, "Zu Schopenhauers Lehre vom Erhabenen," 1.

44. Moses Mendelssohn and Immanuel Kant represented two opposing yet related directions within eighteenth-century thought. We can get a sense of this tug-of-war of the mind from two essays Kant and Mendelssohn submitted to an essay contest of the Berlin Royal Academy. Alexander Altmann wrote that in 1761, "the Academy invited entries for a prize essay on the question: 'Whether metaphysical truths in general, and the first principles of natural theology and morality in particular, are susceptible of the same evidence as mathematical truths, and in case they are not, what is the nature of their certitude; which degree can it attain; and whether this degree is sufficient to impart conviction?' " Mendelssohn was awarded first prize, but Kant followed as a close second, after three votes. "According to the minutes of the meeting, the treatises number twenty (Mendelssohn's) and number twenty-eight (Kant's) received the same number of votes on the first and second ballots." The tie was

broken by the decision of the chairman of the philosophical class in favor of Mendelssohn. See Alexander Altman, *Moses Mendelssohn: A Biographical Study* (Philadelphia: Jewish Publication Society of America, 1973), 112–16.

45. Buber, "Zu Schopenhauers Lehre vom Erhabenen," 6, 3.

46. See Alexander Altmann, *Moses Mendelssohns Frühschriften zur Metaphysik* (Tübingen: Mohr, 1969); and Johann Wolfgang von Goethe, "Iphigenie" (1787), in *Goethe's Werke*, Vol. 6 (Leipzig: Philipp Reclam jun., n.d.).

47. Buber, "Zur Geschichte des Individuationsproblems (Nicholaus von Cues und Jakob Böhme)," Jerusalem, National Library, Buber Archives, Ms. Var. 350 A/2. In his dissertation, Buber spelled Cusa's name "Cues." Cusa's name is also spelled "Kues" and "Cusanus."

48. Buber, "Geschichte des Individuationsproblems," Preface.

49. Dilthey wrote on many of the thinkers and problems that also interested Buber: Schiller, Lessing, Goethe, Novalis, and Hölderlin, as well as on the meaning of history; he also contributed essays to a systematic philosophy of culture.

50. See Biographical Note by Emma Gurney Salter, in Nicolas of Cusa, *The Vision of God* (1928; reprint, New York: Ungar, 1969), xviii–xxvii. Cusa was a very interesting writer. It is easy to see why Buber was attracted to his ideas. Following are a few examples that shed light on Cusa's attitude and method beyond Buber's dissertation. In *Drei Schriften vom Verborgenen Gott*, ed. Elisabeth Bohnenstädt (Hamburg: Verlag von Felix Meiner, 1958), Cusa commented on seeking God. His method was direct. He wrote, "Man came into the world to seek God and to cling to Him when he has found Him. . . . But when the human being is not able to discover God in this physical world which we experience through the senses . . . then man would have been sent into the world for the purpose of finding God. Therefore, the world has to offer the seeker assistance" (8).

Similarly, in another work between an orator and a lay person, *Der Laie über die Weisheit*, ed. Elisabeth Bohnenstädt (1936; reprint, Hamburg: Verlag von Felix Meiner, 1954), Cusa argued through the mouth of the lay person that "wisdom calls from the streets." The orator almost mocked the lay person's claim to wisdom, to which the lay person responded, "Maybe that is the difference between you and me: you consider yourself knowing, although you are not; hence you are mischievous. I recognize that I am ignorant; hence I am humbler. In this respect I am wiser [than you]" (43).

Finally, in a discourse again in the form of a Socratic dialogue, *Vom Globusspiel*, trans. Gerda von Bredow (Hamburg: Verlag von Felix Meiner, 1952), between the Cardinal and John, the Cardinal explained, "We cannot deny that we call man a microcosm, that is, a little world 'with a soul.' " After a long series of explanations and counterqueries, John summed up the Cardinal's disputation in his own words: "If I understand all of this correctly, all things are contained in God, and there they exist in truth, no more, no less; but there they are contracted and undeveloped, like the circle in the dot. And all things are contained in the motion, but they exist as they evolve, like a dot that evolves into a circle through the tip of the circle, for then the dot unfolds the circle previously folded together. All things exist in their potential like the circle in the matter which can become a circular figure. And all things are in the potential exactly as is the actual circle" (37).

51. Buber's note refers to *Archiv für Geschichte der Philosophy IV*.

52. Buber, "Geschichte des Individuationsproblems," 2. On Schleiermacher, see Richard Crouter, *Friedrich Schleiermacher on Religion: Speeches to Its Cultured Despisers* (New York: Cambridge University Press, 1988), and on Emerson, see Edward L. Ericson, ed., *Emerson on Transcendentalism* (New York: Ungar, 1986).

53. Buber, "Geschichte des Individuationsproblems," 2, 1.

54. Buber, *Erzählungen der Chassidim*, 5.

55. Buber, "Geschichte des Individuationsproblems," 2. This was a neoplatonic idea that, according to Buber, was revived by Kurd Lasswitz in his *Geschichte der Atomistik vom Mittelalter bis Newton* (History of atomism from the Middle Ages to Newton) (1890). Kurd Lasswitz, born in Breslau, was a high school teacher and a writer of utopian novels. He published a book, *Wirklichkeiten* (Berlin: Verlag von Emil Felber, 1900), which includes an interesting essay, "Die Persönlichkeit," 161–70. See also Lasswitz, *Seelen und Ziele* (Leipzig: Verlag von B. Elischer Nachf., 1908).

56. Buber, "Geschichte des Individuationsproblems," 2.

57. Ibid., 8.

58. Duns Scotus and Occam are two Scholastic philosophers. For a comparison of Duns Scotus with Thomas Aquinas, see Otto Pfleiderer, *The Development of Christianity*, trans. Daniel A. Huebsch (New York: B. W. Huebsch, 1910), 149.

59. Buber, "Geschichte des Individuationsproblems," 8.

60. Ibid., 7, 9.

61. Ibid., 18, 15, 12.

62. Ibid., 12.

63. Ibid., 15, 18, 22.

64. Ibid., 17.

65. Ibid., 18.

66. Ibid., 20, 21. See also Eucken, *Geistige Strömungen der Gegenwart*, 192–227, on the topic of *Entwicklung*. Eucken points out that *Entwicklung* was introduced into the German language at the end of the seventeenth century. The older term is *Auswicklung*, whose use Eucken first attributes to Jakob Böhme. Buber then applied it also to Cusa.

67. Buber, "Geschichte des Individuationsproblems," 21.

68. Ibid., 22, 17.

69. Buber, "Über Jakob Boehme," 251–53. Also manuscript, "Pantheismus und Renaissance," Jerusalem, National Library, Buber Archives, Ms. Var. 350 B/7.

70. Buber, "Geschichte des Individuationsproblems," 24. Paracelsus, whose real name was Philippus Aureolus Theophrastus Bombastus of Hohenheim, endeavored to advance the applicability of medicine and pharmacology. He was a chemist and philosopher who experimented with alchemy, performed daring surgery, and invented new methods and techniques of treatment. His contemporaries had a difficult time accepting him as a scientist, and he was perceived primarily as a pseudo-scientist. See Walter Pagel, *Paracelsus: An Introduction to Philosophical Medicine in the Era of the Renaissance* (Basel: Karger, 1982).

71. Buber, "Geschichte des Individuationsproblems," 25, 3.

72. Ibid., 29, 27. Böhme and Weigel became models for the German romantics, especially for Novalis. For an excellent study of Novalis, see John Neubauer, *Novalis* (Boston: Twayne, 1980), 64–67. Sais and its goddess were a great inspiration to Friedrich Schiller, who wrote a poem, "Das verschleierte Bild zu Sais" (The veiled image at Sais). In turn, Novalis appropriated Schiller's model for a work which he called "Die Lehrlinge zu Sais" (The apprentices at Sais). The significance of the image, however, is succinctly conveyed by a poem Novalis wrote in 1798:

> Lucky are those who have become wise and no longer worry about the world,
> those who are desirous of the stone of wisdom in themselves.
> Only reasonable men are true adepts—they transform
> everything into life and gold—need elixirs no longer.
> In them the holy retort is steaming—kings reside in them—
> Delphi too and they finally grasp the *Know Thyself.*
>
> (1:404, translated in Neubauer, *Novalis*, 66–67)

73. Goethe's connection to the notion of the microcosm became famous through an incident that became one of the most celebrated of human encounters in German cultural history. For an account, see Emil Staiger, ed., *Der Briefwechsel zwischen Schiller und Goethe* (Frankfurt a.M.: Insel-Verlag, 1966), 13. In 1791, Goethe and Schiller, who had maintained a strained professional relationship without being able to develop a personal friendship, met at a literary gathering. Afterward, they walked home together, in animated conversation. The bone of contention for many years had been their difference of approach. Schiller had explained things philosophically; he had *ideas*. Goethe described things poetically, calling his representations *experiences*. During that evening's conversation, Goethe described to Schiller an experience he had had—the experience of the *Urpflanze* (first plant). With vivid strokes Goethe unfolded before Schiller's inner eye this organic creation. Schiller listened to him attentively, nodding agreement. When Goethe finished, Schiller said calmly that this was not an experience but an idea. Goethe

was outraged, but he held his temper, responding instead that he didn't mind having an idea without even knowing it and being able to see it with his eyes. That was the beginning of a warm and productive friendship until Schiller's death in 1805. Thus Goethe's notion of the original plant was merely a variation of an eternal theme: the organic nature of the microcosm. See also Eucken, *Geistige Strömungen der Gegenwart*, "Mechanisch-organisch," 127–53, and Lasswitz, *Seelen und Ziele*, on Goethe and Spinoza, 246–65.

74. Buber, "Geschichte des Individuationsproblems," 26.

75. This is the synopsis of the contents of the book by Weigel.

76. Ronald Levao, *Renaissance Minds and Their Fictions: Cusanus, Sidney, Shakespeare* (Berkeley and Los Angeles: University of California Press, 1985), 52. The author explains that the work which carries this diagram was "Cusanus' second major work, *De coniecturis* (1440–44), which continues to develop a positive theory of mental effort against the background of the negative way. The admitted inadequacy of our concepts no longer demands their effacement, but asserts their value *as* conjecture" (49). About the actual diagram, Levao writes: "The most ambitious conjecture in the work, an architectonic that includes themes from the others, is the *figura universi*. A single large circle surrounds three smaller circles placed vertically down its axis. Within each of these is another set of three smaller circles, and within these still another set of three, so that when completed, the image shows twenty-seven small circles strung like beads, grouped into threes by nine larger circles, which are in turn grouped by three larger circles, and all included in the 'grossest,' for a total of forty circles. The diagram allows Cusanus to demonstrate his mastery over intellectual traditions that become for him a repertoire of metaphors that can be evoked and combined at will. Important doctrines can be visually grasped and interrelated . . . every specific thing contains within itself a version of the whole. . . . Later Renaissance thinkers would admire the inclusiveness and elegance of the figure and adapt it to illustrate their own versions of cosmic harmony" (52).

77. Buber, "Geschichte des Individuationsproblems," 6.

78. Buber, "Über Jakob Boehme," 253.

79. Buber, "Geschichte des Individuationsproblems," 34–35.

80. Ibid., 29, 30.

81. Buber, "Über Jakob Boehme," 251.

82. Ibid.

83. Ibid., 252.

84. Ibid., 251, 253.

85. Ibid., 252.

86. See Friedrich Wilhelm Joseph von Schelling (1775–1854), *Von der Weltseele* (1798) and *System des transcendentalen Idealismus* (1800), trans. Peter Lauchlan Heath, *System of Transcendental Idealism* (Charlottesville: University Press of Virginia, 1978).

87. Friedrich Schleiermacher, *Über die Religion, Reden an die Gebil-*

deten unter ihren Verächtern (1799), with a postscript by Carl Heinz Ratschow (Stuttgart: Philipp Reclam Jun., 1969), 5; translation mine. See also Crouter, *Friedrich Schleiermacher on Religion.*

88. Schleiermacher, *Über die Religion,* 118–19.

89. Ibid., 59, 160–61.

90. Dorothy Reich, ed., *A History of German Literature,* by J. G. Robertson, 6th ed. (Edinburgh: William Blackwood, 1970), 383.

91. Ericson, ed., *Emerson on Transcendentalism,* 3–4, 38.

92. Ibid., 95, xi.

93. Ibid., 3.

3. Kadima! Apprenticeship in Jewish Culture, 1898–1905

1. Howard M. Sachar, *A History of Israel from the Rise of Zionism to Our Time* (1979; reprint, New York: Knopf, 1986), on "Chovevei Zion," 16–17. See also Ahad Ha-Am, "The Law of the Heart," in Arthur Hertzberg, ed., *The Zionist Idea* (New York: Atheneum, 1977), 251–55.

2. See Moshe Leib Lilienblum, "The Way of Return," in Hertzberg, *Zionist Idea,* 168–70.

3. Samuel Hayyim Landau, "Toward an Explanation of Our Ideology," ibid., 434, 435.

4. Sachar, *History of Israel,* 67. The prototype of the Mizrachi movement, properly called Merkaz Ruchani, was founded by Rabbi Samuel Mohilever (1824–98) in 1893. Rabbi Isaac Jacob Reines reconstituted the movement in 1901. He perpetuated both secular and religious studies in his Yeshiva. Later Rabbi Abraham Isaac Kook, first Ashkenazi chief rabbi of Palestine, followed the same synthetic model.

5. "Protocol of Vienna meeting," May 4, 1901, Jerusalem, National Library, Buber Archives, Ms. Var. 350 F/36. Convened by Matthias Acher (Vienna), who chaired the meeting, Davis Trietsch (Berlin), and Franz Kobler (Jungbunzlau), secretary, the group represented the interests of a segment of Galician Jewry. In addition to Acher, Trietsch, and Kobler, the meeting was attended by Dr. Alfred Kral (Plan), Leopold Sitzmann (Vienna), and lecturer Dr. Friedrich Welleninsky (Prague). Invitations were also sent to Martin Buber (in Switzerland), Dr. Max Diamant (Czernowitz), Fabius Schach (Karlsruhe), Jacob Schorr (Vienna), Bernard Tag (Vienna), and Alfred Nossig (Berlin). The agenda included both a discussion of internal Jewish affairs and responses to various critiques. The committee urged the creation of "Palestine courses" and reported on the principles, progress, and current state of affairs of the Jüdische Orient Colonisations Gesellschaft located in Berlin. There was discussion of a "Palestine Congress" sponsored by such organizations as the Jewish Colonization Association, the Alliance Israelite, Hovevei Zion, Esra, Bnai Brith, and others regarding a possible fusion. The idea of a "comprehensive Yiddish [*jargon*] dictionary and a grammar" was suggested by Matthias Acher, but discussion of Hebrew and Yiddish language was

postponed because of the absence of experts on the topic. The idea of a Jewish college was discussed. The publication of a comprehensive scientific history of the Jewish movement, especially Zionism, was proposed and adopted. Questions of physical fitness also surfaced as the discussants reviewed the issue of how to introduce physical exercise "to the lowest physically fit groups." Another issue of concern was Western Jewish understanding of Jewish culture, though its discussion was seen as premature, as was the discussion of the Jewish theater, "especially one producing plays in Yiddish." Under the general heading of good and welfare, "cooperation for the sake of the general well-being" was discussed, but all participants in the conference agreed "not to take specific action to fight anti-Semitism and to initiate counteraction [*Abwehr*]." The members did support a suggestion by Acher to organize the Jewish social democrats of Galicia as a separate national group of social democrats, to make them *bundistisch* (Bund-like), and then to support a *bundistisch* organization of the East European Workers in Vienna.

6. Buber, "Herzl und die Historie," *Die Jüdische Bewegung* (1916), 167. See also *Jüdische Bewegung*, 105–6. The essay "Renaissance und Bewegung" (ibid., 95–108) was a combination of two essays Buber had published separately, "Die jüdische Renaissance" and "Die jüdische Bewegung." He explained that the two are complementary and hence he published them once more, together. See also "Renaissance," Jerusalem, National Library, Buber Archives, Ms. Var. 350 F/21. This 1911 manuscript is a direct response by Buber to what he perceived to be Max Nordau's "narrow and inadequate definition" of renaissance. Translation mine.

7. Buber, "Herzl und die Historie," 167.

8. For the distinction between inherited Jewishness and consciously chosen Jewishness, see the Epilogue.

9. Buber, "Renaissance," 8.

10. Buber, "Renaissance und Bewegung," 95, 100; translation mine.

11. Ibid., 95–96, 101. In Buber's time, there was a great deal of interest in and scholarship about Spinoza. A number of German scholars mentioned him in the same breath with the German poet Johann Wolfgang von Goethe.

12. Buber, *Drei Reden*, 49–51; translation mine.

13. Ibid.; Buber, "Renaissance und Bewegung," 97–98.

14. Buber, "Renaissance und Bewegung," 97, 98, 106.

15. Ibid., 98–99. The Haskalah was originally a German-Jewish phenomenon. Its beginning, following the European Enlightenment, is generally attributed to the thought of Moses Mendelssohn.

16. Ibid., 106–7.

17. Ibid., 103–5.

18. Ahad Ha-Am, "Slavery in Freedom," in Leon Simon, trans., *Selected Essays by Ahad Ha-Am* (Philadelphia: Jewish Publication Society of America, 1912), 171–94.

19. Buber, "Renaissance und Bewegung," 101–2.
20. Ibid., 9.
21. Buber, "Jüdische Renaissance," 16, 8.
22. Ibid., 15, 11, 12.
23. After 1901, the congresses met every other year and then intermittently.
24. *Stenographisches Protokoll der Verhandlungen des III. Zionisten Congresses*, 190–93; translation mine.
25. Ibid., 191.
26. Ibid., 193.
27. Ibid. See also "Weltzionistentag," in *Die Welt* (September 20, 1901): 1–2. In 1901, Buber proposed that the Weltzionistentag, which was proclaimed the day before the Fifth Zionist Congress, might serve as such a day of union. He, in fact, expected the Weltzionistentag to be a counterpart to the Zionist Congress, a day of "synthetic criticism," which would review the totality of Jewish renaissance work and criticize "in order to help construct that which is developing." He felt that analytical criticism "deconstructs, shreds, breaks down, dissolves, negates" and that such an activity was not conducive to production and the productive fire of a great life. Courtesy of Margot Cohn, Buber Archives.
28. *Stenographisches Protokoll der Verhandlungen des III. Zionisten Congresses*, 193.
29. Ibid.
30. "Die Congresstribüne," *Die Welt* 36 (November 6, 1901): 1–2. Courtesy of Buber Archives.
31. Buber, "Ein Wort zum fünften Kongress," *Jüdische Volksstimme* 2 (January 15, 1902): 2–3; 3 (February 15, 1902): 2–3; translation mine.
32. According to the agenda printed in *Die Welt*, Nordau was scheduled to speak on physical, economic, and spiritual elevation, but he seems to have singled out economic elevation to the exclusion of all else.
33. See Buber, "Von jüdischer Kunst," *Jüdische Bewegung* (1916), 58–67.
34. Buber, "Jüdische Kunst," Jerusalem, National Library, Buber Archives, Ms. Var. 350 F/71, 1.
35. Buber, "Ein Wort zum fünften Kongress," *Jüdische Volksstimme* 2 (January 15, 1902): 3. Courtesy of Buber Archives.
36. Buber, "Jüdische Kunst," Buber Archives, 1.
37. Buber's open complaint did not help for future congresses. In the minutes for the Sixth Zionist Congress, August 23–28, 1903, in Basel, we read that Buber, as always, had difficulty getting recognized to speak. Dr. Max Bodenheimer, a vice-president, intended to adjourn even though he promised Buber the floor. Buber protested, and after some more debate he was given the floor. It was once more a question of the order of business. Apparently those in charge tried to weaken the presentations of the Agitations Comite by splitting up the speakers, having some speak that night, the others the next day. Buber saw the danger to their effectiveness.

In addition, Herzl was not present, and Buber strongly objected to having important issues discussed in Herzl's absence. He therefore requested a postponement of the entire session and discussion until the next day, which was granted.

38. Buber, "Ein Wort zum fünften Kongress," *Jüdische Volksstimme* 3 (February 15, 1902): 2. From the minutes we learn that they were Rabbis Reines and Rabbinowitsch.

39. Buber, "Ein Wort zum fünften Kongress," *Jüdische Volksstimme* 2 (January 15, 1902): 2.

40. Buber, "Ein Wort zum fünften Kongress," *Jüdische Volksstimme* 3 (February 15, 1902): 2–3.

41. Ibid., 3.

42. See Ahad Ha-Am, "Altneuland," *Ost und West* 3 (April 1903): cols. 227–44; Max Nordau, "Ahad Haam über 'Altneuland,' " *Die Welt* 7 (March 13, 1903): 1–5.

43. Buber, "Ein Wort zum fünften Kongress," *Jüdische Volksstimme* 2 (January 15, 1902): 2.

44. Buber, "Wege zum Zionismus," in *Jüdische Bewegung* (1916), 39–44; translation mine.

45. Ibid., 42.

46. See Buber, "Die Entdeckung von Palaestina" (The discovery of Palestine), *Ost und West* 2 (1905): cols. 127–30. Courtesy of Buber Archives.

47. Buber, "Ein geistiges Zentrum" (A spiritual center) in *Jüdische Bewegung* (1916), 80, 89–91.

48. Buber, "Zionistische Politik" (Zionist Politics), *Jüdische Bewegung* (1916), 120–21.

49. Buber, "Bergfeuer—Zum fünften Congresse," *Die Welt* 35 (August 30, 1901): 2–3. Courtesy of Buber Archives.

50. Buber, "Was ist zu tun?" *Jüdische Bewegung* (1916), 125.

51. Buber, "Die Entdeckung von Palaestina," 127.

52. Buber, "Was ist zu tun?" 126.

53. Ibid.

54. Buber, "Ein geistiges Zentrum," 87.

55. Ibid., 87–88.

56. Buber, "Gegenwartsarbeit," *Jüdische Bewegung* (1916), 20–22.

57. When Franz Rosenzweig became ill in the 1920s, Buber took on the leadership of the Lehrhaus in Frankfurt, which was a facility for adult Jewish education. In 1933, when the Nazis dismissed Buber from his *Lehrstuhl* at the University of Frankfurt, the Lehrhaus became a central place of encouragement and spiritual resistance.

58. This exploratory meeting was approved by the Fifth Zionist Congress in 1901. See the document *Eine jüdische Hochschule* (Berlin: Jüdischer Verlag, [1902]). Courtesy of Margot Cohn, Jerusalem, National Library, Buber Archives.

59. Ibid., 31, 22.

60. Buber, "Ein geistiges Zentrum," 79–80.

61. Ibid., 86–87.

62. To give a few examples, in 1904 Buber published a poem, "Elijahu," based on 1 Kings 19:11, 12, in *Ost und West*; in a collection of "young Judaic" poems called *Junge Harfen* (Young Harps), published by Buber's friend Berthold Feiwel in the Jüdische Verlag, Berlin, in 1903, Buber published several poems. Also in *Jüdischer Almanach 5663* (Jewish Almanac 5663), edited by Feiwel and Ephraim Moshe Lilien (Berlin: Jüdischer Verlag, 1902), Buber published a translation of a poem from the Hebrew by Saul Tchernichowsky (Heidelberg), titled "Do You Remember?" In addition, a Buber original, "Der Daimon," and two poems from a cycle, "Geist der Herr" (The Lord is *Geist*)—"The Disciple" and "The *Magier*." In the *Kadimah Kalender für das Jahr 5667* [1906/7] Buber republished one verse of "Elijahu," originally published in *Junge Harfen*. Also in *Ost und West*, June 1902, Buber published two poems from his cycle, "*Acher*," one titled "The Flame," the other "Redemption." Courtesy of Buber Archives.

63. "Gebet," *Die Welt* 5 (June 28, 1901): 13. Courtesy of Buber Archives.

64. "Unseres Volkes Erwachen," *Die Welt* 3 (November 17, 1899): 14–15. Courtesy of Buber Archives.

65. The thought of the awakening of the people existed long before Buber. See the poem "Awake, My People," by Judah Leib Gordon in Michael Stanislawski, *For Whom Do I Toil? Judah Leib Gordon and the Crisis of Russian Jewry* (New York: Oxford University Press, 1988), 45–67.

66. "An Narcissus," in *Jahresbericht der Lese- und Redehalle jüdischer Hochschüler in Wien über das Vereinsjahr 1901* (Vienna, 1901), 17. Courtesy of Margot Cohn, Buber Archives.

67. In "Über das Marionettentheater" (On the puppet theater) (1801), see Helmut Sembdner, *Kleists Aufsatz über das Marionettentheater* (Berlin: E. Schmidt, 1967), the young German is ridiculed for sitting in front of a mirror day and night, admiring himself, to the exclusion of all else. Kleist criticized the shallowness and self-aggrandizement that may come with the attempt at selfhood if one does not watch out for such obstacles.

68. The cover of the Jewish yearbook, *Die Stimme der Wahrheit* (The voice of truth) (Würzburg: Verlag N. Philippi, 1905), depicted a noble [Jewish] savage with wild hair, naked but for a loincloth, clenched fist raised in victory, a primordial being, who can be held up as the contrast to the *verzärtelte* (effeminate) type portrayed in the poem.

69. In this image Buber is acting out the dramatic devices of Schiller, in whose poem "Der Alpenjäger" God thunders at a human being who persecutes His creatures in the Alps. See *Schiller Dramen und Gedichte*, 1102.

70. Buber, "Was ist zu tun?" 136–37.

71. David Pinski, "Das Erwachen—Eine Skizze," translated from

Yiddish by Martin Buber, *Jüdischer Almanach* (Berlin: Jüdischer Verlag, 1902), 209–15. Courtesy of Buber Archives.

72. "I. L. Peretz, Ein Wort zu seinem fünfundzwanzigsten Schriftsteller-Jubiläum," *Die Welt* 5 (May 3, 1901): 9. See Grete Schaeder, *Martin Buber Briefwechsel aus sieben Jahrzehnten* (Heidelberg: Lambert Schneider, 1976), 2: 152. Buber's son Raphael went to Worpswede in 1923 to live in Vogelers Siedlung, a communal settlement established by Heinrich Vogeler, a German communist. Raphael then made aliyah and for a time lived on a kibbutz.

73. Buber, "I. L. Peretz," 9.

74. Ibid.

75. See Buber, "Kunst und judentum," *Jüdische Bewegung* (1916; 2d ed., 1920), 245–51.

76. Buber, *Jüdische Künstler* (Berlin: Jüdischer Verlag, 1903), Preface.

77. Ibid., 4–5.

78. Only in the preface to *Jüdische Künstler*, not in the reprint.

79. Buber, "Was ist zu tun?" 128–29.

80. Buber, *Jüdische Künstler*, Preface.

81. Buber, "Was ist zu tun?" 129.

82. Ibid., 136.

83. Ibid., 129–30.

84. Buber, "Ein geistiges Zentrum," 93–94.

85. Buber, *Jüdische Künstler*, Preface.

86. Ibid.

87. Buber, "Ein geistiges Zentrum," 91–92.

88. Buber, "Die Schaffenden, das Volk und die Bewegung—Einige Bemerkungen," in *Jüdischer Almanach* (Berlin: Jüdischer Verlag, 1902), 19–24; also in *Jüdische Bewegung* (1916), 68–77, quote on 69.

89. Ibid., *Jüdische Bewegung* (1916), 70.

90. Buber, "Was ist zu tun?" 127–28.

91. Buber, "Die Schaffenden, das Volk und die Bewegung," in *Jüdische Bewegung* (1916), 70–71.

92. Ibid., 72–73.

93. Ibid., 73–74.

94. See Buber, "Die Entdeckung von Palaestina," *Ost und West* 2 (1905): cols. 127, 130.

95. "Jüdische Kunst," *Die Welt* 46 (November 15, 1901): 10. Courtesy of Buber Archives. Buber also included an essay on Lesser Ury in his 1903 book on Jewish art. In *Die Welt* 37 (May 13, 1901): 9–10, Buber wrote about the artist Maria Janitschek, whose poems, he felt, evolved "from the mouth of the Bible." He published two of her poems, one of which also dealt with Jeremiah. Courtesy of Buber Archives.

96. Buber, "Die Schaffenden, das Volk und die Bewegung," *Jüdische Bewegung* (1916), 76–77.

97. "Eine jungjüdische Bühne," *Die Welt* 45 (November 8, 1901): 10–11. Courtesy of Buber Archives.

98. Ibid., 10.

99. Ibid., 11.
100. Sachar, *History of Israel*, 38.
101. Buber, "Theodor Herzl und die jüdische Bewegung," Jerusalem, National Library, Buber Archives, Ms. Var. 350 F/25; translation mine.
102. Buber, "Theodor Herzl," *Jüdische Bewegung* (1916), 143.
103. Buber, "Herzl und die Historie," *Jüdische Bewegung* (1916), 164, 166.
104. Buber, "Theodor Herzl," 167.
105. Buber, "Theodor Herzl und die jüdische Bewegung," Buber Archives.
106. Buber, "Herzl und die Historie," 167.
107. Buber, "Theodor Herzl," 143.
108. Buber, "Wege zum Zionismus," 41.
109. Buber, "Theodor Herzl," 144.
110. Buber, "Herzl und die Historie," 167, 169. See also Avraham Shapira, "Martin Buber: The Cause and the Person," *Modern Judaism* 8 (October 1988): 287–95.
111. Buber, "Theodor Herzl," 141.
112. Buber, "Herzl und die Historie," 169, 173. Buber's portrayal of Herzl apparently aroused controversy, and he felt compelled to respond publicly in *Die Jüdische Rundschau* to the criticism of one "Veritas," justifying his assessment with the very quote from *Das Palais Bourbon* cited earlier. See "Zur Aufklärung," *Jüdische Rundschau* 48 (December 2, 1904): 417–18; courtesy of Buber Archives.
113. Buber, "Theodor Herzl," 145, 147–48.
114. Ibid., 148–50.
115. Ibid., 151–52. On the Uganda scheme, see also Sachar, *History of Israel*, 59–63.
116. Buber, "Er und Wir," *Die Welt* 20 (May 20, 1910): 445–46; also in *Jüdische Bewegung* (1916), 196–204.
117. Ibid., *Jüdische Bewegung* (1916), 196–97.
118. Ibid., 197–99. Please see Buber's ultimate disagreement with Friedman's statement in Maurice Friedman, *Martin Buber's Life and Work: The Early Years, 1878–1923* (London: Search Press, 1982), 65.
119. Buber, "Er und Wir," *Jüdische Bewegung* (1916), 200–203.
120. Ibid., 200–202.
121. See Leon Simon, *Ahad Ha-Am* (Philadelphia: Jewish Publication Society of America, 1960), 171.
122. Hertzberg, *Zionist Idea*, 251. For Ahad Ha-Am's texts, see Hertzberg, *Zionist Idea*; Jacques Kornberg, ed., *At the Crossroads: Essays on Ahad Ha-Am* (Albany: State University of New York Press, 1983); and Simon, trans., *Selected Essays by Ahad Ha-Am*. The term *secular protest rabbi* had been applied to Ahad Ha-Am by Nordau during the *Altneuland* controversy. See Friedman, *Martin Buber's Life and Work*, 62–64.
123. Jehuda Reinharz, "Ahad Ha-Am, Martin Buber, and German Zionism," in Kornberg, ed., *At the Crossroads*, 148.

124. Ahad Ha-Am, "The Law of the Heart," in Hertzberg, *Zionist Idea*, 253, 252.

125. Ahad Ha-Am, "Flesh and Spirit," ibid., 258–60.

126. Ahad Ha-Am, "The Jewish State and the Jewish Problem," ibid., 264, 267.

127. Buber, "Der Wägende," reprinted in *Jüdische Bewegung* (1920), 68–73. Buber had proposed the journal *Der Jude* in 1903 but was unsuccessful in securing the funding from his friends. In 1916, Buber funded the journal through subscriptions and with a good bit of his own money through the Jüdische Verlag. Earlier, Gabriel Riesser had published a journal by the same name.

128. Ibid., 71.

129. See Hertzberg, *Zionist Idea*, 251; also Sachar, *History of Israel*, 57.

130. Buber, "Der Wägende," 72.

131. Ibid., 73.

132. Buber, *Drei Reden*, 68.

133. Buber, "Der Wägende," 73.

134. Buber, "Gegenwartsarbeit," *Die Welt* 6 (February 8, 1901): 4–5. Also in *Jüdische Bewegung* (1916), 17–22.

135. Ibid., 19.

4. Hasidism: Apprenticeship in a Life of the Communal Spirit, 1905–1908

1. Martin Buber, *Die Legende des Baal-Schem* (Frankfurt a.M.: Rütten and Loening, 1908), II.

2. Martin Buber, *Die Geschichten des Rabbi Nachman* (Frankfurt a.M.: Rütten and Loening, 1906), 41. According to Buber, Nachman did not write down his teachings because he was too busy. We therefore have no true and direct message. Rather, the stories were written down from memory by Rabbi Nachman's students, especially by his favorite, Nathan of Niemirov. Although they were completely distorted and fragmentary, the maxims nevertheless reflected the spirit and language of the master. Approximately five years after the master's death, they were published in Yiddish with a Hebrew translation.

3. Martin Buber, "Mein Weg zum Chassidismus," in *Martin Buber Werke* (Munich: Verlag Lambert Schneider, 1963), 3: 969.

4. This is not to be confused with an "Epigone" or imitator, a charge leveled against nineteenth-century artists in general.

5. Buber, *Legende des Baal-Schem*, II.

6. Buber, *Rabbi Nachman*, Preface.

7. See Buber, "Der Geist des Orients und das Judentum," in *Vom Geist des Judentums* (Munich: Kurt Wolff Verlag, 1916), 12.

8. See Aschheim, *Brothers and Strangers*, 55.

9. See ibid. on Berdichevsky, 123–25; also Hertzberg, *Zionist Idea*,

on Rabbi Abraham Isaac Kook, 416–31, and on Aaron David Gordon, 368–87.

10. Buber's work in Hasidism, though initially lauded by Gershom Scholem was later severely criticized by Scholem for ignoring scholarly conventions, such as citing the sources. Buber did not wish to write in this way, yet the criticism of his use of the sources continues in our day. See especially "Martin Buber's Misuse of Hasidic Sources," by leading critic Steven T. Katz, *Post-Holocaust Dialogues: Critical Studies in Modern Jewish Thought* (New York: New York University Press, 1983), 52–93.

11. Martin Buber, Bar Mitzvah Address, Jerusalem, National Library, Buber Archives, Ms. Var. 350 A/1a; translation mine. Buber's thesis was based on Hoshea 2:21–22:

> I will betroth you to Me forever.
> I will betroth you with righteousness,
> with justice, love, and compassion.
> I will betroth you to Me in faithfulness
> And you shall love the Lord,

the prayer recited when laying tefillin. Many of the later components for a Jewish way of life which Buber considered important were first expressed in this statement, for example, the concept of reciprocity. God reminds the human being that He has a covenant with him and that the human being is bound to God in loyalty and in truthfulness through the attributes of virtue, justice, mercy, and loving-kindness. Buber explained that one who follows these maxims cannot go wrong in life, not as a young man, not as an adult, and not as an old man. He concluded that virtue and justice, love and mercy, loyalty, faith, and the knowledge of God are indeed beautiful when they are united in brotherly fashion.

12. Rather than quoting additional Talmudic or biblical proofs, Buber supported his argument by quoting the German poet Friedrich Schiller, who knew the value of virtue as well, albeit in humanistic guise. In the poem "Die Worte des Glaubens" (The words of faith), Schiller wrote:

> Virtue is no empty word,
> The human being can practice it in life,
> And even if he struggles
> He can nevertheless strive,
> And that which no intellect can grasp
> Is practiced by a simple mind.
> (In *Schiller Dramen und Gedichte*, 1068; translation mine.)

Justice is as important as virtue, for God is a judge. Justice does not mean "wrath," as it is often interpreted in Christian conceptions of the Jewish God. Buber stressed that justice also means love, for the two qualities which the sages attributed to God, "emet harachamim" and "emet hadayan," which he interpreted as "deepest loving-kindness," and "strictest justice," are not contrasts, but closely intertwined opposites.

It is the love of God that unites these two qualities. Here we see a Buberian tendency not only to bring out the kindness of God—countering the contemporary image that the Jewish God Jehovah was a terrible God—but also to reconcile opposite terms.

The person who alters the Law defiles the Divine name; every attack on the Law is an attack on God's holiness. Buber explained that "emet" (truth) is the "sela" or "amen" of God. Justice is truth and is closely connected to peace. The three virtues of justice, truth, and peace form a single unit, and the world rests on these three pillars, as we see in Zachariah 8:16.

In Buber's assessment, love is the spirit of the Jewish religion, hardly the perception of his Christian fellow human beings. Already at this early stage, Buber's interests involved finding explanations for the great disparities of life. He wrote, "Our religion commands love and mercy for the stranger and for the Jew, loving-kindness and mercy for all of God's creatures." That is why we are commanded to "Love your neighbor as yourself." Thus there is no fundamental difference between human beings. This is a notion Buber worked out theoretically in his dissertation, in which he focused on the ideas of Nicolas of Cusa, who asserted that creation is an emanation of God. In fact, Divine love extends to all of God's creation, not only to humans but to animals as well as inorganic nature. Hence, like God, we shall also have mercy on all of God's creatures, or we shall attempt to become ever more like God. We shall learn to know God, for to know God elevates the human being. Again, quoting Schiller, Buber admonished:

> And there is a God, a sacred Will,
> even if the human will wavers,
> that Will lives high above time and space,
> and weaves the most noble thoughts.
> (Schiller, 1069; translation mine.)

This idea later reemerged in Buber's varied explorations of all types of mystical experiences. He contemplated that "only Christianity [in addition to Judaism] used the right combination of reason and emotion in its formulation of the idea of God. The heathens relied only on the emotions, while the philosophers used only reason." But just as one needs both justice and mercy, so one needs a conception of God which includes reason as well as emotion. And he further interpreted loyalty to mean that we not only say what we will do but actually do what we promise. Again, these are ideas whose implementation he pursued with vigor and conviction in his Zionist work and throughout all of his mature writing.

Buber concluded with a personal prayer in which he asked God to fulfill his innermost wishes, hopes, and desires and to give him strength and support so he would not disappoint his parents and grandparents who had guided him thus far. He prayed that he might increase in wisdom and virtue and become better, purer, and more complete to the honor and joy of his loved ones, as well as to his own good.

13. "Mein Weg zum Chassidismus," Jerusalem, National Library, Buber Archives, Ms. Var. 350 D/31, printed in Buber, *Werke*, Vol. 3, *Schriften zum Chassidismus*, 959–73. References are to printed text; translation mine.

14. Buber, "Mein Weg zum Chassidismus," 966. See also Chapter 3 on rootedness.

15. Ibid.

16. Ibid., 967.

17. Ibid.

18. This is Buber's spelling. Also spelled *Zavva'at ha-Rivash*, by Isaiah of Janow (1794). According to the *Encyclopedia Judaica*, however, this work does not include the testament of the Baal Shem Tov, but only a selection of his statements.

19. Buber, "Mein Weg zum Chassidismus," 967.

20. Ibid., 968.

21. In *Drei Reden*, Buber wrote: "But this alone is not enough. For now we know the innermost sickness of the uprooted people, and its abysmal fate. We know that its absolute and its relative life are sundered; that what constitutes the summit and the eternal for the absolute life is wholly, or almost wholly, unperceived by the relative life, or is at best looked upon as a quickly-to-be-forgotten episode. Hence, renewal must also mean this: that the battle for fulfillment encompass the entire people; that the ideas penetrate the day's reality; that the spirit enter life" (98–99). "At the present time, the Jewish people knows only a relative life; it must regain its absolute life, it must regain living Judaism" (96). "In the absolute life of the Jewish people, it betokens the greatest triumph of the deed-idea achieved so far; in their relative life, Hasidism, too, remained only an episode" (89). Quoted from Glatzer, *On Judaism*, 53, 54, 49.

22. On the history of Hasidism, see Simon Dubnow, *Geschichte des Chassidismus* (Berlin: Jüdischer Verlag, 1931); Dubnow, *History of the Jews in Russia and Poland* (Philadelphia: Jewish Publication Society of America, 1916); Raphael Mahler, *Hasidism and the Jewish Enlightenment* (Philadelphia: Jewish Publication Society of America, 1985); Gershom Scholem, *The Messianic Idea in Judaism and Other Essays on Jewish Spirituality* (New York: Schocken Books, 1971), 325–50; Bernard Dov Weinryb, *The Jews of Poland* (Philadelphia: Jewish Publication Society of America, 1973), 262–303; H. H. Ben-Sasson and S. Ettinger, eds., *Jewish Society Through the Ages* (New York: Schocken Books, 1971), 251–66; Jacob Katz, *Tradition and Crisis* (New York: Schocken Books, 1971), 231–44.

23. Buber, *Rabbi Nachman*, 9.

24. Ibid., 10.

25. See Scholem on Messianism, *Messianic Idea in Judaism.*
26. Buber, *Rabbi Nachman,* 10.
27. Ibid., 10–12.
28. Ibid., 12.
29. These are images which the romantic poet/artist William Blake expressed in his art. See also, interestingly, Buber, *Ekstatische Konfessionen,* 55.
30. Shabbatai Zvi, when confronted by the Islamic rulers, chose conversion to Islam over death for Judaism.
31. Buber, *Rabbi Nachman,* 13. The numbers vary. Ben Zion Dinur states that there were one thousand (*Israel and the Diaspora* [Philadelphia: Jewish Publication Society of America, 1969/5279], 90). Sachar mentions fifteen hundred, stating that five hundred of them died before even reaching Palestine (*History of Israel,* 20).
32. Buber, *Rabbi Nachman,* 13.
33. Ibid.
34. See Buber, *Ecstatic Confessions,* ed. Paul Mendes-Flohr, trans. Esther Cameron (San Francisco: Harper & Row, 1985).
35. Buber, *Rabbi Nachman,* 14. We might also remember that this is what interested Buber in Schleiermacher—not the private personal God experience, but the God experience realized in society. See Chapter 2.
36. Ibid.
37. Ibid., 18.
38. Ibid., 18–19. According to Buber, eventually Hasidism became spoiled. The aspect of the messenger between the two worlds ("shaliah zibur" or *Mittler*), who carried the prayer upward and returned with the blessing, originally only one part of the Hasidic ethos, became ever more important and gradually overpowered all else. He thereby impaired the most important human quality: the independence of the soul that was capable of seeking and desiring on its own.
39. Ibid., 5–6.
40. See his poem "An Narcissus," in Chapter 3.
41. Buber, *Rabbi Nachman,* 6–7.
42. Ibid., 7–8.
43. Ibid., 32.
44. Ibid., 8.
45. Buber, "Mein Weg zum Chassidismus," 968.
46. Buber, *Legende des Baal-Schem,* I.
47. Ibid., I and note. Buber acknowledged that before him, only Simon Dubnow had written a history of the Hasidim, but now two other scholars—S. A. Horodezky and M. Y. Berdichevsky—also wrote on the subject. These works existed only in Hebrew, however, and were virtually inaccessible to German-speaking Jews. Today, these Hebrew works are accessible to many Jewish scholars but, alas, not to English-speaking readers.
48. Buber, *Legende des Baal-Schem,* I.

49. Buber, *Rabbi Nachman*, 15.
50. Ibid. Compare also Schelling's idea of the world soul.
51. Ibid., 15–16.
52. Ibid., 16.
53. Ibid.
54. Buber, *Legende des Baal-Schem*, 2–4.
55. Ibid., 7. See German romanticism for notions of *Fremdling*, especially Novalis.
56. Ibid., 8–9. For the *hasid*, the door to the Divine is not closed. In contrast to the modern human being, he is capable of entering the Divine realm any time he has a mind to.
57. Ibid., 9.
58. See Avraham Shapira, "Work," in Arthur A. Cohen and Paul Mendes-Flohr, *Contemporary Jewish Religious Thought* (New York: Free Press, 1987), 1055–68.
59. The Hasidim were not generally seen to be Zionists, although some were lovers of Zion.
60. Buber, *Legende des Baal-Schem*, 10–12.
61. Ibid., 22, 24–25.
62. See Chapter 2 for the philosophical concept of dualism.
63. Buber, "Christus, Chassidismus, Gnosis," in *Werke*, 949–58. See also Gedaliahu Guy Stroumsa, "Gnosis," in Cohen and Mendes-Flohr, *Contemporary Jewish Religious Thought*, 285–90.
64. Buber, *Legende des Baal-Schem*, 25, 27–28.
65. Ibid., 31. This is a notion Buber highlighted in his study of Cusa; see Chapter 2.
66. Ibid., 32–33.
67. Ibid., 40.
68. Buber, *Rabbi Nachman*, 16–17.
69. Ibid., 17.
70. Ibid.
71. *Sippurei Ma'asiyyot*, Berdichev, 1815.
72. Buber, *Rabbi Nachman*, 5, 20.
73. Ibid., 20.
74. Ibid., 20–21.
75. Ibid., 27. Buber did not hesitate to mention two men he considered to be two great Jews, Rabbi Nachman and Jesus, in one breath. See Buber in Bar Kochba, *Vom Judentum* (Leipzig: Kurt Wolff Verlag, 1913).
76. Buber, *Rabbi Nachman*, 28.
77. For comparison, see Arthur Green, *Tormented Master: A Life of Rabbi Nahman of Bratslav* (University, Ala.: University of Alabama Press, 1979).
78. Buber, *Rabbi Nachman*, 21, 23.
79. Ibid., 24.
80. Ibid., 23–24.
81. See Chapter 2 on Nietzsche's early influence on Buber.

82. Buber, *Rabbi Nachman,* 25–26. Nachman actually dated his life from this journey (27) in 1791 (see Green, *Tormented Master,* 283).

83. Buber, *Rabbi Nachman,* 32.

84. Buber, letter "Eingesandt," in *Generalanzeiger* 36 (September 3, 1905): 6. Courtesy of Buber Archives.

85. Buber, "Der Mythos der Juden," in Bar Kochba, *Vom Judentum,* 21.

86. Buber, letter in *Generalanzeiger* 36 (September 3, 1905): 6.

87. Ibid. See Goethe, "Das Märchen," in *Goethe Werke,* Vol. 2 (Frankfurt a.M.: Insel-Verlag, 1965), 524–50.

88. Here one thinks especially of Ludwick Tieck. Dorothy Reich writes, "It was Wackenroder also who opened Tieck's eyes to the wealth of poetry that lay in 'Märchen' and 'Volksbücher'; and to Tieck's interest in such things we owe three volumes of *Volksmährchen* (1797), which, besides *Der gestiefelte Kater* and a dramatic 'Ammenmärchen,' *Ritter Blaubart,* contained two tales, *Der blonde Eckbert* and *Die schöne Magelone*" (*History of German Literature,* 378).

89. See Chapter 3 on Zionism.

90. Buber, "Der Mythos der Juden," 24, 22.

91. Ibid., 24–25, 22–23. Buber reminded his readers that not only Jewish redactors tried to demythologize the Bible, but in the nineteenth century Christian scholars continued to try to de-Judaize the text, by their use of philological methods. These efforts were an extension of the early Christian desire, including that of the Gnostics, to de-Judaize Christianity. In Buber's view, the entire historical argumentation that allows such thinking was a colossal mistake (23).

92. Ibid., 25.

93. Buber, *Rabbi Nachman,* Preface. Nineteenth-century Western biblical commentary in general was philological.

94. Buber, *Die Erzählungen der Chassidim,* 7.

95. Aschheim, *Brothers and Strangers,* 125.

96. Buber, *Legende des Baal-Schem,* II.

97. For a comparison of the function of language, see Buber, *Ecstatic Confessions.*

98. Buber, "Der Mythos der Juden," 31.

99. Ibid.

100. Buber, *Rabbi Nachman,* 29, 28, 29.

101. Ibid., 29.

102. Ibid., 29, 30.

103. Paul Mendes-Flohr and Jehuda Reinharz, eds., *The Jew in the Modern World* (New York: Oxford University Press, 1980), 241.

104. Buber, *Erzählungen der Chassidim,* 11.

105. Ernst Simon, "Martin Buber on His Centennial: A Tribute and an Evaluation," *Judaism* 27 (Spring 1978): 148–61.

106. Buber, "Der Mythos der Juden," 23.

107. Buber, *Legende des Baal-Schem,* II, III.

Epilogue: Toward a Synthesis of All Syntheses

1. See Sachar, *History of Israel*, 180: "The Brith Shalom was an ideological, not a political group."

2. See Paul Mendes-Flohr, ed., *A Land of Two Peoples: Martin Buber on Jews and Arabs* (New York: Oxford University Press, 1983).

3. Buber, *Drei Reden*, dedication page, Friedman, *Martin Buber's Life and Work*, 336–40, and many other places.

4. Buber, *Drei Reden*, Preface.

5. Buber organized his work from 1909 to 1915 into a second stage in his efforts for the Jewish movement. He put the second three essays, *Vom Geist des Judentums* (On the spirit of Judaism), published in 1916, in the middle between his famous *Drei Reden über das Judentum* (Three speeches on Judaism), 1911, and the seventh speech, *Der Heilige Weg* (The sacred way), 1918. For the complete texts in English, see Glatzer, ed., *On Judaism*. This volume is a translation of Buber's *Reden über das Judentum*, 1923, and also includes Buber's later speeches. The three original speeches were, however, not new, except for the essay "Der Geist des Orients und das Judentum" (The spirit of the Orient and Judaism) (1913), but rather a revival of the 1906 and 1908 essays on spirituality and myth in *Rabbi Nachman* and the *Baal Schem*. In viewing these seven essays as a unified work, Buber let us know that he found a way to integrate Zionist peoplehood and Hasidic enthusiasm into a unified force that would work together for the renewal of Judaism.

6. "Die Hebräische Sprache," in *Jüdische Bewegung* (1916), 184.

7. Buber, *Drei Reden*, 54–55.

8. For comparison see Arthur A Cohen, ed., *The Jew: Essays from Martin Buber's Journal* Der Jude, *1916–1928* (University, Ala.: University of Alabama Press, 1980).

9. See my forthcoming translation of Rosenzweig's 1925 Yehuda Halevi poems, edited by Richard Cohen, which Rosenzweig dedicated to Buber.

10. Buber, *Jüdische Bewegung* (1916), 184.

11. Buber, *Drei Reden*, 11, 23.

12. Ibid., 30, 44, 56.

13. Ibid., 101.

14. Buber, "Vor Sonnenaufgang," *Jüdische Rundschau* 14 (April 2, 1909): 165. Courtesy of Buber Archives.

15. In 1941, the Nazi establishment revoked Buber's doctorate and his German citizenship. See Jerusalem, National Library, Buber Archives, Ms. Var. 350 A/10a.

Appendix

1. Buber, *Matrikelschein*, Jerusalem, National Library, Buber Archives, Ms. Var. 350 A/5.

2. Ibid., 350 A/6.
3. Ibid., 350 A/6-1c.
4. For comparison, see Friedman, *Martin Buber's Life and Work*, 22.
5. Buber, *Matrikelschein*, Jerusalem, National Library, Buber Archives, Ms. Var. 350 A/5–6.
6. Ibid., 350 A/5.
7. Ibid.

SELECTED BIBLIOGRAPHY

Books by Martin Buber

Eine jüdische Hochschule. Berlin: Jüdischer Verlag, 1902.
Jüdische Künstler. Berlin: Jüdischer Verlag, 1903.
Die Geschichten des Rabbi Nachman. Frankfurt a.M.: Rütten and Loening, 1906.
Die Legende des Baal-Schem. Frankfurt a.M.: Rütten and Loening, 1908.
Ekstatische Konfessionen, Gesammelt von Martin Buber. Jena: E. Diederichs, 1909.
Ekstatische Konfessionen, Gesammelt von Martin Buber. 5th ed. Edited by Paul Mendes-Flohr. Heidelberg: Verlag Lambert Schneider GmbH, 1984.
Ecstatic Confessions. Translated by Esther Cameron. Edited by Paul Mendes-Flohr. San Francisco: Harper & Row, 1985.
Drei Reden über das Judentum. Frankfurt a.M.: Rütten and Loening, 1911.
Daniel. Leipzig: Insel-Verlag, 1913.
Die Jüdische Bewegung. Berlin: Jüdischer Verlag, 1916. 2d Edition, 1920.
Vom Geist des Judentums. Munich: Kurt Wolff Verlag, 1916.
Die Jüdische Bewegung. Berlin: Jüdischer Verlag, 1920.
Die Erzählungen der Chassidim. Zürich: Manesse Verlag, 1949.
The Way of Man According to the Teachings of Hasidism. London: Routledge & Kegan Paul, 1950.
Tales of the Hasidim. Commentary Classics. New York: Schocken Books, 1958.
"Mein Weg zum Chassidismus" (1918). In *Martin Buber Werke,* Vol. 3, Schriften zum Chassidismus. Munich: Verlag Lambert Schneider, 1963.
Encounter. Translated by Maurice Friedman. La Salle, Ill.: Open Court, 1967.

Articles by Martin Buber

"Unseres Volkes Erwachen." *Die Welt* 3 (November 17, 1899): 14–15.
"Ein Wort über Nietzsche und die Lebenswerte." *Die Kunst im Leben* 1 (December 1900): 13.
"Über Jakob Boehme." *Wiener Rundschau* 12 (June 15, 1901): 251–53.
"Bergfeuer—Zum fünften Congresse." *Die Welt* 35 (August 30, 1901): 2–3.

"Gebet." *Die Welt* 26 (June 28, 1901): 13.
"An Narcissus." *Jahresbericht der Lese- und Redehalle jüdischer Hochschüler in Wien über das Vereinsjahr 1901*, 17. Vienna, 1901.
"Eine jungjüdische Bühne." *Die Welt* 45 (November 8, 1901): 10–11.
"Die Congresstribüne." *Die Welt* 36 (November 6, 1901): 1–2.
"I. L. Peretz, Ein Wort zu seinem fünfundzwanzigsten Schriftsteller-Jubiläum." *Die Welt* 18 (May 3, 1901): 9.
"Jüdische Kunst." *Die Welt* 46 (November 15, 1901): 10.
"Ein Wort zum fünften Kongress." *Jüdische Volksstimme* 2 (January 15, 1902): 2–3; 3 (February 15, 1902): 2–3.
Translation of David Pinski, "Das Erwachen—Eine Skizze." In *Jüdischer Almanach*, 209–15. Berlin: Jüdischer Verlag, 1902.
"Zur Aufklärung." *Jüdische Rundschau* 48 (1904): 417–18.
Letter, "Eingesandt," in *Generalanzeiger für die gesamten Interessen des Judentums* 36 (September 3, 1905): 6.
"Die Entdeckung von Palaestina." *Ost und West* 2 (1905): cols. 127–30.
"Vor Sonnenaufgang." *Jüdische Rundschau* 14 (April 2, 1909): 165.
"Die Hebräische Sprache" (1909). *Die Jüdische Bewegung* (1916), 175–91. Berlin: Jüdische Verlag.
"Das Land der Juden" (1910). *Die Jüdische Bewegung* (1916), 192–95.
"Ein geistiges Zentrum." *Die Jüdische Bewegung* (1916), 89–91.
"Die Schaffenden, das Volk und die Bewegung." *Die Jüdische Bewegung* (1916), 68–77.
"Er und Wir." *Die Jüdische Bewegung* (1916), 196–204.
"Gegenwartsarbeit." *Die Jüdische Bewegung* (1916), 17–22.
"Herzl und die Historie." *Die Jüdische Bewegung* (1916), 153–74.
"Jüdische Renaissance." *Die Jüdische Bewegung* (1916), 7–16.
"Renaissance und Bewegung." *Die Jüdische Bewegung* (1916), 95–108.
"Theodor Herzl." *Die Jüdische Bewegung* (1916), 138–52.
"Von jüdischer Kunst." *Die Jüdische Bewegung* (1916), 58–67.
"Was ist zu tun?" *Die Jüdische Bewegung* (1916), 122–37.
"Wege zum Zionismus." *Die Jüdische Bewegung* (1916), 39–44.
"Zionistische Politik." *Die Jüdische Bewegung* (1916), 109–21.
"Der Wägende." *Die Jüdische Bewegung* (1920), 71–73.
"Kunst und Judentum." *Die Jüdische Bewegung* (1920), 245–51.

Manuscripts by Martin Buber at the National Library, Buber Archives, Jerusalem

"Alte und Neue Gemeinschaft." Ms. Var. 350 B/47.
Bar Mitzvah Address. Ms. Var. 350 A/1a.
Course registrations. Ms. Var. 350/A5, 350/A6.
"Daniel." Ms. Var. 350 B/8.
"Das Ewige Drama." Ms. Var 350 B/52.
"Das Gestaltende." Ms. Var. 350 H/41a.
"Die Romantik in Briefen." Ms. Var. 350 B/1.

Document revoking Buber's German citizenship. Ms. Var. 350 A/10a.
Ex libris "Mein ist das Land." Ms. Var. 350 A/7a.
"Jüdische Kunst." Ms. Var. 350 F/71.
"Kultur und Civilisation, Einige Gedanken zu diesem Thema." Ms. Var. 350 B/171.
"Mein Weg zum Chassidismus." Ms. Var. 350 D/31.
"On Viennese Literature" (typescript). Ms. Var. 350 B/174. Translated by Robert A. Rothstein, edited by William M. Johnston, University of Massachusetts, Amherst, 1974.
"Pantheismus und Renaissance." Ms. Var. 350 B/7.
Protocol of Vienna Meeting, May 5, 1901. Ms. Var. 350 F/36.
"Renaissance." Ms. Var. 350 F/21.
"Theodor Herzl und die jüdische Bewegung." Ms. Var. 350 F/25.
"Zarathustra." Ms. Var. 350 B/7b.
"Zu Schopenhauers Lehre vom Erhabenen." Ms. Var. 350 B/7a.
"Zur Geschichte des Individuationsproblems." Ms. Var. 350 A/2.

Secondary Sources

Altmann, Alexander. *Moses Mendelssohn: A Biographical Study*. Philadelphia: Jewish Publication Society of America, 1973.
———. *Moses Mendelssohns Frühschriften zur Metaphysik*. Tübingen: Mohr, 1969.
Aschheim, Steven E. *Brothers and Strangers*. Madison: University of Wisconsin Press, 1982.
Barth, Paul. *Die Philosophie der Geschichte als Soziologie*. Leipzig: O. R. Reisland, 1897.
Beardsley, Monroe. *Aesthetics from Classical Greece to the Present*. New York: Macmillan, 1966.
Benjamin, Walter. *Das Kunstwerk im Zeitalter seiner technischen Reproduzierbarkeit*. Frankfurt a.M.: Suhrkamp Verlag, 1963.
Ben-Sasson, H. H., and S. Ettinger, eds. *Jewish Society Through the Ages*. New York: Schocken Books, 1971.
Burke, Edmund. *The Works of the Right Honourable*. Vol. 1. 1906. Reprint. Introduction by Judge Willis. Oxford University Press, 1925.
Cohen, Arthur A., ed. *The Jew: Essays from Martin Buber's Journal* Der Jude, *1916–1928*. University, Ala.: University of Alabama Press, 1980.
Cohen, Arthur A., and Paul Mendes-Flohr. *Contemporary Jewish Religious Thought*. New York: Free Press, 1987.
Cohn, Margot, and Rafael Buber. *Martin Buber: A Bibliography of His Writings, 1897–1978*. Jerusalem: Magnes Press, 1980.
Crouter, Richard. *Friedrich Schleiermacher on Religion: Speeches to Its Cultured Despisers*. New York: Cambridge University Press, 1988.
Cusa, Nicholas of. *Der Laie über die Weisheit*. Edited by Elisabeth

Bohnenstädt. 1936. Reprint. Hamburg: Verlag von Felix Meiner, 1954.
——. *Drei Schriften vom Verborgenen Gott.* Translated by Elisabeth Bohnenstädt. Hamburg: Verlag von Felix Meiner, 1958.
——. *The Vision of God.* Translated by Emma Gurney Salter. Introduction by Evelyn Underhill. 1928. Reprint. New York: Ungar, 1969.
——. *Vom Globusspiel.* Hamburg: Verlag von Felix Meiner, 1952.
Der Grosse Herder. Reference Work for Knowledge and Life. 5th rev. ed. of the Herder Encyclopedia, Vol. 1. Freiburg: Verlag Herder, 1952–56.
Dinur, Ben Zion. *Israel and the Diaspora.* Philadelphia: Jewish Publication Society of America, 1969/5279.
Dubnow, Simon. *Geschichte des Chassidismus.* Berlin: Jüdischer Verlag, 1931.
——. *History of the Jews in Russia and Poland.* Philadelphia: Jewish Publication Society of America, 1916.
Dufner, Max, and Valentine C. Hubbs, eds. *German Essays III Schiller Über Anmut und Würde, Über das Erhabene.* New York: Macmillan, 1964.
Erdman, David V., ed. *The Complete Poetry and Prose of William Blake.* Newly Revised Edition. Garden City, N.Y.: Anchor Books, 1982.
Ericson, Edward L., ed. *Emerson on Transcendentalism.* New York: Ungar, 1986.
Eucken, Rudolf Christof. *Geistige Strömungen der Gegenwart.* Leipzig: Verlag von Veit & Co., 1909.
Flohr, Paul, and Bernard Susser. "*Alte und Neue Gemeinschaft*: An Unpublished Buber Manuscript." *Association for Jewish Studies Review* 1 (1976): 41–56.
Friedman, Maurice. *Martin Buber's Life and Work: The Early Years, 1878–1923.* London: Search Press, 1982.
——, ed. *Martin Buber and the Theater.* New York: Funk and Wagnalls, 1969.
Glatzer, Nahum, ed. *On Judaism.* New York: Schocken Books, 1967.
Goethe Werke. Vol. 2, "Das Märchen." Frankfurt a.M.: Insel-Verlag, 1965.
Goethe's Werke. Selection in 16 vols. Vol. 6. Leipzig: Philipp Reclam Jun., n.d.
Goethe, Johann Wolfgang von. *Elective Affinities.* Translated by Elizabeth Mayer and Louise Bogan. 1963. Reprint. Westport, Conn.: Greenwood Press, 1976.
——. *Faust.* Edited by Erich Trunz. Munich: Verlag C. H. Beck, 1976.
——. *Wilhelm Meisters Lehrjahre.* Munich: Wilhelm Goldman Verlag, 1964.
——. *Wilhelm Meister's Years of Apprenticeship.* London: Calder, 1977.
Gordon, Haim, ed. *Martin Buber.* Beersheva: KTAV, 1984.

Green, Arthur. *Tormented Master: A Life of Rabbi Nachman of Bratslav.* University, Ala.: University of Alabama Press, 1979.
Grunsky, Hans. *Jacob Boehme.* Stuttgart: Fr. Frommanns Verlag Guenther Holzboog, 1956.
Hertzberg, Arthur. *The Zionist Idea.* New York: Atheneum, 1977.
Horwitz, Rivka. *Buber's Way to I and Thou.* Heidelberg: Verlag Lambert Schneider, 1978.
Idel, Moshe. *Studies in Ecstatic Kabbalah.* Albany: State University of New York Press, 1988.
Janik, Allan, and Steven Toulmin. *Wittgenstein's Vienna.* New York: Simon and Schuster, 1973.
Johnston, William M. "Martin Buber's Literary Debut: 'On Viennese Literature' (1897)." *German Quarterly* 47 (November 1974): 556–66.
Jüdisch-Nationaler Akademischer Verein 'Emunah' Czernowitz. *Heimkehr.* Berlin: Verlag Louis Lamm 5672/1912.
Kant, Immanuel. *Observations on the Feeling of the Beautiful and Sublime.* Translated by John T. Goldthwait. Berkeley and Los Angeles: University of California Press, 1960.
———. *Prolegomena to Any Future Metaphysics.* New York: Liberal Arts Press, 1950.
Katz, Jacob. *Tradition and Crisis.* New York: Schocken Books, 1971.
Katz, Steven T. *Post-Holocaust Dialogues: Critical Studies in Modern Jewish Thought.* New York: New York University Press, 1983.
Kellner, Leon, ed. *Heimkehr.* Czernowitz: Emunah, 1912.
Killy, Walter, ed. *Zeichen der Zeit.* Darmstadt and Neuwied: Hermann Luchterhand Verlag GmbH, 1981.
Kornberg, Jacques, ed. *At the Crossroads: Essays on Ahad Ha-Am.* Albany: State University of New York Press, 1983.
Lasswitz, Kurd. *Seelen und Ziele.* Leipzig: Verlag von B. Elischer Nachf., 1908.
———. *Wirklichkeiten.* Berlin: Verlag von Emil Felber, 1900.
Leibniz, Gottfried Wilhelm, Freiherr v. *G. W. Leibniz's Monadology: An Edition for Students.* Pittsburgh: University of Pittsburgh Press, 1991.
Lessing, Gotthold Ephraim. *Nathan der Weise.* Stuttgart: Philipp Reclam Jun., 1983.
Levao, Ronald. *Renaissance Minds and Their Fictions: Cusanus, Sidney, Shakespeare.* Berkeley and Los Angeles: University of California Press, 1985.
Lovejoy, Arthur O. *The Great Chain of Being.* Cambridge, Mass.: Harvard University Press, 1966.
Macquarrie, John. *Twentieth-Century Religious Thought.* 1963. Reprint. London: SCM Press, 1988.
Mahler, Raphael. *Hasidism and the Jewish Enlightenment.* Philadelphia: Jewish Publication Society of America, 1985.

Manheim, Werner. *Martin Buber*. Twayne World Authors Series. New York: Twayne, 1974.

Mann, Thomas. *Death in Venice and Other Stories*. Translated and with an introduction by David Luke. London: Secker & Warburg, 1990.

Meister Eckhart. New York: Harper & Brothers, 1957.

Mendes-Flohr, Paul. *From Mysticism to Dialogue*. Detroit: Wayne State University Press, 1989.

———. *Von der Mystik zum Dialog*. Königstein/Taunus: Jüdischer Verlag, 1978.

———, ed. *A Land of Two Peoples: Martin Buber on Jews and Arabs*. New York: Oxford University Press, 1983.

Mendes-Flohr, Paul, and Jehuda Reinharz, eds. *The Jew in the Modern World*. New York: Oxford University Press, 1980.

Moore, Donald J. *Martin Buber, Prophet of Religious Secularism*. Philadelphia: Jewish Publication Society of America, 1974.

Mosse, George L. *German Jews beyond Judaism*. Bloomington: Indiana University Press, 1985.

———. *Germans and Jews*. New York: H. Fertig, 1970.

Neubauer, John. *The fin-de-siècle Culture of Adolescence*. New Haven: Yale University Press, 1992.

———. *Novalis*. Boston: Twayne, 1980.

Nietzsche, Friedrich. *The Birth of Tragedy* [1872] and *The Genealogy of Morals* [1887]. Translated by Francis Golffing. Garden City, N.Y.: Doubleday, 1956.

———. "Schopenhauer als Erzieher." In *Unzeitgemässe Betrachtungen*, Vol. 2. Stuttgart: Alfred Kröner Verlag, 1964.

———. *Schopenhauer as Educator*. Chicago: Regency, 1965.

———. *Thus Spoke Zarathustra*. Translated by R. G. Hollingdale. 1961. Reprint. New York: Penguin Books, 1969.

Pagel, Walter. *Paracelsus: An Introduction to Philosophical Medicine in the Era of the Renaissance*. Basel: Karger, 1982.

Peuckert, Will-Erich, ed. *Jacob Boehme, Sämtliche Schriften*, Vol. 8. *Mysterium Magnum*. Stuttgart: Fr. Frommann's Verlag Günther Holzboog, 1958.

Pfleiderer, Otto. *The Development of Christianity*. Translated by Daniel A. Huebsch. New York: B. W. Huebsch, 1910.

———. *The Development of Theology in Germany*. Translated by J. Frederick Smith. 1890. Reprint. London: George Allen & Unwin, 1923.

———. *Vorbereitung des Christentums in der griechischen Philosophie*. Tübingen: J. C. B. Mohr, 1906.

Reich, Dorothy, ed. *A History of German Literature*, by J. G. Robertson. Edinburgh: William Blackwood, 1970.

Rozenblit, Marsha L. *The Jews of Vienna, 1867–1914*. Albany: State University of New York Press, 1983.

Sachar, Howard M. *A History of Israel, from the Rise of Zionism to Our Time*. 1979. Reprint. New York: Knopf, 1986.
Schaeder, Grete. *The Hebrew Humanism of Martin Buber*. Translated by Noah J. Jacobs. Detroit: Wayne State University Press, 1973.
———. *Martin Buber Briefwechsel aus sieben Jahrzehnten*, Vol. 1, 1918–38. Heidelberg: Verlag Lambert Schneider, 1976.
Schelling, Friedrich Wilhelm Joseph von. *System of Transcendental Idealism*. Translated by Peter L. Heath. Charlottesville: University Press of Virginia, 1978.
———. *Von der Weltseele* (1798). Munich: C. H. Beck and R. Oldenbourg, 1927.
Schiller Dramen und Gedichte. Stuttgart: E. Schreiber Graphische Kunstanstalten, 1955.
Schiller, Friedrich. *Saemtliche Werke*. Vol. 1. Munich: Carl Hauser Verlag, 1965.
———. *Schiller Werke*. Edited by Benno von Wiese. National ed., Vol. 21, Philosophische Schriften, part 2. Weimar: Hermann Böhlaus Nachfolger, 1963.
———. *Über die ästhetische Erziehung des Menschen*. Stuttgart: Philipp Reclam, 1965.
Schleiermacher, Friedrich. *Über die Religion, Reden an die Gebildeten unter ihren Verächtern* (1799). With a postscript by Carl Heinz Ratschow. Stuttgart: Philipp Reclam Jun., 1969.
Schmidt, Gerda C. *From Turmoil to Unity: Martin Buber's Efforts towards a New Type of Jewish Community, 1897–1915*. Ann Arbor: UMI, 1990.
Schneider, Wilhelm, ed. *Meister des Stils, Über Sprach- und Stillehre*. Leipzig: B. G. Teubner, 1923.
Schön, Lazar, ed. *Die Stimme der Wahrheit*. Würzburg: N. Philippi, 1905.
Scholem, Gershom. *Major Trends in Jewish Mysticism*. New York: Schocken Books, 1961.
———. *The Messianic Idea in Judaism and Other Essays on Jewish Spirituality*. New York: Schocken Books, 1971.
———. *From Berlin to Jerusalem*. New York: Schocken Books, 1980.
———. *Kabbalah*. New York: Quadrangle/New York Times Book Co., 1974.
Schorske, Carl E. *Fin-de-siècle Vienna: Politics and Culture*. New York: Knopf, 1980.
Schweitzer, Albert. *The Quest of the Historical Jesus*. New York: Macmillan, 1910.
Sembdner, Helmut. *Kleists Aufsatz über das Marionettentheater*. Berlin: E. Schmidt, 1967.
Shapira, Avraham. "Dual Structures in the Thought of M. M. Buber." Ph.D. dissertation. Tel-Aviv University, 1983.

———. "Growing Communities and the Mending of the World: The Social Utopianism of Martin Buber." Typescript. Translated by Esther Cameron from the Hebrew edition of *Martin Buber Paths in Utopia*.

———. "Martin Buber: The Cause and the Person." *Modern Judaism* 8 (October 1988): 287–95.

———, ed. *Martin Buber Pfade in Utopia*. Heidelberg: Verlag Lambert Schneider, 1985.

Silberstein, Laurence J. *Martin Buber's Social and Religious Thought*. New York: New York University Press, 1989.

Simon, Ernst. "Martin Buber on His Centennial: A Tribute and an Evaluation." *Judaism* 27 (1978): 148–61.

Simon, Leon. *Ahad Ha-Am*. Philadelphia: Jewish Publication Society of America, 1960.

———, trans. *Selected Essays by Ahad Ha-Am*. Philadelphia: Jewish Publication Society of America, 1912.

Staiger, Emil, ed. *Der Briefwechsel zwischen Schiller und Goethe*. Frankfurt a.M.: Insel Verlag, 1966.

Stanislawski, Michael. *For Whom Do I Toil? Judah Leib Gordon and the Crisis of Russian Jewry*. New York: Oxford University Press, 1988.

Stenographisches Protokoll der Verhandlungen des III. Zionisten-Congresses. Vienna: Verlag des Vereines "Erez Israel," 1899.

Stenographisches Protokoll der Verhandlungen des VI. Zionisten-Kongresses. Vienna: Verlag des Vereines "Erez Israel," 1903.

Tal, Uriel. *Christians and Jews in Germany*. Ithaca: Cornell University Press, 1975.

Verein Jüdischer Hochschüler, draft of letter to the editor, Jerusalem, National Library, Buber Archives, Ms. Var. 350 Z/110a.

Verein Jüdischer Hochschüler Bar Kochba in Prague, ed. *Vom Judentum*, 1st ed. Leipzig: Kurt Wolff Verlag, 1913.

Vermes, Pamela. *Buber*. New York: Grove Press, 1988.

Wagenbach, Klaus. *Franz Kafka*. Reinbek bei Hamburg: Rowohlt Taschenbuch Verlag GmbH, 1964.

Weinryb, Bernard Dov. *The Jews of Poland*. Philadelphia: Jewish Publication Society of America, 1973.

White, Horatio Stevens, ed. *Selections from Heine's Poems*. Heath Modern Language Series. Boston: D. C. Heath, 1890.

Wistrich, Robert. *Socialism and the Jews*. Rutherford, N.J.: Fairleigh Dickinson University Press, 1982.

Wundberg, Gotthard, ed. *Die Wiener Moderne: Literatur, Kunst, und Musik Zwischen, 1890 und 1910*. Stuttgart: Philipp Reclam Jun., 1981.

INDEX

Index

ABOUT THE AUTHOR

Gilya Gerda Schmidt is Judaic Scholar of Religion, Religious Studies Department, The University of Tennessee. She received a B.A. in Liberal Studies and an M.A. in Germanic Languages and Literatures from the University of Pittsburgh. A recipient of the Mellon Pre-Doctoral Fellowship, she was awarded the Ph.D. after studying Comparative Religion with a concentration in Judaic Studies.